Life and Death in the Ancient City of Teotihuacan

LIFE and DEATH
in the ANCIENT CITY
of
TEOTIHUACAN

A
MODERN
PALEODEMOGRAPHIC
SYNTHESIS

Rebecca Storey

The University of Alabama Press
Tuscaloosa & London

designed by zig zeigler

∞

The paper on which this book is printed
meets the minimum requirements of
American National Standard
for Information Science-Permanence
of Paper for Printed Library Materials,
ANSI Z39.48-1984.

Library of Congress Cataloging-in-Publication Data

Storey, Rebecca, 1950–
Life and death in the ancient city of Teotihuacan : a modern
paleodemographic synthesis / Rebecca Storey.
p.   cm.
Includes bibliographical references and index.
ISBN 0-8173-0559-9 (alk. paper)
1. Teotihuacán Site (San Juan Teotihuacán, Mexico). 2. Indians of
Mexico—Population. 3. Indians of Mexico—Anthropometry.
I. Title.
F1219.1.T27S76   1992
972'.52—dc20   91-17942
                                                    CIP

British Library Cataloguing-in-Publication Data available

Contents

Tables and Figures

Tables

Figures

Preface

IN 1980 DR. WILLIAM T. SANDERS of the Pennsylvania State University began the project entitled "A Reconstruction of a Classic-Period Cultural Landscape in the Teotihuacan Valley," funded by the National Science Foundation. The main concern was to excavate potential irrigation canals on the southern edge of the city, which were thought to date to the Middle Horizon, the period of Teotihuacan's florescence. Compounds near the irrigation canals were to be tested for contemporaneity with the irrigation system. A paleodemographic project mounted in conjunction with this project was intended to expand the excavation of one of the tested compounds and conduct a systematic, complete excavation of it. In the course of excavation a special effort would be made to recover a sufficient skeletal sample for a paleodemographic study, because, as discussed below, Teotihuacan is a very important archaeological site that is virtually unknown demographically.

The paleodemographic project, including as it did a complete excavation of an apartment compound, had three prime objectives. First, the intention was to excavate one of the small (30 m x 30 m) compounds lined up on a potential irrigation canal. It was felt that one of these compounds was small enough to be completely excavated in a six-month field season. Also, each compound would likely be linked directly with the canal and thus may have housed farmers. Perhaps two-thirds of the Teotihuacan population were farmers during the history of the city (see Millon 1976), so information from a farming compound would be a first step in understanding the status and internal organization of this large sector of the city of Teotihuacan, as well as the nature of the farmers' relationships to the agricultural resources of the city and to the full-time nonagricultural specialists.

Second, the project would afford an opportunity to excavate completely and systematically a Teotihuacan apartment compound by the use of modern archaeological excavation strategies for the recovery of many types of artifacts from a wide range of contexts. It was intended that screening and flotation of soil matrices would be done and that an attempt would be made to excavate, where feasible, all areas to sterile bedrock or soil. It was hoped that these methods would provide, for the first time, information that would allow a Teotihuacan apartment compound to be analyzed for activity areas and room functions. It would also allow fine-grained investigation of the subsistence and economic features, which had not previously been done on the basis of an extensive excavation of a compound.

The goal was to be able to document and study the specific character of the residential layout, social composition, status differentiations, demographic features, ritual features, activity areas, degree and type of craft specialization, and subsistence base. Also, it was hoped that the characteristics and changes through time in an apartment compound might be related to the larger context of the centralized urban polity of Teotihuacan.

A third, and very crucial, objective was the systematic and careful recovery of sufficient human skeletal remains for paleodemographic and paleopathological analyses. Although Teotihuacan skeletal samples often seem to be poorly preserved, it was felt these problems could be overcome by careful recovery techniques and a commitment to locating burials. Although many remains were expected to be fragmentary, most researchers realize that this does not preclude analysis of a past population (see Ubelaker 1989). Thus, it was assumed that a sufficient skeletal sample could be recovered and that it would yield valuable information on the health and quality of life in the densely populated urban center.

Conditions encountered early in the field season did cause some changes in the objectives. However, these changes did not compromise the main purposes of the research and, in certain ways, even enhanced the value of the excavated material. The main change was in the choice of the compound to be excavated. The compound originally selected for excavation could not be used, and the one that was excavated was in fact no longer directly related to the canal excavations. Between the time the grant proposals were submitted and the beginning of field operations, the original compound site chosen for full excavation had been enclosed within a new cemetery and was no longer available. Because of the reluctance of land tenants to give permission for excavation that would destroy a maize crop, an alternate site with no maize crop on it was obtained in the Tlajinga area. This site was quite removed from the canals, although it was in the same south-central area of the ancient city. The Tlajinga compound turned out to be a felicitous choice, as it yielded a good skeletal sample and information on craft specialization.

The shift to a Tlajinga compound had relatively little effect on the second and third objectives of the project. There would be changes because of the larger size of the selected site, in comparison with the one that had been proposed, and a shorter field season. It was hoped that, for the burial sample, the larger compound would yield more individuals, and as the Tlajinga area did not appear to be a very high-status area in general (see Cowgill et al. 1984), the paleodemographic study would still be focused on the less-privileged residents of Teotihuacan, an important point for studying baseline health at the city. Thus, even though conditions beyond the researcher's control forced a change in the location of the excavated compound, the potential for useful information from the project was not diminished.

The main analysis of the Tlajinga 33 skeletal population was done during 1981 and 1982 at Teotihuacan, Mexico, since one cannot bring the material out of that country. The analysis then stressed the population methods based on the assumption of a stationary or stable population that were current in paleodemography, although the results indicated that Tlajinga 33 might have been the site of a declining population. In that original analysis I did calculate a life table employing an estimate of the possible decline, -1% per year, so that even at that time I did not think that the assumption of stationarity was necessarily the best way to do paleodemography. In the 1980s, as paleodemography has undergone its most recent reexamination of its methods and assumptions, I desired to redo the Tlajinga analysis to see if I would still come to the same conclusion about the declining trend and still derive the implications for the history and fate of the preindustrial city of Teotihuacan. To bring the analysis completely up to date, I returned briefly to the collection in January of 1989 to redo the adult aging, according to the updated standards for auricular surface and the multifactorial method of Lovejoy and his associates published in 1985 (Lovejoy et al. 1985a, 1985b). This re-aging was necessary, because the methods that I had originally used I now believed had tended to distinctly underage the older individuals. This impression was borne out by the results of the re-aging, which definitely increased the number of individuals now aged as being over 40, such that a lack of older individuals is now no longer thought to be a weakness of the Tlajinga 33 population.

Reanalyzing the Tlajinga 33 skeletons according to the new methods and understandings of paleodemography was a very rewarding experience. The new methods that have been suggested are, I believe, generally very good and more realistic for interpreting skeletal remains. However, I was disturbed by a tendency in the work being published to not integrate all the possible aspects that are needed to do a paleodemographic study. Such a study must combine archaeological context and information, demography, and paleopathology if one is to be able to interpret what might have been the vital rates in the past. This study is, then, an attempt to do a paleodemographic synthesis. This synthesis is the first one yet attempted for a Mesoamerican complex society and for a non-Western preindustrial urban center. I believe that it is also one of the first to try this type of synthesis using recent paleodemographic techniques and assumptions.

There are many people I would like to thank for their advice, support, and comments on various aspects of the Tlajinga 33 study. I thank George J. Armelagos and Edward E. Hunt, Jr. for the training in paleodemographic analysis and guidance in the application of various methods to the Tlajinga 33 data. I also thank C. Owen Lovejoy and Richard S. Meindl for their instruction in skeletal aging of adults. The influence of all these people is very apparent in this analysis. I also thank William T. Sanders; without his support and intellectual guidance, the Tlajinga 33 project and study would never have been carried out.

I would also like to thank Randolph J. Widmer. His contribution to the Tlajinga 33 excavation and this study is great and much appreciated. Without his care and concern in excavating the skeletal remains, this study would not have been possible. He has given invaluable advice, support, and criticism on all stages of this study. I would also like to thank the other members of my doctoral committee for their comments and suggestions: David Webster, James W. Hatch, and Paul Simkins.

I am grateful to the various members of the Teotihuacan Mapping Project, Rene Millon, George Cowgill, and Evelyn Rattray, who have been generous with their information and comments on the Tlajinga 33 excavation and study, helping us to understand how Tlajinga 33 should be interpreted within the wider data from the city of Teotihuacan. I thank Emily McClung de Tapia and her associates, who are analyzing the plant remains from the compound, for the information presently available from their work. I would also like to thank Glenn R. Storey and the excavators of the Tlajinga 33 project for their help and interest in the project.

Funding for the excavation and analysis of Tlajinga 33 was provided by the National Science Foundation (BNS 8005825 and BNS 82-04862). The project also received support from NSF grant BNS 8005754. I am grateful to the Instituto Nacional de Antropología e Historía, Mexico, for the permission to conduct the Tlajinga 33 excavation. I am grateful, as well, to Teotihuacan Mapping Project for the housing and care of the

Tlajinga 33 artifacts and skeletons in the project facility in Teotihuacan, Mexico.

The anonymous reviewers who have read the various publications on the Tlajinga study and this book have given me very helpful comments. The Tlajinga 33 study has benefited from the input of all of these people. I hope the results are of interest to all those who are concerned with the past and the demographic characteristics of human beings.

Rebecca Storey
University of Houston

Life and Death in the Ancient City of Teotihuacan

CHAPTER 1

Anthropology and Paleodemography

The Problem and Its Theoretical Foundations

ONE OF THE MORE VISIBLE TRENDS in the anthropological literature since the 1970s is the increasing interest in demography (e.g., Baker and Sanders 1972; Swedlund and Armelagos 1976). Although some study of demographic characteristics for anthropological problems was undertaken early in this century (e.g., Carr-Saunders 1922; Krzywicki 1934), it is only recently that demographic anthropology, or alternatively, anthropological demography, has become an important focus of research, with a developing methodology and an increasing body of field studies. The combination of concepts from the disciplines of anthropology and demography is logical, as anthropologists have come to realize that cultural attributes and processes have demographic causes, influences, and results, and that neither culture nor demography can be understood completely without reference to the other.

The areas of overlap are considerable. Demographic characteristics affect traditional anthropological variables such as kin networks, marriage rules, ecology, and settlement systems (Zubrow 1976). Also, it is apparent that demographic variables such as fertility, mortality, and migration are generally influenced by cultural factors (Nag 1962; Polgar 1971). Demography is also important to understanding many other elements of interest in a culture. For example, in epidemiology one must often correlate the study of environment, biology of disease, and size of population. Small populations can be an important focus, as in the studies of the sickle-cell trait and malaria (Wiesenfield 1967) and the diseases of hunter-gatherers (Dunn 1968). Also, often the study of human adaptability is done by anthropologists in contemporary small populations, and demography is an important component of such study (Little and

Baker 1976; Goldstein et al. 1983). Demography also provides information on social structure and village dynamics, as has been seen in the
case of the Yanomamö (Chagnon 1975, 1979), and on land distribution
and the effects of inheritance rules (Netting 1981). Demography is becoming more prevalent in anthropology, precisely because it provides
information bearing on such a wide range of aspects of a culture. Thus,
anthropological fieldwork on living groups has increasingly included demographic censuses and estimations of vital statistics such as numbers of
births, deaths, and migrations. For past cultures, the interest in demography is revealed by the increased attention to the recovery of human skeletal remains and to the improvement of the techniques for their study.

However, anthropologists cannot simply coopt all the methods and
concerns of modern demographers, because the foci of anthropological
investigations tend to be small populations and communities, not large
nation-states. Methodologically, these small populations present different conditions for demographic inference. The main difference stems
from the fact that the numbers of important demographic events, such
as births and deaths, fluctuate greatly from year to year. Thus, estimates
of fertility and mortality rates must be averaged over a number of years if
reasonable figures are to be obtained. Even then, one cannot be sure that
the rates reflect the long-term rates operating on the population and are
not just the product of a few deviant years. That sampling problem and
the great variability inherent in any estimation of rates for small numbers
means that anthropologists have less confidence than do general demographers in the soundness of many of their demographic rate calculations, even if they have accurately enumerated all demographic events in
their small population. Anthropologists also face the problems of defining accurately the individual members of their often mobile populations,
and of determining how influences from neighboring cultures and widespread effects of acculturation might be affecting the target population
(Howell 1979, 1986). The large national populations studied by general
demographers yield rate estimates with much less variability and potential statistical error, although these populations, too, are subject to problems resulting from the underenumeration of minorities.

More recently, there has been a better understanding that much demographic methodology is devoted to compensating for incomplete data
and making estimates of population parameters not directly measured
by available or incomplete written sources (see Brass 1968; Preston and
Bennett 1983). These indirect methods often are very useful to anthropologists, as they allow researchers to maximize demographic inferences on the basis of data they can collect in a field situation, and so
they are being used increasingly by anthropological demographers (e.g.,

Ray and Roth 1984; Gage et al. 1984). Thus, the supposed distinctions between demography and anthropological demography are fewer than many anthropologists had thought. Small populations, after all, have been the norm for most of human existence and still accurately characterize the relevant social and demographic milieu for many of the world's people. Thus, to understand the actual demography of human beings, one must understand the effects and dynamics of small numbers.

Although the problems are far from solved, anthropologists have used various methods to counteract the sampling weaknesses inherent in small-population demography. Since demographic rates estimated for small populations may have large amounts of variance, the main methodological concern has been to define and calculate what might be reasonable estimates for these populations. One important focus has been on the use of model life tables (e.g., Weiss 1973). A life table is a mortality schedule, which allows the quick summation of the mortality rates and demographic characteristics of a population. Model tables are constructs that supposedly cover the whole range of human mortality profiles possible and are internally consistent with the known interrelationships of demographic measures. Weiss's tables were developed by the use of anthropological populations, that is, small populations from non-Western cultures and individual communities from larger premodern societies. The data are from both ethnographic counts of living people and the age and sex information of skeletons recovered archaeologically. Weiss's purpose was to discover what the possible mortality range for these populations was. These model life tables were intended for use with small populations. With Weiss's tables, one can take a few raw calculations from data and fit them to the appropriate table, not only to flesh out demographic information but also to assure that mortality estimates are couched in demographically consistent or reasonable terms.

This model-table methodology has been subject to several criticisms. Weiss's tables are no longer employed often by anthropologists, as much of the anthropological data on which they are based is too flawed to yield useful models. Weiss's accomplishment was an important pioneering effort in anthropological demography, but his tables have been superseded by the large number of model tables of Coale and Demeny (1983). The Coale and Demeny tables are based largely on nineteenth- and twentieth-century European populations, which may mean they are biased toward certain mortality patterns and not representative of all possible mortality patterns that may be encountered in anthropological populations. It is entirely possible, if not probable, that a distinctive pattern would be obscured by its being fitted to a model table, and thus valuable information about a population's situation and characteristics would be lost. If sufficient data are available, it is best to investigate the raw data and compare it to its best-fit model table before accepting only the model. Model tables should be applied carefully to avoid reifying the model mortality patterns as the total reality for anthropological populations.

Another important method for the study of small populations, and one that skirts the pitfalls of overly smoothing raw data to make it fit a model, is computer simulation (Dyke and McCluer 1974; Howell 1979). With computers it is possible to take the calculated rates of a few years, simulate the effects on the demographic profile over many years, and then judge what the reasonable estimates for the population might be. The advantage of this method over the use of model tables is that one is not just dependent on the possibly distorted rates of a few deviant years on which to base the demographic estimates; deviant years can be identified and corrected with simulation. As do model tables, simulation tries to control, somewhat, the variance of small numbers of demographic events and derive demographic estimates that are realistic in terms of population dynamics and reasonable in terms of what is known about that society and other anthropological populations with similar ecological conditions and cultural characteristics. The purpose of the methodologies of model tables and simulation is to yield valid demographic parameters, not just as ends in themselves but as means to generate hypotheses about other aspects of a society.

Traditionally, the techniques of anthropological demography have depended on methods that assume a stable population. The model-table method is one such example. Stable-population theory states that unchanging birth and death rates for a hundred years will yield a stable age structure. Once this age structure is present, the proportion of individuals in each age class will remain constant. The advantage of stable-population methods is that age structure, mortality, and fertility rates are all interrelated, and knowledge of some can be used to estimate others. Thus, for anthropological problems, the lack of written documentation of demographic events does not prevent analysis, as population characteristics and events that could be recorded are analyzed, and calculations are made to estimate missing data. However, an important assumption of stable-population methods is that the vital rates of fertility and mortality have been constant, and the visible age structure of the population is the stable one.

Perhaps one of the most important changes in demography during the 1980s has been the development of methods for nonstable populations (e.g., Preston and Coale 1982). It is obvious that many modern nations are not stable in their demographic characteristics (just think of the changes in mortality and birth rates in the United States in the twentieth century). More appropriate demographic methods were needed for more accurate estimation, especially where demographic records are incomplete. Assuming the existence of stable characteristics where there has not been the necessary stability of vital rates results in errors. Nonstable-population methods, on the other hand, require fewer assumptions but still work to define the relation of the age structure with mortality and growth rates (Gage 1985). The difference is that these methods work on the basis of age-specific mortality and growth rates, rather than on rates for the entire population (Preston and Coale 1982). These methods are highly appropriate for anthropological populations and result in more accurate results (Gage 1985). The development of these new methods is likely to revolutionize anthropological demography. In fact, anthropological demography is presently undergoing a time of ferment and excitement, when newer, as well as more traditional, methods of demographic estimation are applied to small populations.

Although the development of methods for small populations continues, it is not only living populations that are available or at issue in anthropological demography. The skeletons preserved from past populations also are anthropological populations and suffer from the general liabilities already discussed, as well as having certain advantages and disadvantages of their own. Nevertheless, archaeology, as part of the discipline of anthropology, is also concerned with demographic problems and analysis (Hassan 1981). As in the rest of anthropological demography, here, too, there is a lot of ferment and rethinking of methods and goals. Before discussing paleodemography—the application of demographic analysis to past populations based on skeletal analysis—I will examine the importance of demographic study to understanding the past.

The Human Past and Demography

Anthropologists are interested in past populations demographically for two reasons: (1) for theoretical reasons, to understand the demographic characteristics typical of human populations in the past and the ways these may be related to the long-term changes in cultural evolution; and (2) to understand the demographic characteristics of specific cultures in order to understand better why that particular culture had the history it had. Thus, there is interest that is general and theoretical and interest that is pertinent to specific sites and regions. The two cannot be considered completely separate spheres of investigation, as the theoretical level needs examples of specific cases to set up theories, and the specific needs hypotheses generated by theories of the relation of culture and population. What is distinctive is that the methods employed in each differ, and that demography plays a slightly different role at each level. At the general theoretical level demographic processes may be said to have primary causality. At the specific level demographic characteristics are interrelated with other cultural aspects, such as economy, social structure, and ideology, to explain how a society functioned. Discussion of both levels will point out the similarities and slight differences in emphasis on demography in each.

Two basic theoretical questions that anthropologists ask are, how do cultures change and evolve, and are there cross-cultural similarities to the process? Again, one confronts two levels—the overarching pattern of human cultures that started out as small and mobile societies and evolved through millenia to the present industrialized "postmodern" societies, a pattern of increasing organizational complexity through time; and a second level of the actual history of this increasing complexity on regional scales of time and space. What happened on a regional scale should be a reflection of the general evolutionary processes of the overarching pattern, of course, but cannot be expected to be the same everywhere, as history is not a repeatable experiment. Thus, anthropologists have tended to look at both *universal* and *multilinear cultural evolution* (Steward 1955; White 1959; Sanders and Webster 1978). The focus is the general causes and consequences of cultural evolutionary change.

At the most basic level of cultural evolution is the question of how cultural and biological evolution are interrelated. Are similar processes at work, or how do they differ? Is the difference so profound as to make cultural evolution a completely different "animal" than biological evolution? Although the discipline's interest in cultural evolution seems to have waxed and waned over the past hundred years, there presently seems to be a renewed interest in the relationship of biological and cultural evolution. Several writers have urged anthropologists to adopt Darwinian theory and natural selection as explanations for cultural phenomena and cultural evolution. At the same time, some of these writers have attacked the past use of evolution and adaptation in anthropology as being essentially non-Darwinian and thus not able to contribute to theory as biological evolution has (Rindos 1985; Greenwood 1984). Although it is not necessary here to go into great detail about the arguments involved, some of these new cultural evolution theories will be discussed, as then it will be clearer why demography becomes important.

Rindos (1985) presents a strictly Darwinian model of cultural selection. His main point, and criticism of past cultural evolutionary models, is that evolution is not directed or inherently progressive. Darwinian selection works on randomly occurring, heritable, and undirected variation. He finds that the symbolic aspects of culture provide the type of variation suitable for a Darwinian selection. Cultures are then selected in a two-tiered process: individuals are selected because they have a cultural trait, and traits are selected by integration, and the like, within the culture. Of course, Rindos recognizes, as do all writers on this subject, that cultural evolution has important differences from the biological one, most importantly, that it is not analogous to speciation and is reversible in a way genetic evolution is not (1985: 74).

Rindos's formulation has been criticized for misunderstanding that although evolution is not directed, cultural evolution has worked toward greater cultural complexity, and explaining the evolution of this complexity is one of the important tasks facing anthropologists interested in the phenomenon (Carneiro 1985; see also Sanders 1984). He is also criticized for using symbolic variation as a functional equivalent to genotype variability, as symbols are arbitrarily assigned meaning by users and so should be selectively neutral (Richerson and Boyd 1985). That is, the variation is really unimportant, as different symbols should be functionally equivalent. What is probably important for selection is the ability to symbolize, not the variation, so it is inappropriate to use symbols as the source of variation on which evolution works.

A more influential work on the processes of cultural evolution in relation to biological evolution is that of Boyd and Richerson (1985). Theirs is a model of dual inheritance—by cultural transmission and genes—as the way to understand human behavior and evolution. Like Rindos, Boyd and Richerson are concerned with modeling the analogies between neo-Darwinism and cultural evolution. Unlike Rindos, who is concerned solely with variation and selection, Boyd and Richerson are concerned with the interaction of biological and cultural evolution, and more importantly, with determining and modeling the forces of cultural evolution—not just selection, but also the functional equivalents of mutation, drift, and migration. The forces of cultural evolution will be different from their genetic counterparts, and here lies the importance of culture in understanding human beings. However, both genetic and cultural processes are important for understanding how humans evolve and why cultures change.

I have discussed these models, though briefly, because the role of demography in cultural evolution will continue to be debated and, in fact, should become even more theoretically central. Why is that? The models of cultural evolution that are explicitly Darwinian also implicity or explicitly adopt the Darwinian definition of evolutionary success— *greater fitness and differential reproduction*. Populations and cultures that are evolutionarily successful leave more descendants, that is to say, their populations grow. This is one of the points made by another model of the way biological and cultural structure coevolve (Hammel and Howell 1987). Hammel and Howell argue that it is demographic processes and a population's reactions to stress that allow us to understand how cultural evolution occurs. Populations have several options for growth or decline that form regularities in their behavioral and cultural consequences, the regularities of cultural evolution. In this model the successful evolutionary theory will be one "in which demographic events are the central mechanism and leading indicators of the coevolution of bodies, minds, and societies" (Hammel and Howell 1987: 142).

Demography has always been important in the study of cultural evolution and is destined to become more so. The role of demography in the process of cultural evolution revolves around two questions: (1) how valid is the model of the Demographic Transition (a model of the diachronic changes in the balance of fertility and mortality in human populations), and (2) what is the role of population growth or pressure in fueling cultural change? Demographers (e.g., Stolnitz 1964) have modeled the demographic processes underlying population history as essentially high fertility with high mortality (Stage 1). Only recently have societies entered into Stage 2, high fertility with low mortality, which is fueling the high modern population growth rates in many countries, and Stage 3, low fertility and mortality, the demographic profile of fully industrialized nations. The theory that populations move eventually from Stage 1 through 2 to Stage 3 is called the Demographic Transition (Stolnitz 1964). Demographers have been arguing about the inevitability of a demographic transition in all the world's populations, but anthropologists have been concerned with finding evidence for Stage 1, which should characterize past preindustrial and prehistoric populations and the traditional anthropological groups that are extant.

An examination of the trends of the human past reveals that throughout the long Paleolithic period, the overall rate of population growth was very low and the human population of the world fairly small (Dumond 1975). A recent estimate is for 8–9 million at the end of the Paleolithic, with very low yearly growth rates of about 0.00007% during the Lower Paleolithic, increasing to about 0.01% in the Upper Paleolithic (Hassan 1981: 208). Then, with the advent of agriculture, population growth began to rise dramatically, increasing through time and eventually attaining the high rates seen in this century. The rates have increased from an estimate of 0.1% per year during the Neolithic (Carneiro and Hilse 1966) to 2%–3% per year in some countries during the 1960s and 1970s. Thus, population has shown a pattern of exponential growth throughout human history, with an especially steep slope since A.D. 1 (Dumond 1975). The periods of increase in population growth rate also often coincide with milestones in cultural evolution, such as the beginnings of agriculture, the rise of urban centers, and the advent of industrialization.

A high mortality in simpler societies, as contrasted with the low mortality in nations in Stage 3, does seem to be borne out by skeletal studies, historical records, and studies of contemporary nonindustrialized groups. However, in the contemporary groups, infant mortality seems to be the primary source of high mortality figures, whereas the evidence of skeletons and historical records seems to indicate that in the past adult mortality rates were higher and life expectancy lower than for many modern nations. There is some evidence that adult mortality patterns have changed somewhat under industrialization and modernization (see Bocquet-Appel and Masset 1982), but there is no doubt that most of human experience is characterized by significantly higher mortality rates and shorter average life expectancies than are common today.

However, when it comes to high fertility, the picture is much less clear, and here anthropologists have made valuable contributions to the study of human demographic patterns through time. Several studies of simple agriculturalists like the Yanomamö (Neel and Weiss 1975) and the Semai Senoi (Fix 1977) reveal completed fertility measures (the average number of children ever born to a woman during her reproductive years) that are fairly close to the average of the seven most fertile contemporary nations (Hassan 1981: 134). The average of about seven children found in modern fertile nations and in many ethnographic samples is significantly below the theoretical potential of approximately twelve (Hassan 1981), and below the highest recorded completed fertility for an actual population, the Hutterites at about eleven (Eaton and Mayer 1953), although the Hutterites have been below that figure in more recent decades. Therefore, there always seems to be some fertility-dampening factors at work, whether conscious or unconscious, cultural or environmental. These are discussed in more detail below. Nevertheless, the completed fertility found ethnographically in agricultural societies is always much greater than that needed for simple replacement of the population, and so can be characterized as high.

There are indications, however, that fertility has not always averaged seven to eight children per woman. One of the surprises, a somewhat unexpected finding, of anthropological demographic research on ethnographically known hunters and gatherers is that their fertility and mortality can be characterized as moderate, rather than high. In an intensive study of the Dobe San of southern Africa, Nancy Howell (1979) found that, although the numbers of deaths were small enough to cast doubt on their representativeness and so simulation was used as a control, the San have an expectation of life at birth ranging from 37.5 to perhaps 50 years. In the recent past, though, it is more likely to have been about 30, because of the lower survivorship of children born before 1950 (Howell 1979: 116). The higher life-expectancy estimate is better than those calculated for many skeletal samples from past populations (see Weiss 1973 for comparisons) and is compatible with figures from nineteenth-century industrializing populations (Howell 1979).

As for fertility, the evidence is strong that the average completed fertility of women past reproductive age is 4.69, and Howell's tabulated age-specific fertility rates are, as she points out, low for a noncontracepting population (1979: 123). The fertility pattern seems to be a result, according to Howell, of the length of the reproductive span and the length of birth intervals, with the latter probably being the more important. What she finds is that reproductive ability starts slowly and ends early (several years before menopause, although human populations in general show some years of almost no childbearing before the median age of menopause), and that the birth intervals are long. This combination of factors has become the focus of research on the reasons that mobile hunter-gatherers may differ from sedentary agriculturalists, and on the demographic implications of the shift to agriculture and settled habitation 10,000 years ago.

The findings about general low average fertility per woman seem to be borne out by other studies of mobile hunter-gatherers (see Handwerker 1983). However, moderate fertility is not the case for sedentary hunter-gatherers (see Widmer 1988). Thus, the transition to sedentary life, and the subsequent adoption of agriculture, becomes potentially the first turning point in the general demography of human populations. This change can actually be considered the First Demographic Transition, a shift from moderate fertility and mortality, virtually in balance, to the high fertility and mortality regime typically found in sedentary populations, including agricultural ones (Hassan 1981; Handwerker 1983). The shift, of course, raises the question of why fertility is low in mobile foragers and then rises with sedentism and the adoption of agriculture. Also of interest is whether the change at the transition to agriculture and sedentary life involves mostly fertility or mortality rates (Hassan 1981; Handwerker 1983).

A promising theory comes from the work of Rose Frisch and others and is often referred to as Frisch's "critical fat" hypothesis. In a series of studies (Frisch et al. 1971; Frisch 1974) Frisch and associates determined that there was a relationship of height to weight and percentage of body fat to the timing of menarche. This percentage of body fat is "the critical fat" needed to start menstruation. Frisch also found that a minimum weight or percentage of body weight in fat is needed to maintain ovulatory cycles, below which amenorrhea results (Frisch and McArthur 1974). Thus, women need a minimum weight, adjusted for height, with some critical percentage in body fat for the onset and maintenance of the menstrual cycle, that is, to be fertile. The mechanism is very attractive to demographers, as it is a biological one and would be sensitive to problems in the environment. As Howell (1979) points out, the San do not choose to have their lowered fertility, and a mechanism like "critical fat" also would be beyond the conscious control of women. For hunter-gatherers, whose diet is adequate but low in fats and calories and whose mobility brings fairly high caloric expenditure in relation to food collected (Lee 1979), the "critical fat" hypothesis is an apparently appropriate one. Thus, maybe the San, and by extension other mobile foragers, have late menarche and long birth intervals becase it takes time, given their diet and lifestyle, to build up female body fat during adolescence and replenish it after childbirth and lactation.

The hypothesis would also explain why agriculturalists have high fertility. Stored domesticated grains and cereals can have two effects upon fertility and fat. Such grains would provide more steady caloric intake over a year for fat accumulation by women, so the "critical fat" could be reached earlier in adolescence and be better maintained between children. This effect is more likely to occur when women are sedentary than when they have to be highly mobile, and agriculturalists are sedentary. Also, the caloric demands of lactation can be shortened, because the cereals provide an easily digestible gruel, which allows children to be weaned earlier than possible without those foods. This earlier weaning creates a shorter birth interval. Thus, with shorter birth spacing and more calories to recover "critical fat" to shorten the postpartum amenorrhea, females in those cultural conditions would tend to have more children during their reproductive years.

There have been some studies of the effects of sedentism on mobile hunter-gatherers. Among the San, those that have become sedentary with more grain in the diet do seem to show a shorter birth spacing and higher fertility (Kolata 1974), although the information is not such that sedentism and higher caloric foods can be considered the only possible factors (Howell 1979). Binford and Chasko (1976), looking at the recently sedentized Nunamiut Eskimos, also find that fertility has definitely increased under the new lifestyle. Part of the new lifestyle has been the increase in the consumption of imported grains and vegetables because of the year-round contact with a store, thus probably providing the Nunamiut with a steadier supply of more calories than was available to them as nomadic hunters.

Although the "critical fat" hypothesis is attractive, the results of recent research do not seem to support it. As Howell (1979: 211) points out, the San women are too few to provide a rigorous test, and although the data seem to favor the hypothesis, alternative explanations cannot be ruled out. The whole question of the effect of nutrition on fertility is a difficult one, as many studies have not sufficiently controlled for the various cultural factors and the different ways to measure malnutrition, to assure that the length of the postpartum amenorrhea, an important factor in the length of birth intervals, is simply related to nutrition, as the "critical fat" hypothesis suggests (Scott and Johnston 1985). An important factor in the length of postpartum amenorrhea seems to be the duration and daily intensity of breastfeeding (Bongaarts 1980; Menken et al. 1981). For example, among the San, breastfeeding lasts three years, and it is generally the only source of food for children at this time, making lactation a prime candidate for explaining their long birth intervals (Lee 1980). In fact, many studies do not show a good causal relationship of nutrition and fat with fertility (see Scott and Johnston 1985). The hormonal cycle that underlies normal menstruation is affected by multiple factors, and thus it is likely that several behaviors and biological conditions, probably including adequate but not abundant diet, the patterns and length of breastfeeding, and heavy work load, are implicated in lowered fertility among mobile foragers. This example reveals the complex relations between culture and fertility, and how in cultural evolution newly sedentary societies must adapt to increased fertility. The example also reveals how fertility can be affected by many factors in a female's cultural environment.

A second general interest that demography has for the study of cultural evolution is the role that the growth of human populations has in fueling changes and new adaptations. Ever since the economist Ester Boserup (1965) argued that population increase is an independent factor and can lead to pressures that force technological expansion and economic growth, population pressure has become a popular explanation for changes at all sociocultural levels of cultural evolution. In Boserup's model people undertake more intensive agricultural techniques only when they have to, to feed the population. With the use of more intensive subsistence techniques and more people, there are concomitant increases in sociocultural complexity.

The problem that population-pressure models have in both general anthropology and archaeology is defining and quantifying the concept of population pressure, as it is not likely to be just large population numbers or the high rate of population growth, but the numbers of people in relation to resources or carrying capacity that are important. For example, populations may decline in actual number but still be pressured, because resources are even more limited. The concept of carrying capacity has been somewhat hard to define for human groups (Hayden 1975) because of the difficulty of calculating the amount of potential usable food under various technologies and, thus, the population that can be supported. At any rate, it has become obvious from ecological studies in anthropology that human populations are usually well under the maximum that could be supported in their environment (Hassan 1981). Therefore, definitions of population pressure have tried to incorporate measures of possible stress or other limits on a group, and not just use the maximum food potential, because for human groups that maximum does not seem to be a real limiting barrier. Problems seem to arise long before that theoretical threshold is reached.

Harner (1970) defines pressure as occurring when the percentage of the diet from wild terrestrial food resources declines, meaning that resources are being used heavily and that more intensification of land use is under way. For Carneiro (1970), population pressure is what turns an environment from an open to a circumscribed one, whether the barriers that are raised are from geography, resource scarcity, or other competing societies. Sanders et al. (1979) define pressure for agriculturalists as occurring when the per capita work cost increases for the agricultural system under use because the land is filled up, a measure derived from Boserup (1965). Price (1982) defines pressure as occurring when there are increasing energetic costs and diminishing returns in sustaining a given way of life, so the crucial demographic threshold of pressure will depend on the culture ecology and productive system of a population. Hammel and Howell (1987) have recently defined pressure as occurring when the resources are not in balance with the needs of the population, but on the short side, as measured by absolute standards or by the standard of the recent past. Population pressure arises from the scarcity and limits to the resources utilized and valued by a group, and not from the maximum food potential in the environment.

All models relying on population pressure postulate changes in subsistence techniques, usually intensification of some kind, which then necessitate changes in social organization, if the cultures or populations perceive pressure. Well-known models are those of Harner (1970), Sanders et al. (1979), and P. Smith (1972) for general models; Binford (1968),

Meyers (1971), and Cohen (1977) for the rise of agriculture; and Carneiro (1970) and Netting (1972) for the rise of complex societies. The appearance of several more recent models illustrates the continuing theoretical importance of demography to cultural evolutionary theory. Johnson and Earle (1987) have developed a model of social evolution based on economic intensification that says "the primary motor for cultural evolution is population growth" (p. 16). As population increases, the subsistence economy must be intensified; the intensification, in turn, creates opportunities for economic control that ultimately leads to inequality and social stratification. Thus, over time, mobile foragers can evolve into the complex society of the agrarian state. In a very similar model for the evolution of complex societies, Sanders (1984) reiterates his views that population growth is an intrinsic feature of human societies, and that large populations require organizational complexity to integrate successfully and prosper. Thus, population pressure fuels the cultural evolution of complex societies. Hammel and Howell's theory (1987) is also similar in its stress on the effect of population pressure and on the way populations respond as the impetus to cultural evolution. What is distinctive about their theory is its use of reproductive success so explicitly as the measure of evolutionary success. In their view, population can respond to pressure by more integration and complexity, but group fission can also be a powerful impetus to evolutionary change, as long as there is room to fission by increasing the opportunities for change and for favoring communication innovations that make human culture and the human species what it is.

Population pressure models, though, do not lack vociferous critics. The critics question whether human populations just naturally increase, as most pressure arguments do take that for granted. There is, after all, evidence that human populations can regulate themselves culturally, for there are social factors that can influence growth, such as age at marriage, and the like. Therefore, population growth is not truly an independent factor or intrinsic character of humans.

Cowgill (1975) is an influential critic of population-pressure models. He attacks the implication that cultural development was stimulated "by hunger" and that population stress will generally stimulate innovations in cultural development and change. In fact, he feels that the evidence is that stress from shortages may actually inhibit innovation and evolution. Population-pressure theorists underestimate the ability cultures possess to regulate size, and they ignore many other factors that influence development and innovation. Cowgill calls for a model of cultural development and population processes that is more cognizant of the individual decisions and perceptions of new opportunities that affect the demographic behavior of populations. These perceptions are influenced by a variety of economic, political, and social factors involved in the cost or value of another child. For Cowgill, population growth is not an inherent tendency, but a possibility encouraged or discouraged by certain institutional, technological, and environmental circumstances.

In a ten-point critique Hassan (1981: 162–163) attacks population-pressure theories in the most recent and comprehensive treatment of the antipressure position. He makes points that are similar to Cowgill's but also stresses that population increase is only one demographic variable and that others, like dependency ratios and desired family size, are ignored, with the result that the effects of demography on cultural change are distorted and oversimplified. Pressure critics decry the oversimplified causality of a population-pressure model as the prime mover of cultural evolution.

Hassan's points also illustrate the tendency among critics to oversimplify the viewpoint of population-pressure theorists. For example, Hassan and Cowgill criticize the assumption that when it is needed, the right innovation will be present. However, this assumption is not necessarily implied by a pressure model. As in all models where natural selection is operating, obviously stress will not always be met successfully and will not necessarily lead to innovation. Some populations will become extinct, and others may stabilize rather than innovate. However, it is those societies that do successfully cope with stress and continue to grow that are of most concern to the understanding of cultural evolution. That is exactly the underlying point of a pressure model, even if not explicitly stated. It is not that all societies meet growth successfully, but that selection can favor those that do adapt to it. As another example, Hassan feels that population-pressure models tend to be extreme and invoke catastrophic events, such as famines or severe shortages, which often occur when innovation is not possible. However, he is confusing increasing demands with a food crisis. Again, that is an oversimplification, and natural selection should favor populations that adjust before they get into such deleterious situations. A population-pressure model uses the truism of natural fertility with its continued natural increase of population (which is a potential in each generation, even if it is slow, or even if there are strong institutional or environmental checks for a time) as the catalyst of changes, usually through some sort of intensification in subsistence and economic changes that cause changes in political and other social aspects of a culture (Johnson and Earle 1987). Cultural evolution studies those cultures that have intensified over the long run.

Two legitimate, but related, objections can be raised to a population-pressure model, but these are not stressed or really answered by the vociferous opponents. One, of course, is the assumption of increase without any attempt to answer why it occurs, or to elucidate the factors under which it occurs. The population-pressure theorists seem to be somewhat right in that the measured completed fertility of non-contracepting populations, and even prehistoric ones (see Henneberg 1976), is usually significantly higher than is necessary for simple replacement. On the other hand, the opponents are right that obviously most societies have not maintained much growth for very long; they must have stabilized or grown very slowly, or else long-term population growth would have been much higher than it has been. Thus, although there does seem to be a potential for demographic increase in every generation, the extra fertility is to a great extent not translated into growth. Premodern population regulation may exist; how and why it occurs is crucial to the understanding of how demography operates in human experience.

This issue is the crux of the second objection to both the pro and con positions in regard to population-pressure theory. Both positions often make assumptions about population regulation and growth without knowledge of the specific patterns of fertility and population regulation, and their cultural decisions and choices underlying these patterns. In fact, Caldwell et al. (1987) have discussed population regulation among primitive societies as an "anthropological myth." They feel that there is no evidence of an "effective, voluntary fertility control" (p. 33) or the widespread use of infanticide in anthropological populations, or in other populations, before modern times. Natural fertility seems to characterize these populations, and although cultural patterns affect fertility, Caldwell et al. (1987) do not think these indicate deliberate control "unless one wishes to argue that the age at weaning or the propensity of widows to remarry was fundamentally aimed at controlling population size rather than meeting other social ends" (p. 33). Cultural practices do affect demographic rates, but that does not mean that demographic regulation was the population's rationale for these practices. Demographic regulation is not likely to have been consciously practiced, but why populations do or do not grow *is* related to cultural behavior.

Understanding growth is where recent demographic studies are making important contributions to the study of human evolution (Hammel and Howell 1987). Only through studying the relationships of fertility and mortality to underlying ecological and social relations of populations will anthropologists learn how and why populations behave under various circumstances, and thus understand how population-pressure operates to affect cultural evolution. The work that anthropologists and demographers are doing in less-developed countries (e.g., Caldwell and Caldwell 1977; Handwerker 1981) is also refining knowledge of the ways demography and other cultural aspects interrelate.

One finding of the 1980s seems to be that population regulation, as traditionally conceived by anthropologists, is not really present. Cowgill (1975) is correct in insisting that individual demographic decisions should be investigated. What is different is the growing realization that most individuals in most cultures have neither the desire nor the technology to control their fertility. In other words, the demand for children is not the key variable; other social factors, such as age at marriage, and biological factors, such as the potential dampening of fertility brought about by poor nutrition and long lactation with long postpartum amenorrhea (see Handwerker 1983), are what result in high or low fertility. It often makes economic good sense for individuals to have many children for labor and social security under all but a few cultural situations (Caldwell 1981; Sanders 1984), so the trend is for individuals, and by extension, their societies, *not* to control their numbers. Thus, most populations have the potential to grow; if they do not, it is because of cultural and biological regulators of mortality and fertility beyond the control of most individuals, not because of the individual reproductive decisions (Handwerker 1983).

Thus, cultural evolution is indeed the result of decisions and innovations made by populations in response to stress and pressure of some sort. A good criticism made by Hammel and Howell (1987) is that too often only food is looked at as a potential stressor, whereas sex and sociality are also likely to be involved at times. It is the relationships of fertility and mortality, whether these are growing, maintaining stability, or even declining, that affect the history of a population on the specific level. *Ultimately, through time, those societies that were able to intensify, support more people, and integrate them through more complex cultures create the trends seen overall in cultural evolution.* There is nothing in this process that expects all populations to do the same, or even to intensify or respond to stress in the same way. Thus, the understanding of demographic processes is important to an understanding of the ways cultural evolution occurs, the ways cultures become more complex and cope with the problems brought about by increased numbers, and the ways new types of societies appear in the history of a region. It is also important to an understanding of the reasons why societies in a region stop evolving and collapse.

However, because modernization and industrialization seem to be affecting most contemporary populations (see Howell 1979), past populations provide perhaps the only opportunity for studying many important cultural evolutionary transformations, as modern populations may not provide valid analogies. One will have to directly study the past to understand the effect of population on evolutionary transformations. Thus, the development, refinement, and use of paleodemographic methods are essential to the study of cultural evolution. Besides, many theoretical questions about the relationship of population and culture can be answered only from paleodemography (Hammel and Howell 1987).

The Paleodemographic Method

The study of demographic characteristics of nonliving populations depends upon the validity of the results of paleodemographic analysis. Although paleodemography often has the general problem of anthropological demography with small population size, it also has special problems because it is performed largely on the basis of skeletal remains. It is true that other archaeological information can be used to estimate population parameters like size of community, family size, or rates of artifact usage, replacement, and disposal (Cook 1973). Archaeologists can also use ecological information and analogy to model carrying capacities and sizes of populations in the past (Hassan 1981). However, for information on vital events such as fertility and mortality rates, skeletons are the primary source of data.

The study of skeletal remains to extract as much information as possible is relatively recent and, not surprisingly, has paralleled the changing interests in archaeology and biological anthropology (Swedlund and Armelagos 1976). When archaeologists were interested in cultural affinities and history, skeletal remains were studied for racial affinities. With the "new archaeology" has also come a populational, or demographic, orientation in skeletal studies. With this emphasis came an interest in the way inferences on demographic rates could be made from skeletons.

Skeletal remains contain a plethora of information useful for demographic studies but have inherent limitations. Information about causes of death, genetic anomalies, chronic diseases, traumas from accidents or warfare, and biomechanical patterns from habitual work are recorded in skeletal remains (see Ubelaker 1989; Ortner and Putschar 1981). But because the skeletal system is quite well buffered physiologically and is not as sensitive as soft tissue to insults and environmental influences, interesting and important information on disease, trauma, and the like is just not preserved. Bones tend to record the most dramatic insults, and this must be remembered when paleodemographic and paleopathological results are being interpreted. Furthermore, multiple or different diseases produce similar modifications to bone, resulting in inconclusive diagnoses. Also, there is no necessarily direct correlation between the disease or trauma modification to bone and mortality.

Extracting mortality and fertility information, which is the basis of the study of vital rates, from skeletons is an exercise fraught with potential peril. There are certain base conditions that must be met for a paleodemographic study to yield results having any validity (Acsádi and Nemeskéri 1970), but these conditions are necessary for any good anthropological demographic study, and not just those studies using skeletal remains. One problem arises from the question of representativeness. One would like, of course, to have the complete series of deaths that occurred in a past population. As it is unlikely that archaeologically one would have 100% preservation of anything, one must have at least a representative sample of the deaths. This condition can be complicated by fragmentary, incomplete remains and by burial practices that discriminated against the preservation of the remains of certain segments of the population, thereby biasing the sample. Also relevant are the field strategies employed in the archaeological excavation where skeletons are recovered—what kind of sample is it and is it likely to have been biased by the recovery techniques utilized? Is it possible that the excavated sample would be biased toward certain ages and sexes because of differential locations of burial and the grave goods they contain? In other words, archaeologists often seek out certain kinds of burials, those with elaborate grave goods, and ignore more modest interments.

There are two ways to mitigate the problem of representativeness. One concerns archaeological recovery technique and evaluating archaeological context. The excavation methods used should be fine-scaled enough to identify human bone and recover even the smallest bones typical of infants. If proper recovery methods are used, there is no reason why all the bone present in the excavated portion of a site cannot be part of the study. Thus, adequate excavation control and recovery techniques, such as fine-mesh screening, ensures that all human skeletons in the excavation will be recovered. Then, the archaeological context can be evaluated to judge if there might be *a priori* grounds for doubting their representativeness. Is it a formal cemetery of which only a portion could be excavated for a society that segregated burials by age or sex or both? Does it seem that every possible burial location was sampled in the excavation? Is there evidence that significant portions of skeletal remains will not be recovered in the excavation? Are soil conditions similar in all

areas of the site for preserving bone of differing density? If the archaeological context is favorable, then a representative sample of remains can
be recovered.

The next method to judge representativeness is to investigate the age
and sex characteristics to try to identify problems. Sexes should be
evenly distributed, and all ages should be present in the proportion of
deaths that would result from a living population. Age distribution
should have a general J-shape that follows the usual human mortality
pattern (Weiss 1973), with high infant mortality, then a dropping of mortality through childhood to a low in early adolescence, followed by an
increasing rate of mortality throughout the rest of the lifespan. There
should be more infants and young children than older children and adolescents, for example. The numbers of individuals should then rise gradually through the young and middle-age adult years and then rapidly in
older ages. If an age or sex is missing or present in lower percentages
than would be expected in a J-shape pattern, then it is probable that the
sample is biased, and demographic inferences probably cannot be made.
Of course, one must be able to accurately assign age and sex to the skeletal population on the basis of osteological indicators, which is another
potential source of problems.

The difficulties and possible error in making accurate age and sex
assignments on bones have been well discussed in the literature (see esp.
Ubelaker 1989 and Lovejoy et al. 1985a). The question has been raised
whether methods currently used are valid, because they are based on
modern populations and one cannot assume similarity to the past (Bocquet-Appel and Masset 1982). This issue is explored in more depth in
Chapters 5 and 6, but it must be emphasized that the more complete the
skeleton, the better the estimate of age and sex. Thus fragmentary, incomplete remains can undermine the accuracy of age and sex determinations, as well as impact the ability to determine if the skeletal sample is
representative. Theoretically this is not a problem, if fragmentary remains are exhaustively analyzed and controlled by reference to more
complete remains. The populational technique for aging and sexing skeletons from past populations (fully discussed in Chapter 5) is a method to
better age and sex skeletons, so as to determine the representativeness
of the population.

Another condition that must be met so that valid demographic inferences can be made is the careful definition of a population. Demography is performed on populations, individuals who interact and
interbreed. This can be difficult to define in practice, and certainly can be
difficult to define for anthropological groups, because the boundaries
that define populations in time and space are often vague or not solely

culturally defined (Hammel and Howell 1987). For archaeologically derived skeletal populations, this condition necessitates very tight control of the chronology and context of the burials. The shorter the period in which the burials accumulated and the tighter their spatial clustering, the more reasonable the definition as a valid population, for it is more likely the skeletons are the result of a single living population. As the time and space boundaries for the skeletons expand, any demographic information must be critically evaluated in terms of what else is known about the archaeological context to judge whether the skeletons can be considered a population. In practice, paleodemographers have tended to define somewhat liberally what is representative and what is a "true" population, mainly because it is felt that any demographic information that can be gleaned is useful. However, the more rigorous the population control and definition, the greater the validity of the paleodemographic results. It is becoming clearer that when the basic conditions of a population are violated, the demographic information is less useful. The future of paleodemography lies in careful attention to producing valid results on carefully chosen skeletal samples that meet the criteria of a population.

The history of paleodemography has been a somewhat checkered one. Although interest in paleodemographic analysis is relatively recent, it has resulted in a surprisingly large body of information on past populations. There have also been periods of great self-doubt and criticism, first in the 1960s and early 1970s and again in the mid-to-late 1980s. The theory and method of paleodemography, along with the criticisms, are covered in Chapter 6. The ultimate assessment of the reasonableness of paleodemography must be based on what it tells us about the past and whether it fits into the set of uniformitarian assumptions about human demographic capacities (Howell 1976). These assumptions are that the range of demographic factors and biological capacities that condition the situations of modern-day populations should also have worked in the past. In other words, certain fertility and mortality processes are somewhat invariant, like maximum lifespan or the maximum number of children most women in a population are likely to have, no matter what human population is being studied. In addition, fertility and mortality have a definable range of variation, because they fluctuate predictably with varying aspects of the culture and the environment. Howell's examples (1976) of predictable variation include the long birth intervals of the hunter-gatherer San, and the assumption that when mortality is high, it is infants and children that form a large proportion of the deaths. These demographic conditions, understood on the basis of the study of contemporary populations, would be expected in the past.

Thus, paleodemography can measure the reasonableness of its results against the uniformitarian assumptions, and very deviant results from what is known would be called into question.

Starting with Acsádi and Nemeskéri's groundbreaking study *The History of Human Life Span and Mortality* (1970), paleodemographic studies have revealed a series of patterns in the past. Acsádi and Nemeskéri identified the low average life expectancy of humans before quite recent times. Life expectancy at birth is in the low twenties during the Paleolithic and Neolithic and rises to around 30 years with state-level societies. These low figures are mainly due to extremely high infant and child mortality. Even when one looks at life expectancy at age 15, past the high-mortality years, the figures are between 20 and 30 again, which indicates that most adults lived only into their thirties and forties. Thus, it appears that for most of human history, mortality has been high, and few people have lived to old age. Another finding of these paleodemographic studies is that men had a generally longer life expectancy and women a higher mortality rate in the young adult years (Acsádi and Nemeskéri 1970; Hassan 1981). The evidence for this finding contradicts the general contemporary pattern, wherein women live longer and have lower probabilities of death at most ages. There are, however, a few contemporary populations with the former pattern. The pattern is usually explained by reference to the rigors of hard work and childbearing on women, a situation that is ameliorated with better medical care and better general nutrition. These two demographic patterns fulfill uniformitarian assumptions, because they do not violate the biological capacities of populations or the potentialities of known demographic rates and conditions. However, these patterns are currently undergoing some rethinking as new methods are being developed, so that it is premature to list here all the accomplishments of paleodemography. However, the indications are still for shorter lifespans and higher proportions of young women than men in the skeletal samples.

Paleodemography aims to mitigate the inherent limitations of skeletal data through careful control of the archaeological context and continual refinement of techniques for aging, sexing, and diagnosing disease and stress from the bones. It tries to produce demographically valid results by testing for the representativeness of the skeletons recovered and the reasonableness of defining the skeletal series as a true population, valid for demographic analysis. It will provide a means of adding to our knowledge about the history of human populations and the kinds of demographic regimes possible in human cultures if each paleodemographic study meets these conditions and uses valid methods of inference.

The Statement of the Problem

There is a real need in archaeology to incorporate the results of skeletal studies into existing knowledge of the past. Skeletal remains are becoming ever more valued for the information they can yield about various demographic and health conditions, and it is now recognized that even fragmentary remains do not preclude study (Ubelaker 1989). But archaeologists must recover skeletal remains systematically and carefully, as a large number are needed for a demographic study; ten to fifteen individuals found just by chance in the course of excavation do not meet the requirements of the population assumption necessary if one is to draw demographic inferences, although a few burials can provide a surprising amount of biocultural information (Rathbun et al. 1980). Excavation techniques need to yield the maximum recovery of bone, and the recovery of skeletal populations, which requires the recovery of all the burials in a site, should become an integral part of archaeological research designs.

Population and demographic characteristics have basic theoretical importance for understanding cultural evolution, and skeletons are the single most direct means for reconstructing the dynamics of life and death in a past society. As discussed above, the more complex the society, the larger the demographic numbers that are involved, and the more important demographic pressure has been to its evolution. Consequently, wherever a regional archaeological history reveals cultural evolution from small settlements to cities and states, demography is important and necessary in discussing and explaining the changes visible in the archaeological record.

One of the world areas with a trajectory to autochthonous state development and a wealth of complex societies is Mesoamerica. Although skeletal remains have been recovered from archaeological sites in both the Mayan and highland Mexican areas, there have been no studies specifically focused on paleodemography in Mesoamerica, although there have been a number of interesting analyses of the skeletal series (Faulhaber 1965; Haviland 1967; Rathje 1970; Saul 1972; Lopez, Lagunas and Serrano 1976; Márquez 1984; Jiménez and Lagunas 1989; Serrano and Martinez 1989). One study of skeletons from Monte Alban (Wilkinson and Norelli 1981) did use age and period breakdowns to compare tomb and nontomb samples to detect biological differences that might be related to social organization. That study and a later one done on Oaxaca skeletons (Hodges 1987) are the only ones based in highland Mexico that attempt analyses similar to those reported here. Yet, in neither case was the research specifically designed to collect skeletal material that adequately met the requirements of a paleodemographic study. A core of paleodemographic studies must be developed for Mesoamerica if we are to understand and adequately explain the variability of sociopolitical forms found in prehistoric populations there.

In the Valley of Mexico one has the whole range of cultural evolution from small agricultural hamlets to the development of the state, plus the advantage of long-term archaeological research projects and a well-documented population history known from archaeological survey (Millon 1976; Sanders et al. 1979). It is a promising area for paleo-demographic research where practically nothing has been done to date.

One of the truly impressive and important sites in the Valley of Mexico is the pre-Columbian urban center of Teotihuacan, the first city in Mesoamerica. It is a site that is unknown paleodemographically but that could yield groundbreaking information on the demographic features, health, and general quality of life in a New World preindustrial city. With the large population necessary to maintain an urban center, Teotihuacan obviously will require long-term research and the analysis of many skeletons before we will be able to adequately characterize it. However, there must be a beginning, and the excavation of one apartment compound, S3W1:33, hereafter referred to as Tlajinga 33, which yielded a skeletal sample large enough for paleodemographic analysis, provides the first opportunity to characterize this important urban center demographically. The methods and results of the analysis of Tlajinga 33 are reported here.

The main purpose of the study was to reconstruct the demographic characteristics of the apartment compound. However, the paleodemography of Tlajinga 33 has important and direct implications for a wider problem in demography and the study of cultural evolution. The general problem is whether New World pre-Columbian cities like Teotihuacan have demographic characteristics similar to those of other known preindustrial cities. Most demographic knowledge of preindustrial cities is from Europe. But New World cities, which are characterized by a different cultural tradition and the pristine development of urban centers without the influence of Old World patterns, could be quite different. The arid, highland environment of Teotihuacan, so very different from that of European cities, to say nothing of the much higher disease load of the Old World (McNeill 1976), could yield a distinctive and very different demographic profile.

The general hypothesis of this study is that in spite of the potential for differences, the demographic characteristics of a population like that of Tlajinga 33 from Teotihuacan will reveal that the New World city is similar to other known preindustrial cities. Such a finding would be important, because it would support a further hypothesis that there is a *cross-culturally valid preindustrial urban demographic pattern*. The hypothesis could then be used to study the ecological, energetic, and social aspects of urbanism within the framework of cultural evolution. The general demographic urban pattern would emerge, because the aggregation of large and dense populations under preindustrial conditions of sanitation and supported by preindustrial economies dependent largely on human labor are likely to result in predictable demographic characteristics. Whether preindustrial cities have similar demographic characteristics is a question with profound implications for our understanding of the ways population processes work in the maintenance and success of an urban society. Although demography is also obviously very important to the understanding of how the concentration of people into one center would have evolved and an urban society would have been created, that question cannot be addressed here. Unfortunately, the data are not available. However, the role that population issues play in the collapse of an urban center is addressed. In sum, this study can look at only one aspect of the relation of population and cultural evolution, *the maintenance and fall of a New World urban center*.

To begin our investigation of the hypothesis that Teotihuacan demographically resembles other preindustrial cities, Chapter 2 continues the background discussion with a profile of what is known demographically about preindustrial cities and a description of Teotihuacan as an urban center. The differences in the Old World and New World disease loads are also discussed. In Chapter 3 the paleodemographic case study begins with a discussion of the excavation and archaeological context of the skeletal population in the Tlajinga 33 compound. Chapter 4 introduces the individuals who were in relatively undisturbed burial contexts and presents a preliminary analysis of the mortuary patterns and the status structure of the compound. Chapters 5 and 6 examine the general demographic characteristics of the complete Tlajinga 33 skeletal population and, by the use of recent paleodemographic methods, analyzes and compares the demographic profile of the population with other skeletal populations.

Chapter 7 investigates the paleopathological evidence for stress and morbidity. On the basis of just skeletal remains, it is often difficult to diagnose the exact cause of lesions and pathoses on bone (Ortner and Putschar 1981). Nevertheless, through the use of nonspecific indicators of stress preserved in skeletal remains (Huss-Ashmore et al. 1982) that are integrated into a model of biocultural stress (Goodman et al. 1988), it is possible to find age-specific patterns of the occurrence of stress in the population and to relate these patterns to the lifestyle of the population, even though the actual disease processes involved could not be identified. The intention in Chapter 7 is to relate the stress indicators on bone to the characteristics of the demographic profile identified in Chapter 6 and to show how these indicators support certain age-specific mortality patterns. When both demographic information and health indications are considered, it will be possible to understand what life was like in ancient Teotihuacan and how the urban center would have collapsed. This understanding is crucial if one is to know how viable Teotihuacan was as an adaptive system. These issues are addressed in Chapter 8, where the paleodemographic study is evaluated in terms of the hypothesis. The implications of the demographic profile in relation to the known data from European preindustrial cities are also discussed. The Tlajinga 33 study adds unique and important information to anthropological knowledge of the city, no matter whether Teotihuacan resembles other preindustrial cities. The significance of the Tlajinga 33 results for the study of the urban center of Teotihuacan and the ways they enhance archaeological understanding of the demography of preindustrial cities and of the adaptive features of an urban system are discussed in the conclusions of the study.

Paleodemography is still refining its methodology and adding to its body of data. This study is intended to add to *both* the methodology and the corpus of paleodemographic knowledge and, in doing so, to add important new data regarding the cultural processes of an early urban center in the New World. The study will open up a new perspective on the study of urban processes in the New World.

The study shows that despite the different history, the lack of communication with the Old World, and a dearth of the epidemic diseases that characterize the Old World urban centers, Teotihuacan has demographic characteristics that resemble those of Old World preindustrial cities. This finding supports the existence of a *general preindustrial urban demographic profile,* which has cross-cultural validity irrespective of time or place. Such a conclusion could not have been made before this study.

Teotihuacan and the Demography of Preindustrial Cities

THE ARCHAEOLOGICAL SITE of Teotihuacan in the northeastern Valley of Mexico and near Mexico City has long been considered one of the most impressive prehistoric sites in the world (see Figure 2-1). A large-scale project to study Teotihuacan and the Teotihuacan Valley, using primarily surface survey, was initiated in the 1960s. Its results are among the best known and most comprehensive archaeological studies ever undertaken (e.g., Millon et al. 1973; Sanders et al. 1979).

Since completion of the work of the Teotihuacan Mapping Project, with Dr. René Millon as its director, and publication of the map of the site (Millon et al. 1973), the truly urban nature of Teotihuacan is no longer questioned, no matter what definition of a city is used (see Fox 1977). What is impressive about Teotihuacan is its size, the density of its population, and the complexity of its urban organization. It is clear from the Teotihuacan map that the site is highly organized, as there were regular grids of streets and structures orthogonally oriented along a uniform axis (see Figure 2-2). The urban characteristics have been discussed by Millon in several articles (1973, 1976, 1981), which form the basis for the discussion that follows.

The city (c. 150 B.C.–A.D. 750) covered 20 square kilometers (8 square miles) at its height and had a population of at least 125,000 and probably 200,000 (Millon 1973). At the size of 125,000, it was at least the sixth-largest city in the world at A.D. 722, after Constantinople, Changan, Loyang, Ctesiphon, and Alexandria (Chandler and Fox 1974: 268).

Teotihuacan is further distinguished by its position as the earliest urban center in Mesoamerica. Characterized by quick growth, it reached

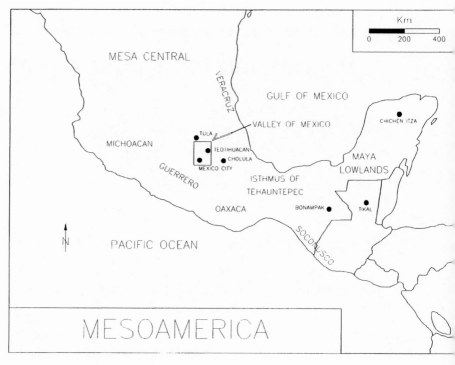

Figure 2-1. Mexico, Showing Location of Teotihuacan

its largest areal extent early in its history and then maintained a stable size for approximately 500 years (Cowgill 1979).

Teotihuacan's urban nature is revealed by the evidence of a stratified society and a state-level sociopolitical organization. The immense size and plan of the public buildings at the site, like the Pyramids of the Sun and Moon (names given to the structures by the later Aztecs), the broad central avenue of the "Street of the Dead" between them, and the large complex of platforms and pyramids called the Ciudadela, have long been considered evidence of the great abilities and power of the Teotihuacan rulers, who controlled enough labor to carry out the construction. However, as Millon (1981) has pointed out, in spite of the power wielded by the rulers, they are nowhere obviously depicted in the iconography of Teotihuacan. It may be that virtual invisibility of these rulers was part of the official policy to emphasize the difference between ruler and ruled.

Archaeologically, defining the rulers' residence or palace has not been straightforward. Millon (1973) identified the large Ciudadela complex as the probable palace of the ruler. Although this conclusion may be true for earlier phases, more recent work indicates that the palace may have had one or more locations in the central district of the city during its history (Cowgill 1983).

Although the highest strata are somewhat ill defined in the Teotihuacan hierarchy, at least six status levels have been identified for the overall city on the basis of differences in residential construction (Millon 1976). The topmost level would include the ruler and other powerful individuals. The next level would also be of quite high status and probably consists of the religious and administrative hierarchy (Cowgill et al. 1984). Millon sees evidence for three intermediate levels exemplified by several of the excavated residential compounds, and a sixth, lowest level represented by two other excavated compounds. Work has been done to refine status definitions, although the high-status distinctions have been stressed (Cowgill et al. 1984). Millon (1973) speculated that people of the lowest status lived in apartment compounds or insubstantial structures. Investigation of surface artifacts revealed that some insubstantial structures were residences but many were outbuildings, and both types were found everywhere in the city (Cowgill et al. 1984). The lower class lived in both apartment compounds and insubstantial structures intermixed in neighborhoods, and it is possible that this status level will be further subdivided in the future. Almost all excavation at Teotihuacan has been around the religious and economically central buildings; the upper and higher intermediate strata are much better known than the lower. Fortunately, more recent work has investigated more modest structures. Not enough will be known about the organization of Teotihuacan until more is known about the majority of the population that would have occupied the lower strata of the city.

What is known about lower-status individuals comes from the study of the economic organization of Teotihuacan. Here, too, Teotihuacan exhibits the urban characteristics of a complex, differentiated economy with evidence of occupational specialization. Millon (1981: 219–220) has listed the five main components of the site's economic base, a base that clearly reveals a state-level type of planning and scope. The components are: (1) the control and management of its local agricultural resources, which probably included large-scale relocation of food producers; (2) the control and exploitation of all the Valley of Mexico and areas to the east and south of the valley; (3) the monopolization of the mining, manufacture, and distribution of obsidian, an important lithic raw material in pre-Columbian Mesoamerica; (4) the control of the distribution of various other artifacts, like Thin Orange ceramics; and (5) the development of Teotihuacan as a religious and cultural center.

Teotihuacan seems to have accomplished much of its economic im-

LEGEND

EXCAVATED ROOM COMPLEX OR OTHER STRUCTURE	
UNEXCAVATED ROOM COMPLEX	
POSSIBLE ROOM COMPLEX	
RM CMPL.-SOME LIMITS UNCLEAR	
TEMPLE PLATFORM	
SINGLE STAGE PLATFORM	
INSUBSTANTIAL STRUCTURES	
MAJOR WALL	
WATER COURSE	
PROBABLE OLD WATER COURSE	
METERS ABOVE MEAN SEA LEVEL	2275
MAPPING PROJECT EXCAVATION	

KEY

PYRAMID OF THE MOON	1	PLAZA ONE	14
PYRAMID OF THE SUN	2	HOUSE OF THE EAGLES	15
CIUDADELA	3	"OLD CITY"	16
TEMPLE OF QUETZALCOATL	4	OAXACA BARRIO	17
"STREET OF THE DEAD"	5	ATETELCO	18
GREAT COMPOUND	6	LA VENTILLA A	19
WEST AVENUE	7	LA VENTILLA B	20
EAST AVENUE	8	LA VENTILLA C	21
"MERCHANTS' BARRIO"	9	TEOPANCAXCO	22
TLAMIMILOLPA	10	RIO SAN LORENZO	23
XOLALPAN	11	RIO SAN JUAN	24
TEPANTITLA	12	RESERVOIRS 25,26,27,51	
MAGUEY PRIEST MURALS	13	ACUMULCO	52

GRID IS ORIENTED CA 15°25' EAST OF ASTRONOMIC NORTH.

SUN PYRAMID
19°4.1'30" N. LAT.
98°50'30" W. LONG.

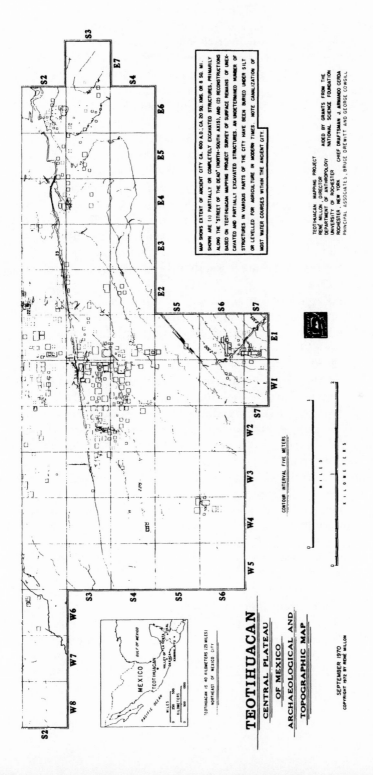

Figure 2-2. Ancient Teotihuacan by the Teotihuacan Mapping Project (from *Urbanization at Teotihuacan, Mexico, vol.* 1 ©1973 by René Millon)

pact by concentrating most of the population of the Valley of Mexico within its borders (see Sanders et al. 1979: 105–129), perhaps by forced resettlement. Teotihuacan was overwhelmingly dominant in the settlement pattern, being much larger than any other settlement in the valley. The process of this great centralization of population began very early in the city's history; by approximately 100 B.C.–A.D. 100, 80%–90% of the population of the Valley of Mexico was at Teotihuacan (Sanders et al. 1979: 107). After some time there was a recolonization of the Valley of Mexico, but Teotihuacan always remained the dominant center of its immediate hinterland. In the fourth century A.D. the process of expansion continued as the city had begun to influence areas outside the Valley of Mexico (Hirth and Swezey 1976; Hirth 1978). In these outer areas Teotihuacan seemed to have organized settlement and ties for the provisioning of articles needed by Teotihuacan and probably also to provide markets for its own production. Although Teotihuacan prestige and influence were felt in more distant areas, like the Mayan lowlands, there is no real evidence that Teotihuacan exerted direct control in the distant areas (Sanders 1974).

Given the large-scale organization of the regional economy, Teotihuacan also had a complex internal structure of occupational specialization. The Teotihuacan Mapping Project found evidence of a variety of craft workshops. The majority of them were involved in the use or production of obsidian tools, apparently the leading industry of the city (Spence 1981; Clark 1986). Teotihuacan seems to have controlled the obsidian from the main source of Cerro de Navajas, which is only 50 km to the northeast, and distributed the raw material to its workshops. Some obsidian workshops were obviously local ones, providing commodities for their neighborhoods, but others were in clusters located near important public buildings, like the Pyramid of the Moon and the Ciudadela. These clustered workshops were probably under state control and produced mostly for export (Spence 1981). Besides obsidian, the survey also identified ceramic, figurine, shell, slate, ground stone, and lapidary workshops. In addition, there were probably some crafts that left no clear remains, such as featherworking or hide tanning, plus there were craft specialists who provided services, such as masons and carpenters (Millon 1973).

Two important questions about the nature of Teotihuacan society is how much of the population was involved with craft and service activity, and was it full- or part-time? Cities are usually filled with nonagriculturalists who are dependent on rural areas for food. The estimation is that about one-third of the inhabitants of Teotihuacan were involved with a craft specialty (Millon 1976), although whether all were full time cannot be determined from surface survey information. It is generally assumed that most of the craft specialists were full time, because the other two-thirds of the residents were farmers or cultivators, who farmed the large areas of nearby agricultural land that fed the city, and which otherwise have little evidence of occupation (Millon 1976, 1981). Thus, nonagricultural workers probably did not form the dominant part of this urban population, unlike many other known preindustrial cities. This characteristic appears to be distinctive of Teotihuacan and related to the extreme centralization of population present at the city (Sanders and Webster 1988). The massing of farmers and nonagricultural specialists in one center undoubtedly strengthened the control of Teotihuacan's rulers (Millon 1976).

Because of the economic heterogeneity of the residents, the hub of the Teotihuacan economy must have been the market, where foodstuffs and crafts were exchanged. If estimates are correct, one-third of the residents would have been dependent on the market for most of their food, and the farmers in turn would have been dependent on it for nonagricultural products. The Teotihuacan Mapping Project identified the Great Compound, a large plaza with platforms in the center of the city opposite the Ciudadela, as the probable location of the main market (Millon 1973).

Besides the local exchange that went on for daily living, Teotihuacan was also involved in long-distance trade for foreign goods and raw materials. A variety of materials found in the residences came from some distance. There were probably long-distance merchants of some kind, but their relation to the state or the amount of autonomy they enjoyed is presently unclear. Popular Teotihuacan imports included mica, cinnabar, hematite, jadeite, slate, and marine shell. Marine shell was an especially common item and has been found both as ornaments and ritual objects. It seems that enormous quantities of shells were imported from both the Gulf and Pacific coasts, and it is reasonable to assume that the city controlled this trade (Starbuck 1975). The Teotihuacan central market was most likely a place with a variety of goods from both local and long-distance places, fairly similar to the Aztec markets recorded by the Spanish at Conquest.

The Teotihuacan population lived in a distinctive type of residential structure well suited to urban living. The Teotihuacan map is dominated by large rectangular structures that are called apartment compounds (Millon et al. 1973). These structures were the main residential units and consisted of large, self-contained buildings with complex interior plans of rooms, patios, platforms, and passageways. Usually, a compound was subdivided into units that appear to be suites of rooms with a small patio, an apartment, to house a family. Each compound also seemed to have had at least one temple in a prominent courtyard for ritual activities. Each excavated compound has had a different plan, so the buildings were apparently tailored for their residents. Compounds were occupied for several hundred years and rebuilt several times. The size varied, but 60 m on a side was common, and a building this size would have housed 60–100 people (Millon 1976).

The compound unit comprising several households is an efficient way to house a large population in an urban setting. It would also have provided a good way to organize the population at a local level. It was apparently the unit of craft specialization, and it performed ritual functions as well. Compounds were not constructed until Tlamimilolpa times, c. A.D. 200 (Millon 1973), after the city was already established and had almost reached its stable size. The form disappeared with the fall of the city. Thus, the apartment compound was a distinctive residential plan for the city of Teotihuacan.

The organizational level above the compound seemed to be the *barrio* or neighborhood (Millon 1981). Craft workshops seemed to cluster into areas that might be defined as neighborhoods. Also, early in the study, an ethnic *barrio* of people from Oaxaca was identified, and it may have been a common pattern to have outsiders moving into the city and into their own ethnically defined neighborhoods (Millon 1973). Such neighborhoods defined by ethnicity and occupation are typical of many preindustrial cities (Sjoberg 1960), and their presence in Teotihuacan is further evidence of its urban character. Further investigation, using multivariate techniques, of the survey information from the Teotihuacan Mapping Project has identified some possible neighborhoods within the city, although the heterogeneous status, occupational, and artifactual remains of many possible neighborhoods indicates the complexity of the internal organization of Teotihuacan (Altschul 1987; Cowgill et al. 1984).

Teotihuacan was, therefore, a large, complex settlement having clearly urban characteristics in its plan, density, and economic organization and offering ample evidence of a powerful central organization. Its growth and development were quite rapid and dramatic, as similarly, was its fall around A.D. 750 (Cowgill 1979; Millon 1981). The center of Teotihuacan was burned, probably as a kind of ritual desanctification. Whether the destruction was by insiders or invaders is not clear. The destruction was probably relatively bloodless, and many of the apartment compounds were apparently still occupied for some time. There are no archaeologically detectable indications that the city was obviously declining or had special problems when it was burned (Millon 1981). Interestingly, the fall appears to have been so rapid and sudden that the investigators have assumed that the deterioration of the effective power of the Teotihuacan polity was also fairly rapid (Millon 1981), although the processes of economic and social deterioration had probably been brewing for some time. After A.D. 750 Teotihuacan remained a large settlement until Conquest, but much reduced in scale compared with its florescence. The ritual center around the pyramids and Ciudadela was never occupied again.

This brief description has been able to touch only on a few high points about the ever-increasing knowledge coming out of Teotihuacan about this ancient and pioneering urban society of Mesoamerica. However, there are several interesting aspects of this city yet to be explored in any detail. These include its demographic characteristics and the related questions of its nutritional and health conditions. These subjects have not been studied for any prehistoric New World city, but they are necessary to the understanding of the Teotihuacan state. Understanding the demography will help researchers evaluate how well Teotihuacan adapted to its environment and just how successfully it supported its large, dense population.

Teotihuacan was an urban center in an arid highland basin in the New World. It presents a very important subject for demographic analysis because of its pioneering urban status; its large, dense population in a pre-Columbian and therefore preindustrial society; and its exclusive reliance on human labor, in lieu of any domesticated draft or transportation animal. Although there have been paleodemographic studies of North American pre-Columbian populations (e.g., Ubelaker 1974; Asch 1976; Blakely 1977; Lovejoy et al. 1977), not much has been done for Mesoamerica. Given the size and density of Teotihuacan's population, it would be expected to differ demographically from North American skeletal populations that represent smaller, less dense groups, *if* size and density have demographic effects.

The Demography of Preindustrial Cities

The general features of preindustrial urban demography in Europe have become virtually axiomatic in historical inquiry and seem to support the idea that size and density can have dramatic demographic effects. In a general summary of background characteristics of preindustrial populations, Wrigley (1969: 96–97) starts with the differentiation of town from country. His point is that before the Industrial Revolution and concomitant advances in medicine and public health, life expectancy was shorter and mortality higher in cities than in rural areas. The reasons fall into two general categories: (1) where public hygiene and sanitation are not good, dense populations create conditions where diseases flourish and take a high toll of life; and (2) city dwellers are often completely dependent on grain from the countryside, which can cause serious problems when harvests fail and food is scarce. The problems also seem to escalate as towns or cities increased in size. Epidemics that had high death rates, like the plague in Britain during the seventeenth century, occurred mostly in the large towns and hardly affected the rural areas at all (Wrigley 1969: 96).

These demographic characteristics have been summarized as the "Law of Natural Urban Decrease" (de Vries 1984: 179), because the high mortality meant that urban populations could not replace themselves and were dependent on migration from rural areas not only for growth but just to sustain themselves (Wrigley 1969; Davis 1973). As evidenced by the 1662 treatise *Natural and Political Observations and Conclusions Made upon the Bills of Mortality* by John Graunt, the fact that burials outnumbered christenings was evident to the seventeenth-century London resident. The effects of this natural urban decrease would be felt in the countryside and in a nation's population. The cities provide a significant proportion of the national deaths, 14.8% for Amsterdam c. 1800, even though the city totaled only 11.6% of the entire Dutch population (de Vries 1984: 194). The rural areas then must provide the migrants to sustain the population of cities. Thus, during the seventeenth century, London was probably yearly absorbing half the natural increase of the population of England as migrants to make up the intrinsic urban shortfall and fuel the city's growth (Finlay 1981). The impact was felt in every corner of the realm, as one-sixth of all surviving English births were destined to become Londoners (Wrigley 1969: 97). Cities required a rural hinterland that produced not only a surplus of food to feed urban dwellers but, more importantly, a surplus of children to migrate to cities (McNeill 1976). The dynamics of cities, then, cannot be understood in isolation from their supporting rural areas.

The main reason cities were unable to maintain their population intrinsically was that the disease burden was just too great (McNeill 1976: 55–58). In populations with dense concentrations of people, communicable diseases, especially infections like measles or respiratory viruses, were easily transmitted from individual to individual. In addition, cities would have had a strong circulation of diseases maintained and transmitted through both bacterially and parasitized contaminated water supplies and vermin, both resulting from poor and limited sanitation systems, which would continually infect and then reinfect portions of the population. Cities were also vulnerable to local crop failures, which could cause famine and disruptions of supplies from long-distance sources. All these would be sources of morbidity likely to cause mortality beyond what fertility could replace. These conditions would have been present until the Industrial Revolution created enough wealth, so that public sanitation and dietary nutrition was improved, and medical knowledge advanced enough to deal with the disease burden. It is probable that only in the early twentieth century were the adverse conditions sufficiently mitigated to allow cities to become demographically self-sufficient and maintain their population size through intrinsic growth (Davis 1973).

Although the "Law of Natural Urban Decrease" seems to be self-evident, quantitative data measuring the demographic parameters of preindustrial urban mortality and the magnitude of population shortfall are lacking (de Vries 1984). This is due partly to the large number of records needed to study an urban center and partly because the mobility and immigration of many urban residents make them difficult to trace and control through demographic documents, such as birth and death registers. However, recent historical demographic work has provided quantitative information to support the urban-decrease model.

Perhaps the most detailed information available is for preindustrial London, based on a recent study by Roger Finlay (1981). The main source used was the record of baptisms, marriages, and deaths noted in parish registers from A.D. 1580 to 1650. Finlay used the technique of family reconstitution on the parish entries to try to obtain accurate mortality and fertility rates, so as to investigate the relationship between them in this preindustrial city. He wanted to verify that the death rate was actually higher than the birth rate in London, and to find out how high the death rate really was.

To estimate the normal underlying level of mortality undistorted by the effects of epidemics, Finlay concentrated mortality calculations on measuring life expectancy at birth and during childhood in nonplague years. Adult measures were not estimated, because the pervasive effects of migration make it likely that adults will die in but not be born in a parish. Adult records, therefore, tend often to be incomplete, whereas those of children tend to be complete within a parish. Finlay's calculations were based on infant and child deaths in four parishes of the same size, two defined as wealthy and two, poor. The survivorship estimates, the proportions surviving to a given age, and the death rate per 1,000 individuals of a given age are presented in Table 2-1.

Fitting the mortality calculations to model life tables, Finlay estimated the life expectancy at birth, which is the average number of years

TABLE 2-1
Mortality Calculations for Four London
Parishes (per 1,000 individuals), A.D. 1580–1650

	Age	Survivors	Death Rate	Life Expectancy at Birth
Wealthy				
St. Peter	0	1,000	200	34–36
Cornhill	1	800	148	
	5	682	46	
	10	651	31	
	15	631		
St. Michael	0	1,000	203	29–31
Cornhill	1	797	156	
	5	673	83	
	10	617	34	
	15	596		
Poor				
St. Mary	0	1,000	265	21
Somerset	1	735	246	
	5	554	93	
	10	502	69	
	15	467		
All Hallows	0	1,000	242	24–26
London Wall	1	758	208	
	5	600	104	
	10	538	56	
	15	508		

Source: Adapted from Finlay 1981: Tables 5.7 and 5.15.

lived by an individual born alive into a population. Immediately evident is the loss of 20%–25% of the individuals in the first year and the generally short life expectancies compared with modern populations.

All calculations for the London parishes were compared with those of English villages during the same time. Here, infant death rates were

12%–15% with life expectancy at birth 41–46 years (Finlay 1981: 91–92). A further comparison was that whereas 75% of all individuals born survived to their fifteenth year in the villages, the London figures (Table 2-1) were considerably less, only 47%–63%. Comparing the baptisms and burials in ten London parishes, Finlay found there were on average 0.87 baptisms per burial in London (1981: 59). The gap generally found between burials and baptisms indicates that the resident London population was declining. Finlay's conclusion was that mortality was considerably higher in London than elsewhere in England, and that the growth London experienced in the seventeenth century could have been maintained only by migration.

Amsterdam in the eighteenth century reveals a similar pattern: a baptism-burial gap that yields an estimated rate of natural decrease of 5 per 1,000 per year (de Vries 1984: 193). Mortality, especially of children, appears to have been the most likely cause. Comparing the age-specific death rates for Amsterdam from 1777 to 1797 with a model life table, de Vries found that the rates for infants and children conform to a life expectancy at birth of 23.5 years, with a measured death rate in the first year of 29% (de Vries 1984: 359). After age 10 mortality ameliorates, an indication that it is the high mortality of infants and children, not that of adults, that causes urban deaths to outpace the fertility of the urban residents (de Vries 1984: 193). The life expectancy and infant mortality estimates for Amsterdam are similar to those discussed above for London.

A third example is Geneva. Using both family-reconstitution techniques and aggregation measures from a death register, Perrenoud (1975, 1978, 1982) estimated death rates from the seventeenth to early nineteenth century. The overall pattern is one of decreasing mortality through time, but during the seventeenth century the figures are similar to those for London: life expectancy at birth was 24 to 27.6 years with infant mortality rates of 25%–35% (Perrenoud 1978: 219–223). The net reproduction rate at the end of the seventeenth century was 0.83, where replacement would be equal to 1.0 (Perrenoud 1982), very reminiscent of London's baptism shortfall. Here, too, the city was not able to reproduce itself but was declining internally.

However, urban populations are characterized by economic and social heterogeneity. Perrenoud (1975) was able to study Genevan mortality by social class (defined by occupation) and found a great difference in infant and child mortality and life expectancy between rich and poor. For example, life expectancy at birth averaged 35.9 years for the upper class but only 18.3 years, almost one-half that of the upper class, for the lowest class from 1625 to 1684 (Perrenoud 1975: 236). Finlay (1981: 83–110) found a similar pattern for London: the differences between wealthy and poor parishes translate into at least 5 and possibly to 15 more years' life expectancy at birth (see Table 2-1). Infant and child mortality rates are 20% the first year, with 60%–63% of the children ever born surviving to age 15 for wealthy parishes, and 24%–26% losses the first year and 47%–51% surviving childhood in the poorer. Furthermore, the ratio of baptisms to burials was around 1.0 for wealthy parishes but only about 0.70 for many poor ones (Finlay 1981: Table 3.3).

Finlay also investigated why St. Mary Somerset had lower life expectancy than Allhallows London Wall, even though both parishes were very poor. Further study revealed that riverside parishes had higher infant mortality rates than inland parishes, regardless of the wealth of the parish (1981: 103). His hypothesis was that the problem might have been due to differences in quality of the water supply, because there is evidence that the riverside parishes drew their water directly from the Thames, which may have been a more polluted water source than the wells often used by more inland parishes. Thus, there is some evidence that London mortality may have varied for more reasons than just socioeconomic wealth and was probably affected by problems with public sanitation.

Imperial Rome, the urban center of the Roman Empire (A.D. 0–400), is an interesting case study, as it exemplifies an ancient city, perhaps likely to be more similar to Teotihuacan than the postmedieval cases. We have historical information about Rome that can be used for demographic inferences, not only for the city but for some of the cities in the empire's provinces as well. Here, information has been compiled from thousands of epitaphs, mostly done by researchers in the past hundred years (e.g., Beloch 1886; MacDonnell 1913). Other explicitly demographic information was generally not collected (Russell 1985). Several attempts have been made to calculate demographic measures from these data (Russell 1958; Durand 1960).

The Roman epitaph data do pose problems as a demographic source. They probably underestimate deaths of infants, because often no epitaph would be constructed for individuals who did not live long, and they tend to round people's ages at death into numbers like 25 and 40, rather than 23 or 38; the result is a lumping or clustering in some ages and the absence of others. The latter is a common problem of censuses in anthropological populations as well, where people do not really know how old they are (e.g., Fix 1977). In the Roman epitaphs there is apparently the further problem of even greater rounding off of older adult ages to a convenient number like 60, or if very old, of ages like 90 or 100 (Russell 1958). Also, the mortality of women age 15 to 40 seems to have been abnormally high. Thus, the distributions of ages at death are biased by underreporting of infants and young children, older-age exaggeration, and overestimation of deaths of young women (Durand 1960). Some researchers have tried to remedy these shortcomings by using models based on preindustrial populations measured in the twentieth century, such as India (Russell 1958), or by fitting only the adult males 15–42 to the United Nations series of model life tables, as they are likely to be the least biased sector of the population (Durand 1960).

Comparisons of demographic measures estimated for Rome and some of its provinces by Russell (1958) are given in Table 2-2. These measures are based on the assumption of a stationary population, that is, it was not growing or declining, a condition that has not been substantiated by other information. Regardless of this shortcoming, for general demographic observations it is readily apparent how much lower life expectancies and how much higher the yearly death rate in Rome, and even its surrounding province of Latium, were in comparison to more distant provinces. *The low expectancies at birth in Rome and Latium occurred even with underrepresentation of infant mortality.* Russell notes the generally high level of infant mortality in Roman times, revealed by the drastic improvement in life expectancy between birth and one year, especially in the city. Russell concludes that Rome was the unhealthiest location in the empire on the basis of mortality rates of 65%–75% for young men and women, and child mortality losses of 17%–26% (Russell 1958: 25). Durand's study, based mostly on urban groups of the western part of the empire, also yields estimates of generally high mortality, such that average life expectancy at birth was 15–25 years, with losses in the first year about 30%–40% (1960: 371–372).

The mortality estimates for Rome and other Roman Empire urban populations are higher than for the postmedieval European cities, although revealing a similar trend of very high mortality, especially for infants, and correspondingly low life expectancies. In fact, the measurement of mortality from the epitaph inscriptions is higher than any seen in modern or historically known populations. This result may indicate either the difference between ancient and modern demographic patterns (Durand 1960) or the great deficiencies of the data (Hopkins 1967). It is probable that the age-at-death distribution of epitaphs tells more about the cultural practices of commemoration than about the actual age structure of death in Rome (Hopkins 1967). Epitaphs reflect grieving survivors rather than demography, and young widowers and the parents of young children were probably more likely to erect epitaphs than other age groups (Hopkins 1967). Thus, one cannot really estimate Roman urban mortality accurately enough to conclude that it is higher than that of London or Amsterdam. Sadly, there is not the same demographic infor-

TABLE 2-2
Life Expectancies of the City
of Rome and Roman Provinces

	Life Expectancy at:			
Population	Birth	1 yr.	15 yrs.	30yrs.
Rome, males	15.3	22.5	20.8	20.0
Rome, females	16.3	21.3	15.5	15.2
Latium	14.5	21.2	19.3	20.7
Cisalpine Gaul	20.7	26.0	20.1	20.5
Gaul, Narbonne	23.0	27.4	21.1	20.5
Amelia, Umbria, Etruria	28.4	32.2	24.9	20.8
Asia, Greece Illyricum	29.2	33.1	25.3	19.6
Africa, males	42.9	47.7	39.8	33.0

Source: Russell 1958: 25–29

mation for Rome as for those cities. In general, the pattern seems to be one of high mortality and short life expectancy, but quantitative data are lacking.

However, on the basis of the postmedieval cities, it appears that pre-industrial urban demography was characterized by high mortality, especially of infants and children, and a declining population that was kept growing by migrants from rural areas. In addition, there were internal differences of wealth and sanitation that affected demographic rates. In fact, wealthier segments of the population were replacing themselves, although perhaps barely, while the very high mortality of the poor seems to be the most important factor in causing a declining urban population (Finlay 1981; Perrenoud 1982). Preindustrial cities on the whole would be expected to show adverse patterns of mortality and life expectancy because of the effects of density, disease, and poor sanitation. These problems overburden the urban fertility potential to replace the population.

The Demographic Characteristics of the New World

In contrast to the Old World pattern, the pre-Columbian Americas are considered to have been relatively free of diseases (McNeill 1976).

Long isolated from the Old World, the New World was also protected by the cold screen of the Bering Strait migration route, which prevented both the transfer and subsequent invasion of many microbes (Stewart 1960). This protection was revealed when European contact transferred many diseases, including smallpox and measles, that caused severe epidemics among the Native Americans, who apparently had no previous immunity to any of these (Newman 1977). In return, syphilis seems to have been the only New World disease transferred to the Old World (Baker and Armelagos 1988).

These facts have led to an interest in what kind of diseases that could create similar demographic impacts were present before contact. Studies from the paleopathology of human bones, mummies from the Andean area, and some ethnohistorical sources indicate that gastrointestinal and respiratory infections, various tropical fevers (including probably yellow fever), parasites, nonvenereal syphilis, tuberculosis, strep and staph bacteria, salmonella, and other food-poisoning agents were present and endemic among Native Americans (Cook 1946; Newman 1977). Aztec accounts of epidemic death because of famine occur, and associated with famine were respiratory infections, nutritional deficiencies, skin rashes, and the like—those that might be expected because of the weakened state of the people (Cook 1946). Although these are not inconsequential diseases, Mesoamerica does seem to lack the epidemic "crowd-type" infections (Newman 1977), and there is no evidence of the great variety of diseases typical of the Old World.

Because the pre-Columbian New World was free from many epidemic-type diseases that occurred in dense populations of the Old World, it has been suggested by one researcher, Dobyns (1983: 42), that pre-Columbian populations would then have grown to the limits of the food supply. Following this line of reasoning, one might conclude that the disease environment, in general, had little dampening effect on the growth and increasing density of pre-Columbian populations.

The picture painted by McNeill (1976: 176–180) is of populations in the New World that are relatively free of infectious disease and lacking the strong epidemic patterns found in many dense population concentrations in the Old World. Although Mexico and Peru did have populous settlements (like Teotihuacan) with sufficient density to sustain infections endemically, they just did not suffer from the heavy disease burdens characteristic of cities in the Old World. McNeill believes that the reason few infections seem to have become established is that the New World lacked the disease-variant reservoirs of domestic animal herds, which seem to have been important in the etiology of diseases in the Old World. The few domesticated animals of Mesoamerica, principally turkey and dog,

may make this statement generally true for Mesoamerica and Teotihuacan, but the statement certainly would not seem to hold for Peru,
where the importance of camelids and guinea pigs in daily life could
have provided suitable vectors for disease. Yet, there is no more evidence for disease there than in Mesoamerica. Therefore, though many
researchers agree on the distinctive pre-Columbian epidemiological environment of the New World, it is probably more the result of isolation
and the Bering cold screen than just the lack of domesticated animals.

Thus, perhaps it would seem reasonable to expect that New World
pre-Columbian cities differed somewhat in their demographic characteristics from their preindustrial counterparts in the Old World. A reasonable expectation is that mortality would not be particularly elevated
among the dense population of a city like Teotihuacan. One benefit of a
demographic study of Teotihuacan is that it might indicate how similar a
New World city is to Old World counterparts in demographic characteristics. If different, preindustrial cities are not a uniform demographic
type, but instead vary on the basis of their overall disease load. Dense
concentrations of population could have differing health effects, depending on geography and history. However, as will be demonstrated, such
difference is not the case.

CHAPTER 3

The Tlajinga 33
Apartment Compound

The Background of the Project

THE EARLY URBAN CENTER of Teotihuacan was characterized by the distinctive residential unit called the apartment compound. These compounds are large structures with complex plans of rooms, patios, and central courtyards that could have housed populations up to 100 people (Millon 1976), perhaps organized into 15–20 families. These are intriguing structures, but how they functioned as residences and what their domestic and craft functions were are poorly known.

Several excavations of Teotihuacan compounds have been conducted in the past. These include the compounds named Xolalpan (Linné 1934), Tlamimilolpa (Linné 1942), Zacuala Palace (Séjourné 1959), Tetitla (Séjourné 1966), and La Ventilla B (Vidarte 1964). These excavations were fairly extensive, and in most cases the entire compound was exposed to the uppermost preserved structure. However, these excavations did not attempt to recover artifacts and organic remains from a wide range of contexts, such as general fill, middens, features, and earthen floors. Most excavations also did not document shifts in architecture through time by investigating all phases present at the site.

The Teotihuacan Mapping Project systematically excavated a number of test pits in various compounds. The results indicated that an extensive range of artifactual and organic remains could be recovered by the use of screening and flotation (Millon 1973; Starbuck 1975). Tests also demonstrated that apartment compounds had complex, elaborate stratigraphy with numerous superimposed floors of both earth and "Teotihuacan concrete," an aggregate of crushed volcanic stone and mud mortar (Millon

1973: 27). However, these tests were small and could hardly be expected to reveal much about an entire compound.

The Tlajinga area is a distinctive concentration of mounds on the southern edge of the ancient city, just south of the Barranca San Lorenzo, one of the intermittent streambeds within the bounds of the city. It has been identified as a ceramic craftworking *barrio* (neighborhood) in the latter part of the city's history, the Late Xolalpan phase (Altschul 1987; Krotser and Rattray 1980; Krotser 1987). Its product was the San Martin Orange ware found throughout the city. The Tlajinga ceramic workshops seem to have specialized in mass production of two large forms: craters, large and deep bowls for cooking, and amphoras, tall bottles with handles (Krotser 1987). Thus, the excavation of a Tlajinga compound promised the opportunity to investigate ceramic production in Teotihuacan. It was also thought that perhaps residents of Tlajinga may have been farmers before the Late Xolalpan and perhaps were part-time farmers during the Late Xolalpan. If so, the excavation of a Tlajinga compound could provide insight into the farmers of Teotihuacan, who were thought to compose the majority of the population (Millon 1976). As it turned out, the excavated area of the compound does not seem ever to have been occupied by farmers and was always the residence of full-time craft specialists.

The Excavation Strategy

The apartment compound chosen for excavation was site 33 in grid square S3W1 on the Teotihuacan map in the Tlajinga area (Millon et al. 1973) (see Figure 2-1 for the location of the grid square within the city). The site has been named Tlajinga 33 for convenient reference, although it is not the only site numbered 33 by the Teotihuacan Mapping Project in the Tlajinga area. Figure 3-1 shows the location of the site in the grid square. Initial surface inspection revealed ubiquitous ceramic remains, no exposed architecture, and very low density of architectural rubble, particularly when compared with other nearby sites.

During a field season from September to December of 1980, shorter than originally planned, an area of approximately 1,250 square meters was excavated, but, unfortunately, it was not possible to excavate the compound completely. On the basis of the excavation, the compound is estimated to have had a maximal area of 2,280 square meters. Thus, 55% of the possible area had been opened. Most of the area opened was excavated to sterile soil or to the *tepetate* (the local name for the volcanic ash bedrock), but about 20% was not. Thus, only an estimated 44% of the compound was completely excavated.

It is felt that most of the site area was adequately sampled. Although not all outer boundaries of the structure were definitely located, portions of the outer compound wall, complete with entrances, were found in the western, southern, and northern areas. Although these walls do not have the usual *talud* form (that is, with sloping sides) found in outer walls in other excavated Teotihuacan apartment compounds, these Tlajinga 33 walls are generally more carefully constructed and slightly more massive than the interior walls.

The eastern area is the only one that may have been inadequately sampled. Only one trench 15 m long was excavated here, and rooms definitely continued on the northeast and southeast corners for an unknown distance. Surface artifact density, however, indicates that the compound is unlikely to extend more than 10 m beyond any excavated portion. Coverage is felt to be adequate for other areas within the estimated compound area.

Since the focus of the excavation was on the recovery of skeletal remains, any possible burial pit, indicated by holes or breaks in "concrete" floors or looser fill in soil matrices, was separated out as a provenience for special excavation. The fill was carefully removed and screened until bone or offerings were reached. After careful cleaning of all bone present, the burial was photographed and mapped. In addition, before removal, elevations and other descriptive information such as orientation, pit size, and the like were recorded. Bones were carefully removed and placed in bags according to body part. Pit fill around skeletons was screened. For adults, quarter-inch screen was sufficient to recover most elements, but for the bones of children and infants, fine-screening through 1-mm mesh was used. A soil sample was taken from near the bones for later chemical analysis of pit fill characteristics. An attempt was made in the field to judge the completeness of the skeleton and to record age and sex indicators *in situ*, in case there was loss or damage in removal and transport to the lab. Given the fragile condition of a few burials, the field observations were crucial, and in general, they were a good complement to the laboratory determinations.

The excavation strategies (to provide maximum recovery of skeletal material) were the explicit concentration on locating and identifying burial pits, the screening of pit fill, and the making of field observations on certain baseline demographic characteristics such as age and sex. More importantly, because of the architectural modification these compounds are known to have undergone, it was anticipated that many burials that took place in the compound would be disturbed and not in their original burial context. This is why many secondary contexts were screened. In addition, workers were encouraged to look for and recover

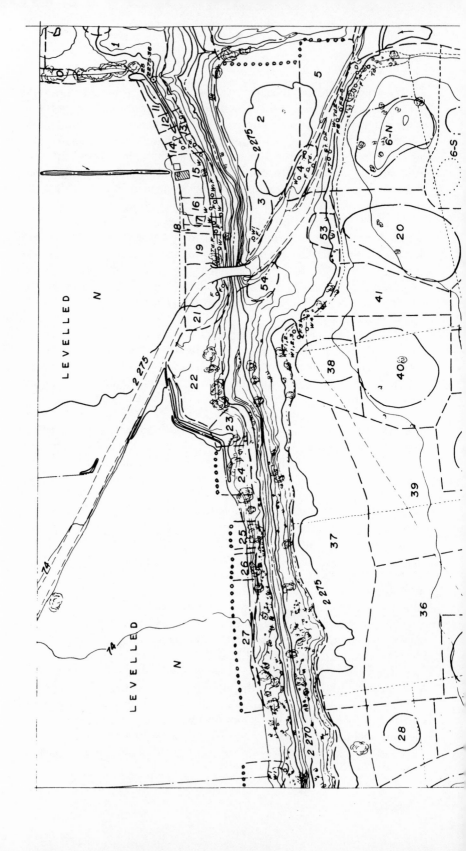

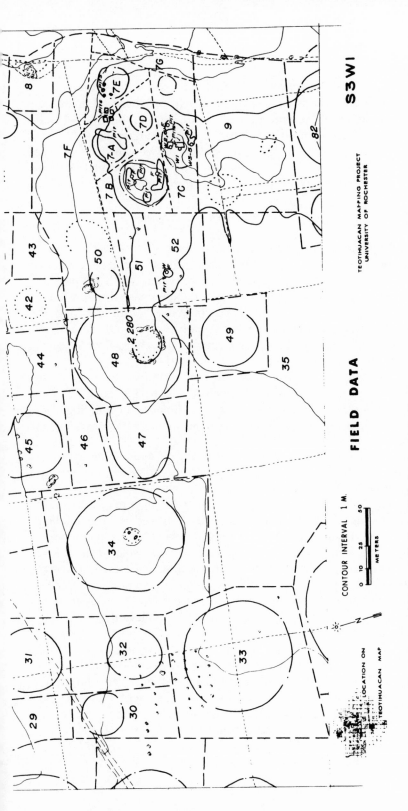

S3WI

TEOTIHUACAN MAPPING PROJECT
UNIVERSITY OF ROCHESTER

FIELD DATA

CONTOUR INTERVAL 1 M.

0 10 25 50
METERS

LOCATION ON
TEOTIHUACAN MAP

N

Figure 3-1. The Location of Tlajinga 33 (from *Urbanization at Teotihuacan, Mexico,* vol. 1, ©1973 by René Millon)

bone. Because of this, recovery of faunal bone and of loose and single pieces of human bone was excellent. It is felt that these explicitly designed techniques allowed recovery of a sufficient number and *adequate representative sample* of individuals for a paleodemographic study, regardless of context or element size. As will be seen, a demographic study would have been impossible without the use of skeletal material from *all* of the site deposit types, not just from burials.

General Compound Characteristics

The Tlajinga 33 excavation revealed that both stone and adobe were used in the construction of the compound. The site occupation was exclusively during the Middle Horizon (Classic period), with nothing before or after, and spanned the Early Tlamimilolpa phase through to the Metepec (see Table 3-1), a period of 450–500 years. During this long occupation the apartment compound was extensively remodeled and rebuilt, with at least twelve sequences of construction change, which seem to fall into three major phases.

All architecture that was uncovered in the excavation, irrespective of temporal assignment, has been mapped in Figure 3-2. Such detailed mapping was done to show the general complexity of building construction and to demonstrate the extent of architectural modification plus recent disturbance.

The site plan also revealed that rebuilding or remodeling episodes had a differential effect on the preservation of earlier architecture. In some cases early architectural features, such as walls and floors, were retained and integrated into the new construction, whereas in other cases the original architectural features were destroyed and the building materials reused. This inconsistency left a number of puzzling architectural remnants, which make no sense, since they are isolated from their original context. Such ambiguity is very frustrating when one is trying to reconstruct earlier phases. However, because the sequence here is likely typical of the construction sequence of most Teotihuacan apartment compounds, much of the architectural information relevant to earlier occupations is only partially understood.

Because natural soil in the area is very shallow, less than 20 cm, shifts in site layout and configuration are compressed vertically. Numerous construction phases are superpositioned within a very thin stratigraphic matrix, resulting in a confusing arrangement of walls and floors. There is no deep stratification of construction buildup, as seen in profiles in reconstructed apartment compounds located near the center

TABLE 3-1
Chronology for the Teotihuacan Period

Archaeological Phase	Teotihuacan Phase	Dates
Terminal Preclassic or First Intermediate phase 3	Patlachique	150 B.C.– A.D. 0
Terminal Preclassic or First Intermediate phase 4	Tzacualli	A.D. 1–150
Classic or Middle Horizon	Miccaotli	150–200
	Early Tlamimilolpa	200–300
	Late Tlamimilolpa	300–400
	Early Xolalpan	400–500
	Late Xolalpan	500–650
	Metepec	650–750

Source: Adapted from Millon 1981: 207.

of the city, such as Zacuala Palace or Tetitla (Angulo 1987). Instead of vertical buildup due to modification and reuse, there is lateral shifting of construction to facilitate compound rebuilding. In no extant area of the site is there a vertical accumulation of culture-bearing stratigraphic deposits of more than 1.40 m. Because earlier building materials and fill are shallow enough to be available for recycling throughout the lifespan of the compound and, more importantly, because construction fill in general is in very short supply, there was a tendency to destroy earlier walls and floors to obtain fill and building materials for later construction. The shallowness of soil and recycling of building materials seem also to have, not surprisingly, disturbed many burials. The evidence for these disturbed burials is discussed in Chapter 5.

To date, 104 rooms have been identified; not all were contemporaneous. This high number is ample testimony to the intense and frequent architectural modification, particularly in the context of the relatively small excavation. Therefore, the reconstructed architectural history of the compound is tentative. There is no complete site layout for any phase, as modification and looting have obliterated parts of the compound. All present phase-specific site interpretations are regarded as approximations, subject to revision as analysis continues.

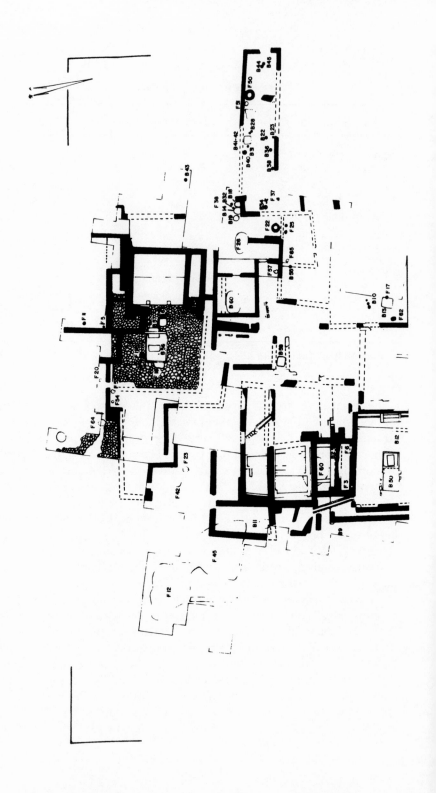

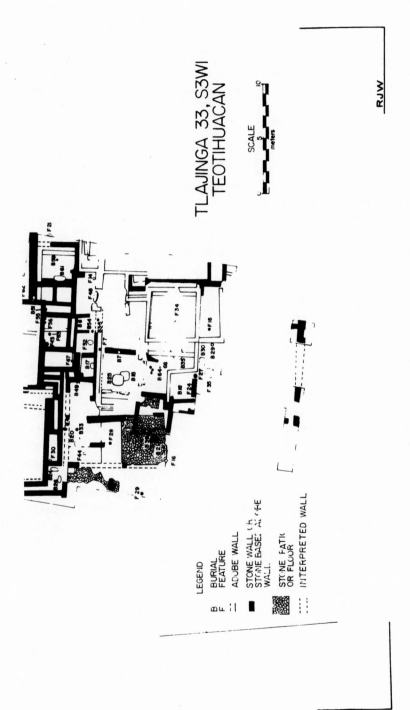

TLAJINGA 33, S3W1
TEOTIHUACAN

SCALE
5 10
meters

RJW

LEGEND

B   BURIAL
F   FEATURE
::   ADOBE WALL

■   STONE WALL OR
    STONE BASED ADOBE
    WALL.

    STONE PATH
    OR FLOOR

:::   INTERPRETED WALL

Figure 3-2. The Excavated Architecture of the Tlajinga 33 Compound

Architecture and Function in Tlajinga 33

A brief description of the changes in size and architectural layout for Tlajinga 33 during its occupational history is necessary for placing the skeletal population in context. More detailed information on the compound's characteristics can be found in other sources (Sanders et al. 1982; Storey 1983; Storey and Widmer 1989).

The Early Tlamimilolpa Phase

The initial occupation at the site, as can be determined from the excavation, dates to the Early Tlamimilolpa (see Table 3-1). The architectural layout, as interpreted to date, has been presented in Figure 3-3.

The courtyard complex is in the center of Figure 3-3, and the occupation, as revealed by walls, floors, and burials associated with this period, appears to have been located mostly in the northern half of the total excavation. The courtyard is large, approximately square, and constructed of river cobbles, which are placed in a leveled, prepared surface (Figure 3-4). On the east margin of the courtyard is probably some kind of public building or temple.

The general compound layout, size, and room functions are poorly known for this earliest period. Though burials and features have been dated to this period, they are into or near the *tepetate*, and much of the architecture associated with them is no longer present. Only the courtyard and a few rooms around it are preserved. Thus, it seems that the compound was probably mostly present only in the northern area of the site during this period. Figure 3-3 reflects present best knowledge of the area of Early Tlamimilolpa architecture and does not purport to reconstruct the limits of the compound at the time, as these have been obscured by later rebuildings at the site.

The time of initial occupation was, however, the wealthiest phase in the compound's history, although apparently the smallest. Relatively rich offerings accompanied the burials from this phase. For example, the richest burial offering of all Tlajinga individuals accompanied the individual buried in the courtyard, Burial 57 (see Chapter 4). Other indications of wealth include the fact that over half of the room floor surface area excavated that can be assigned to this phase is plastered concrete, and this phase had the largest courtyard area.

The Late Tlamimilolpa–Early Xolalpan Phase

The next construction phase crosscuts and includes both the Late Tlamimilolpa and Early Xolalpan phases (Table 3-1). During this period of occupation there was a southward shift in architecture (see Figure

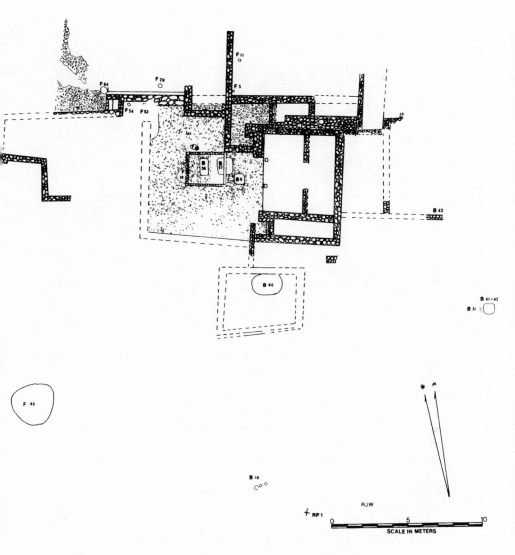

Figure 3-3. The Tlajinga 33 Compound in the Early Tlamimilolpa Phase

Figure 3-4. The Main Courtyard of the Early Tlamimilolpa Phase. The temple or public building is to the right (unexcavated).

3-5). It is not known for certain whether this shift represents a gradual, southerly extension of rooms and patios, or instead an abandonment of the earlier section of the compound and a planned large-scale construction in the southern area. Certainly, there is direct continuity in the inhabitants of the compound, as evidenced by the fact that a single, deep burial pit (with Burials 41 and 42) contains seven individuals belonging to two chronologically distinct burial episodes: the Early Tlamimilolpa (Burial 41) and Late Tlamimilolpa (Burial 42). These associated burials clearly indicate a continuity of mortuary behavior linking the two phases. A continuity in inhabitants is also seen in the continued use of cobblestones for the extant courtyard from the period.

A fairly radical relocation and reconstruction of the compound to the south is implied by the fact that Late Tlamimilolpa and Early Xolalpan burials are found only in the southern half of the compound area. It is not yet certain that the northern area was completely abandoned, but the ceramics seem to indicate that it was not much used again until the Late Xolalpan. It seems clearer that the shift of construction and most intensive use, as revealed by preliminary analysis of middens, is to the southern half. Unfortunately, the crucial central area between the north and south halves of the site has been extensively disturbed by still later aboriginal construction and by recent looting, which has obliterated many possible clues as to the integration of the two halves. Thus, the northern limits for this period are as unclear as the southern limits were for the earlier period.

It appears that a large part of the Late Tlamimilolpa–Early Xolalpan compound did grow by just gradual addition of new rooms and patios to the south, so that the compound at this period can probably be best described as the result of a combination of some deliberate reconstruction plan plus the accretion of rooms as needed. During this phase the compound reached its greatest areal and demographic size, a growth in absolute size over the Early Tlamimilolpa. This growth is ascertained not only by the large area of construction but also by the fact that the greatest number of burials are assigned to this phase (see Chapter 4).

Two distinct characteristics emerge in this phase when it is compared with the earlier phase. First, there is the use of cheaper building materials, that is, adobe walls instead of stone, and earth or crushed *tepetate* floors, rather than "concrete." Second, although the overall plan of the compound is larger, the only courtyard dated to this phase is small and in the southwest corner; in other words, there is now proportionally less public area than domestic rooms than there is in the Early Tlamimilolpa. There was absolutely greater area of courtyard and a greater percentage of concrete floor area in the Early Tlamimilolpa.

The use of cheaper materials and the reduced public area may indicate an overall lower status in the political and economic condition of the compound and a general decline in wealth. This interpretation is somewhat supported by the difference in grave goods associated with the two periods. For example, more shell, a long-distance trade item, is associated with Early Tlamimilolpa burials than with Late Tlamimilolpa burials.

The history of Tlajinga 33 reveals growth from the Early Tlamimilolpa through Late Tlamimilolpa phase, but a decline in the quality of architecture. The compound by the Late Tlamimilolpa–Early Xolalpan phase seems to have matured as a residential unit. The later phase will bring shifts in organization and function, but the compound has stabilized in population size.

The Late Xolalpan–Early Metepec Phase

In the final construction phase, beginning in the Late Xolalpan and lasting into the Early Metepec, the architectural layout and plan of the compound underwent a dramatic shift (see Figure 3–6). The compound

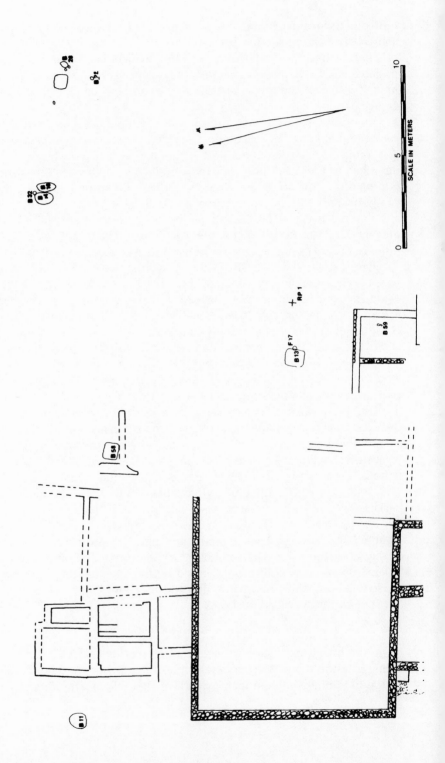

SCALE IN METERS

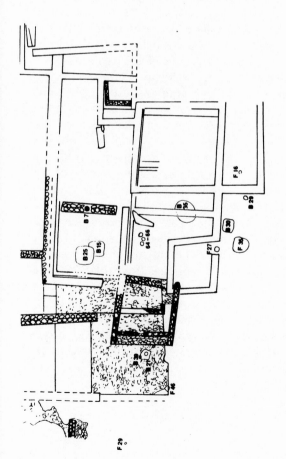

Figure 3-5. The Tlajinga 33 Compound in the Late Tlamimilolpa–Early Xolalpan Phase

shifts from primarily adobe walls with packed earth floors to stone masonry, adobe walls with stone masonry footings, and plastered concrete floors on crushed *tepetate* subfloors several centimeters thick. This is also a shift from a cobblestone courtyard to one with a plastered concrete floor, a plastered central altar shrine, and a platform with balustraded staircase for a temple structure.

The location of the compound seems to again shift, from the southern-focused Late Tlamimilolpa–Early Xolalpan to a more central situation. It is also only slightly larger, although the absence of Late Xolalpan architecture in the southern end could be a result of erosion of upper construction. The compound during this building phase has the best preserved architecture, the clearest residential plan, clearly defined activity areas, and the best knowledge of the use of space in general.

During the Late Xolalpan the typical compound apartment suite, so visible at other more centrally located compounds like Tetitla, is clearly identifiable at Tlajinga 33 (see Figure 3–6, upper right and lower central portions of map). This suite is the basic unit of domestic residence within the compound and usually consists of two or three rooms around a small patio. The unit is architecturally self-contained and usually has only one entrance from other parts of the compound (Hopkins 1987). Domestic refuse is found in conjunction with most of the patios. Five of these can presently be identified around the Late Xolalpan central courtyard. Thus, it seems that each family occupying a suite was responsible for its own domestic functions, while ritual and craft activities were located in both compound-wide use areas, the public areas, and the more localized areas, like large patios, that may have been shared by several families.

Estimating the population of the Tlajinga 33 compound from the number of identified apartment suites depends on an estimate of the average family size in each suite at Teotihuacan. No matter what figure is chosen, the population should be slightly underestimated, as there are probably more apartment suites to the southeast of the excavations and perhaps in the northeast as well. The figure for mean household size for prehistoric Mesoamerica has been set at 5.5 individuals, although polygamous and extended households would be larger (Kolb 1985). Such a household figure would give a population of around 28 people for the excavated portion of the compound. With several rooms around a patio, it is quite possible that an extended family of seven or eight was the basic unit of production, yielding a population of 35–40. In any case, if one assumes that there was a functioning corporate group, organized by either lineage or craft, at the compound, then a population of less than 35–40 would appear to have been less than economically viable, as there would not have been enough adults to carry out the craft specializations that have been identified for this phase.

The Late Xolalpan–Early Metepec occupation was the last at Tlajinga 33. The compound was apparently abandoned some time before the "fall" of the city in A.D. 750. The abandonment was deliberate: before the inhabitants left, they apparently removed most of the burial offering from the shaft tomb under the altar of the central courtyard (see Figure 3-7). This shaft tomb, 2 m deep, had been broken into through a sealed concrete floor, but the bones of five individuals (Burial 50) had been fairly carefully replaced at the bottom. The removal of the burial goods probably had two purposes: ritual desanctification and the reclamation of these artifacts, which could function in some capacity at a new residence after this site was abandoned. Where the residents went cannot be determined, but the Tlajinga 33 site was never occupied again.

Subsistence

A wealth of fine-grained subsistence data was recovered from the quarter-inch screening plus fine screening of soil samples. Many new perspectives on Teotihuacan subsistence have been generated from the investigation of Tlajinga 33. Some are site specific, but some have implications for Teotihuacan as a whole. All statements must be considered preliminary and may change as analysis proceeds.

Tlajinga 33 apparently was not involved in agricultural production of any kind, because no evidence of hoes or other clearly agricultural tools were found. Thus, the residents made their living by craft specialization and would have been dependent upon some form of market exchange for most of their subsistence. It is possible, if not probable, that they may have had small gardens, especially as the Tlajinga *barrio* compounds have open spaces between them, unlike the more block-like arrangements in most of the city. Although these spaces were used for craft work, especially during the Late Xolalpan (Krotser 1987), part may have been used for crops.

Specific identifications and numbers are not yet available, but preliminary sorting indicates that smaller birds such as pigeon, quail, and duck were the most frequent faunal element in the diet. Rabbit was also very common and without question the most common mammal. The most striking aspect of the faunal material from Tlajinga 33 is the general rarity of deer and the domesticated dog and turkey. This finding contrasts with the faunal analysis done for selected pits of the Teotihuacan Mapping Project (Starbuck 1987: Table 1), where deer, dog, and turkey

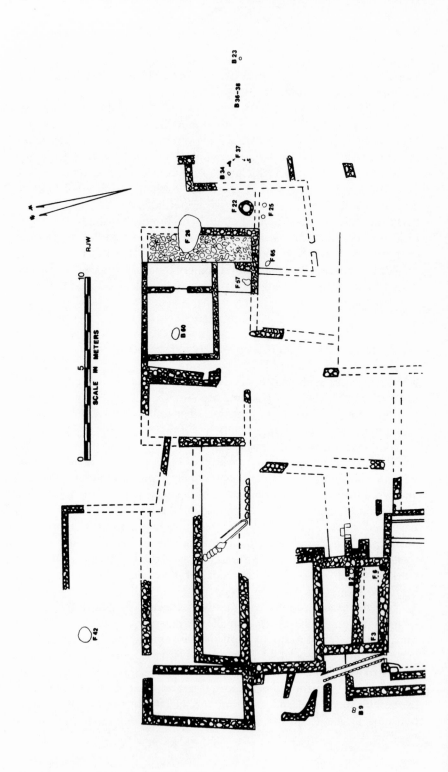

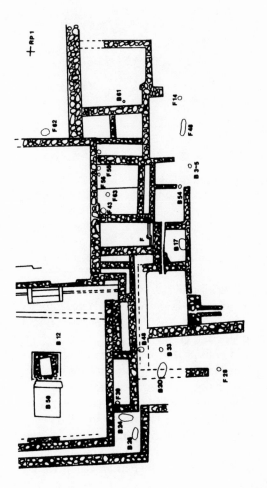

Figure 3-6. The Tlajinga 33 Compound in the Late Xolalpan-Metepec Phase

Figure 3-7. The Altar, Shaft Tomb Entrance, and Temple of the Late Xolalpan Courtyard. In the rear is the balustrated staircase and *talud* wall of the temple.

generally were found most frequently and apparently provided the bulk of the meat.

The difference could be largely attributable to wealth differences, as Tlajinga 33 is among the poorest compounds excavated to date. Rabbits and small birds might perhaps have been the least expensive animal foods available to Teotihuacan residents. Although these animals may have been semi-domesticated, wild ones also probably were common in agricultural fields and open spaces near the city and easily trapped by residents for their own use or to exchange. Other protein resources are indicated by plentiful remains of turkey eggs and small freshwater fish.

The analysis of floral resources at Tlajinga 33 is continuing. Domesticated and wild species both have been found in samples taken by the Teotihuacan Mapping Project (McClung de Tapia 1987), indicating maize, beans, squash, amaranth, chenopodium, hot peppers (*Capsicum*), acacia, and various cacti. The best identification so far is of eight species of cacti (Scheinvar and Gonzalez 1985). Tlajinga 33 residents probably used a wide variety of wild or semi-domesticated resources, besides the usual domesticated staples.

The subsistence items available to the residents of Tlajinga 33 were varied and sufficient to provide a nutritionally adequate diet. Whether the actual daily diet of the residents was adequate is a more difficult question. The archaeological remains are subject to preservation and sampling vagaries, which make them only general guides to diet. In many ways, the skeletons to be discussed in later chapters provide the best answers. The bone chemistry could provide more direct evidence of dietary intakes (see Wing and Brown 1979; Klepinger 1984), but this has not yet been done for the Tlajinga 33 skeletons.

The importance of the Tlajinga 33 project is its evidence for the life-ways and conditions in the lower-status, artisanal compounds of Teo-tihuacan, especially those dependent on the market for most of their subsistence. In other preindustrial cities these individuals have marginal diets (see Frisch 1978) and are most affected by food shortages (McNeill 1976). The Tlajinga 33 residents are hypothesized to have had dietary insufficiencies, because their food supply would have been contingent on the value of their craft products in trade. The skeletal data are expected to indicate that chronic undernutrition was a health hazard for the residents of Tlajinga 33.

Craft Specialization

Until now, little mention has been made of the evidence for the occupational specialization during the history of the compound. The fill of middens and rooms contained a wealth of information that could be used to identify what the inhabitants were doing during the time of occupation of the compound and how it changed through time. Soil samples were retrieved from 214 proveniences, including earthen floors, middens, and subfloor fill deposits. Separation of artifacts by wet screening through 1-mm mesh provided information that was simply missed or poorly represented in the quarter-inch screening.

The evidence from the southern half of the site suggests that during the Late Tlamimilolpa–Early Xolalpan phase the occupants were jewelers and lapidaries working in a number of media, including greenstone, the painting and working of slate, the production of fine-grained travertine bowls and dishes, and shell jewelry. This supposition was supported by the discovery of partly finished artifacts and, most dramatically, by the debitage present in the soil samples.

The best evidence is from the frequency of debitage of fine stone and other exotic materials recovered from the soil samples (data from Widmer 1983). Slate was the most frequent class of imported raw material, appearing in 90.9% of the samples, mostly as small flakes. Mica and shell are the next most frequent, appearing in more than half the samples. Greenstone pieces are found in 42.6% of the samples, for a total of 132 chips, which compares favorably with the 120 chips recovered from the lapidary *barrio* in the northeast quadrant of the city (Turner 1987), although the density in Tlajinga is lower. These pieces are difficult to identify accurately because of their size, but they definitely include small pieces of jadeite, serpentine, and malachite, all of which were imported into the city from outside the Basin of Mexico.

Not only is this identification of craft specialization supported by the debitage, but also by the 45 partly finished products of shell, greenstone, and slate. Only two completely finished objects resulting from the craft production were found at Tlajinga 33, but this low number is consistent with the interpretation of lapidary and jewelry production, since finished products would have been exchanged in the market and not produced solely for compound consumption. According to a behavioral interpretation, the items left at the site should be either broken in production and of no market value, or else found in a context indicative of normal consumption patterns, as in ritual offerings, for example. Given that such materials represent valuable long-distance trade items, one would expect to find few, if any, raw materials or blanks awaiting production.

The foregoing evidence argues that the economic specialization of the occupants during the construction phase was general lapidary, jewelry, and the painting of frescoes on ceramic vases. It also suggests that this was a full-time occupational specialization, although agriculture cannot be totally ruled out as part of the compound's economic activities. There is presently no evidence that even some of the occupants were engaged in agricultural activities on a full- or part-time basis. No artifacts such as basalt hoes or distinctive assemblages of tools have been found that could be linked to agriculture.

The craft specialization was definitely practiced from the Late Tlamimilolpa into the Late Xolalpan or Early Metepec phases. Some debitage is found in Early Tlamimilolpa contexts, but not as much domestic and midden space has been preserved as for later phases, so the evidence is not as clear. However, it is likely that this had been the craft activity since the founding of the compound. It might be the case that the larger number of earth floors and adobe walls and the generally poor architectural construction in the southern area of the site relates mostly to the concentration and restriction of craft-production activities to this area, especially from the Late Tlamimilolpa on.

During the Late Xolalpan phase the northwest and north-central areas of the site were also intensively, and apparently exclusively, used for craft specialization. The craft was ceramic production, and more specifically, the production of the specialized market ware, San Martin Orange. The Tlajinga area has been recognized as an area of specialization in the production of San Martin Orange in the form of craters and amphoras (Krotser and Rattray 1980; Krotser 1987). The fill of this area of the site contained large numbers of misfired and burned San Martin Orange sherds. There is little doubt, on the basis of excavation, that this craft activity was engaged in by the inhabitants of the site, and ceramic production probably overtook lapidary work as the main craft of the residents during the Late Xolalpan phase.

An interesting and important question is why there was a shift in occupational specialization between the Late Tlamimilolpa–Early Xolalpan and the Late Xolalpan phase. Although there was not a complete change in specialization between the two periods, ceramic production was clearly added to the compound's repertoire. Ceramic production appeared during the Late Xolalpan, or perhaps the end of the Early Xolalpan, and probably became dominant, as the whole northern area of the site was given over to it. The evidence for the lapidary work at this time is found in one room and one small patio. The reason for the shift probably has to do with the appearance of the *barrio* organization for the San Martin production, whereas the lapidary specialization has not been identified for any neighboring compounds, although it would not be easily identified by surface indications. That is, although the evidence from other Tlajinga compounds is not conclusive, it is possible that the lapidary craft was organized only on the individual compound level. The change was probably from semi-autonomous lapidary production to *barrio*-based ceramic production.

Tlajinga 33 simply became one of several nodes of production organized at a higher *barrio* level, whereas earlier the compound had perhaps been an autonomous node of production. The lapidary craft continued, however, and this would seem to have made good economic sense. The residents probably had stronger and more dependable market power with more than one craft actively pursued. A hypothesis about Teotihuacan economy is suggested by the Tlajinga excavation: perhaps there was a shift through time from compound autonomy in production to the clear grouping of specialists into *barrios*, from a pattern of dispersed and somewhat random locations of craft compounds to more patterned locations, perhaps as the state control of crafts and their markets increased. Additional craft specialist compounds must be excavated before we can judge whether craft specialization in Teotihuacan generally changed levels of organization, from compounds to *barrios* and state-controlled workshops.

Summary

The excavation of Tlajinga 33 has revealed that the history and evolution of the Teotihuacan apartment compound was a complex and involved process, with continuous remodeling and shifting of rooms and walls. At Tlajinga 33 this process probably had a strong lateral component rather than just a vertical buildup of architecture. There were three primary building phases, which crosscut ceramic phases, an interpretation that is based on dated, well-preserved courtyard complexes.

It is important to note that compounds such as Tlajinga 33, on the margins of the city of Teotihuacan, do not have well-defined quadrilateral compound boundaries. It appears that these compounds are more loosely organized in spatial form. There was a gradual accretional buildup and addition of rooms and architectural units, at least during the Early Tlamimilolpa through Early Xolalpan phases.

There was also during these phases a modest energetic expenditure for architecture, with the use of cobblestones for courtyards and earthen floors and adobe wall for most domestic architecture. It does appear, however, that concrete floors and masonry walls were utilized during the Early Tlamimilolpa phase for some domestic architecture but not during the Late Tlamimilolpa–Early Xolalpan phase. During the Late Xolalpan–Early Metepec phase concrete floors and masonry-footed walls were used for domestic architecture, indicating a return to better building materials for more parts of the compound. There was, however, a general decline through time in compound wealth and status (see Chapter 4).

The Early Tlamimilolpa through Early Xolalpan represent a distinctive occupational period at Tlajinga 33. The occupants were apparently engaged in a craft specialization of lapidary and jewelry production in a number of media, including slate, travertine, greenstone, and also possibly frescoed tripod vases. There is no evidence of agriculture during this phase.

During the subsequent Late Xolalpan–Early Metepec phase there was a dramatic shift in architectural layout, construction technique, and occupational specialization. During this period the complete reorganization of site architecture was accomplished to focus on the central courtyard and balustraded *talud-tablero* temple building. Concrete floors and masonry-footed walls become the standard architectural forms. Even the courtyard for this last period had a concrete floor (at least two), instead of the earlier cobblestone pavement. A new craft specialization, ceramic production, was added and became the dominant craft.

A significant finding of the excavation at Tlajinga 33 is that there may have been a considerable shift in occupational specialization for an apartment compound through time at Teotihuacan. Many of these shifts may not be recognizable from surface survey alone. For example, at Tlajinga 33 the ceramic specialization of the last occupational phase was recognized from the surface, but the specialization of the earlier phases was not. What this suggests is that there may be considerable changing of economic specialization over time in Teotihuacan apartment compounds and that surface survey is not sufficiently precise to detect or chronologically organize such shifts. Detecting such shifts is particularly important when two specializations are present, one of which is very visible on the surface, ceramic production, and the other, lapidary, is not. A lapidary specialization could leave behind only the debitage of the precious and exotic materials worked and would rarely leave the obvious large fragments. This is a problem for future study at Teotihuacan.

Although surface survey and collection can accurately identify craft specialization and the location of site boundary, as was the case for Tlajinga 33, it does not provide the detail of changes in site layout, demography, and craft specialization through time. Only through more extensive excavations of compounds using specific, sophisticated fine-scale recovery techniques can site functions be specifically identified and architectural layout known.

One of the purposes of a compound excavation like that at Tlajinga 33 is to allow comparisons with other previously excavated examples. Tlajinga 33 appears in architectural layout and construction materials to be smaller and more poorly built than all of the other excavated compounds, except perhaps La Ventilla B. Most of the excavated La Ventilla B compound is from the earlier Tlamimilolpa phase; because the upper building levels had been removed by bulldozers (Vidarte 1964; Millon 1976), it cannot be known how it would compare in the Xolalpan phase. On the basis of information from La Ventilla B (Vidarte 1964), one can conclude that Tlajinga 33 had more adobe and earthen floor construction during its Tlamimilolpa phase and thus might arguably have been of lower status. According to René and Clara Millon's scheme of six status levels of excavated compounds (Millon 1976), the lowest one contains La Ventilla B and Tlamimilolpa, and this seems to be where Tlajinga 33 would fit. Thus, Tlajinga 33 is perhaps the compound of lowest status yet excavated at Teotihuacan. It certainly was the first with a craft specialty clearly identified. Tlajinga 33 stands alone as the only compound extensively investigated by the use of sophisticated excavation techniques; yet it is probably more representative of Teotihuacan life than any other excavated compound. That is, since wealth is hierarchical, poor compounds like Tlajinga outnumber wealthy ones. Demographic patterns derived from Tlajinga thus will reflect the demographic characteristics of the majority of the inhabitants of the city, even though the compound is but one of 2,000.

The Tlajinga 33 excavation already has provided a wealth of information on the archaeological contexts of the Tlajinga 33 skeletal population, although more analysis is needed. Information on layout, occupational specialization, subsistence, and the changes through time is essential to an understanding of the characteristics of the Tlajinga 33 population as revealed by paleodemographic analysis. The Tlajinga 33 excavation is one of the few windows archaeologists presently have into the characteristics of the distinctive residential unit of the urban center of Teotihuacan, the apartment compound.

CHAPTER 4

The Tlajinga 33 Skeletons

A PRIME OBJECTIVE of the Tlajinga 33 compound excavation was the recovery of all human skeletal material present, no matter how fragmentary. Although complete, well-preserved skeletons are preferred and are more informative about past populations, paleodemographers and osteologists realize that fragmentary material can also yield valuable information and must not be ignored (Ubelaker 1989).

Pre-Columbian Mesoamerica in general and Teotihuacan in particular are poorly known paleodemographically or paleopathologically. Teotihuacan is an interesting and important subject, because it is necessary to know if this preindustrial city resembled European ones in health and mortality conditions. Was it characterized by the "Law of Natural Urban Decrease" (de Vries 1984)? The Tlajinga 33 excavations revealed a compound of modest architectural and artifactual features compared with other excavated compounds; it was in essence a lower-class artisanal compound. Thus, its residents should provide valuable information concerning life in the city of Teotihuacan for the poorer sectors of the city.

Previous Skeletal and Demographic Study in Teotihuacan

The problem for Teotihuacan is that not much has been excavated that can be studied demographically. There have been fairly extensive, although shallow, excavations of the public buildings in the ritual and administrative center of the city, especially along the northern end of the Street of the Dead, and in several apartment compounds. However, the human skeletal remains recovered, the basis for any demographic study, were few, even from the residences. For example, only 7 burials were recovered from the Xolalpan compound (Linné 1934), 27 from Zacuala Palace (Séjourné 1959), and 34 (33 burials plus one called an offering) from the Tetitla compound (Séjourné 1966). These are obviously small numbers for compounds that held as many as a hundred residents at a time for several centuries. However, part of the answer is that excavations were usually only of the initial levels, so that many burials would have been below the level of excavations and thus missed.

Although burial under the rooms and patios of a compound was a common practice (Séjourné 1959), the paucity of burials led to the suggestion that only part of the residents were buried in the compounds (Séjourné 1966). This idea may have been given some credence by the discovery by the Teotihuacan Mapping Project survey of a possible crematorium in the northwest quadrant of the city, a feature identified by the sheer amount of calcined bone fragments present (Spence 1971). However, nothing else like it was found around the city, and Spence concluded that it represented a local, isolated practice.

The burials that came from many compound excavations were cremated and wrapped in cloth as bundles. In fact, on the basis of the burials in Zacuala Palace, Séjourné (1959) believed that the Teotihuacan pattern was very similar to the Aztec and involved cremation, a dog buried as a guide, red ochre, and a jade or shell bead in the mouth. Most burials from Tetitla and Xolalpan were also cremated, and so it was thought that the main treatment of the dead in Teotihuacan was by cremation.

The findings of Linné's and Séjourné's compound excavations and the preponderance of cremations and generally few burials made it doubtful that detailed study of skeletal remains could be done for Teotihuacan. The small numbers of burials meant that a representative sample of the residents of a compound would not be recovered, and the cremation would destroy most of the bones needed for age, sex, and pathological information. However, the salvage excavation in the early 1960s of an apartment compound named La Ventilla B (Vidarte 1964) was an important indication that it would be possible to recover a skeletal sample from Teotihuacan that met the population requirements necessary for demographic purposes. The excavation recovered 174 burials from within and around the compound boundaries. Also, there were only three cremations (Serrano and Lagunas 1974), which indicated that not all burials were necessarily cremated, and more importantly, that only a small percentage were actually cremated.

However, in spite of the potential, no detailed paleodemographic study was performed on the La Ventilla B skeletons. An article by two physical anthropologists (Serrano and Lagunas 1974) discussed and summarized the data from their study. Most of the article is concerned with mortuary patterns, orientation, and the position of the bodies in the graves. Most bodies were flexed, but no dominant orientation for the head or face was found. The most common burial position for adults (65%) was flexed and sitting upright in the grave. Osteological study focused on cranial deformation, dental mutilation, and dental attrition. Many skulls were intentionally deformed, but dental mutilation was little practiced. Pathological observations found dental carious lesions and arthritis, but only 45% of the studied remains showed any lesions at all. Infectious reactions on long bones, an important pathological indicator (see Chapter 7), were quite rare.

To make demographic inferences, researchers divided the La Ventilla B population into general age categories. They noted that the mortality of subadults was low, because children and adolescents together totalled only 18% of the sample, whereas adults were 62%. However, there was a high percentage, 20%, of fetal-age individuals. Many of these were found in altars, and thus Serrano and Lagunas thought these might be ritual abortions or infanticides, interred when the altars were built. They did note that biological factors could be implicated in the prenatal mortality but could not tell what these might be. If the percentage of fetal-age individuals was due to ritual abortion or infanticide, it would mean that a significant proportion of pregnancies might have been deliberately ended. This would be a rare case of population fertility control that was institutionalized on a premodern basis, and the only real evidence for it is suggested by archaeological context alone. Other more probable explanations, like health, are not precluded.

The main importance of the La Ventilla B study was that it suggested that cremation was perhaps not the most common mode of disposal of the dead at Teotihuacan. Burials were similar to those of other contemporary sites in the Valley of Mexico, where a tradition of flexed, uncremated burial in residences was found (see Sanders et al. 1979). The study was the first indication that perhaps most Teotihuacan burials were not cremated but buried deeply under the floors of residences.

Besides the brief discussion of the skeletons in La Ventilla B, there have been three other short notes on Teotihuacan demography, based on what little data existed. One was an overview of Teotihuacan health, which concluded that because there seemed to be a city sewer system and there was an absence of large numbers of skeletons buried together, which is indicative of epidemic disease, public health was probably relatively good (Somolinos-D'Ardois 1968). On the other hand, a study of available skeletal remains from Teotihuacan led at least one researcher to conclude that there was ample evidence of malnutrition and vitamin deficiences (Dávalos 1965), although not much detail for this conclusion was provided. Using the data from La Ventilla B, researchers estimated a crude death rate for Teotihuacan (Sanders et al. 1979: 46). This demographic measure is a general rate for the yearly mortality, and for skeletal populations it is usually determined as the reciprocal of life expectancy at birth under the assumption that a population is stationary (see Chapter 6). For La Ventilla B the calculation, which could only provide a rough estimate because of the very general age breakdowns used, was 3.5 deaths per year for every 100 people in the population. This figure is high for contemporary populations (which are often around 1.0), but it was lower than earlier skeletal samples, where it was 4.03 per 100 per year (Sanders et al. 1979: 47). This work was an attempt to extend the information available from a skeletal sample, and it is known from comparisons with other prehistoric samples calculated the same way (see Chapter 6) that this crude death rate was fairly low. The results from the small samples available for Teotihuacan had painted a fairly rosy picture for a prehistoric population from a dense urban settlement, with quite low juvenile mortality, a low yearly death rate, fairly good health, and only one study showing possible nutritional problems. As will be shown, this solitary study by Dávalos, though at odds with other analyses, turned out to be correct.

Poor preservation was the reason not much demographic study was undertaken on the La Ventilla B skeletons. About thirty skeletons, for instance, were not recovered at all because of their condition. The fragmentary condition of the recovered skeletons militated against almost any demographic and pathological study (Serrano and Lagunas 1974). Poor preservation is a recurrent characteristic of Teotihuacan burials. Séjourné noted the poor condition of burials in Tetitla (1966) and Zacuala Palace (1959). From photographs of Teotihuacan burials *in situ*, it is clear that the epiphyseal ends of long bones are often missing. Poor preservation of even uncremated remains has been another bar to the demographic study of Teotihuacan, and another explanation for why virtually nothing has been done to date.

In spite of the little that had been learned by the early 1980s, the Tlajinga 33 project was based on the belief that a paleodemographic study was feasible for Teotihuacan. La Ventilla B had demonstrated that an extensive excavation could yield a skeletal population of suitable size for paleodemographic study. Although preservation and fragmentary bones were likely to be a problem, new and developing techniques are allowing researchers to dramatically expand the information obtainable from even poorly preserved skeletons. One no longer has to feel as discouraged as Serrano and Lagunas did with the La Ventilla B skeletons.

Also, although La Ventilla B had few cremations, it was the only excavated compound to have that pattern. Cremations would ultimately hinder extensive paleodemographic study. However, it is felt that La Ventilla B is more likely to be representative of the general Teotihuacan pattern than Tetitla or Zacuala Palace. Cremation is probably a fairly high-status treatment because of the extra energy involved in the disposal of the body. Deforestation was probably well advanced in the environs of Teotihuacan during the city's height (Sanders et al. 1979), which would have made fuel a precious commodity. In this situation, fuel would not have been used for widespread mortuary treatment of the dead, which would have diverted it from usual household and ritual activities. It is hypothesized that, with more investigation, it will be seen that cremation is a minority treatment mostly reserved for high-status individuals such as those in Tetitla and Zacuala. Therefore, the impact of cremation on the paleodemographic study of Teotihuacan would be negligible.

Since the time of the Tlajinga 33 excavation, work at the Temple of Quetzalcoatl of the Ciudadela, at the center of the ancient city, has revealed more uncremated human interments associated with a ritual grave complex of sacrificed individuals (Sugiyama 1989; George Cowgill, personal communication). The importance of the recent work is that it is further proof of the possibility of recovering adequate skeletal samples for analysis from Teotihuacan. Also, the ongoing analysis of these skeletons should provide an interesting contrast to the Tlajinga 33 study, as it is the first clearly nonresidential sample from the city.

The Tlajinga 33 Burials

So that health and demography could be investigated, the excavation strategy for the Tlajinga 33 compound was designed to recover as much bone as possible and to excavate as burial contexts any concentration of recognizable human material. The excavation strategy was successful, as 68 burial features, with 110 individuals, were recovered. However, the general instruction to the workers to watch for and save all bone yielded a surprising quantity of human bone fragments from general proveniences. Human bone was separated out in the laboratory from faunal bone, since it had not been recognized as human in the field, even though some complete bones were involved. Thus, the Tlajinga 33 skeletal population is actually derived from two different excavation contexts: from individuals removed as formal burial interments with the methods described in Chapter 3, and from individuals recovered in the general bone collections from nonfeature proveniences. The latter context is an important discovery of the Tlajinga 33 project, as previously published work had not indicated that human bone could be recovered from middens and fill.

The human skeletons are actually found in two different mortuary contexts. The burial category includes individuals deliberately placed in formal graves as well as any concentration of recognizable human bone excavated as a burial. But bone that is indistinguishable in treatment and location from the general provenience collections should be combined with it. Thus, the Tlajinga skeletons can be divided analytically into those recovered from formal graves and those scattered in midden and fill contexts without evidence of grave pits or deliberate deposition. Each mortuary context is discussed separately. Most of this chapter will be concerned with the formal graves; the individuals in secondary deposits, in middens and fill, are discussed in more detail in Chapter 5.

The formal graves contain all information presently available from Tlajinga 33 on mortuary practices and patterns. Though mortuary analysis is an important technique for studying social relationships and organization of past groups (e.g., Brown 1971), a complete and formal analysis of this aspect of a skeletal population is not attempted here. The Tlajinga 33 graves are instead described by types and attributes, and some general information about the mortuary practices and their reflection of the internal organization of this apartment compound is presented.

Burial Types

The 68 burial features can be divided into five types, of which four pertain to formal graves.

1. Primary Interment with Offering—35 burial contexts containing 39 individuals.
2. Primary Interment without Offering—7 burial contexts with 10 individuals.

A primary interment has a skeleton that is still articulated when recovered, indicating that the body was placed in the ground while still with flesh. It is a burial that has not been much disturbed since the original interment. In Tlajinga 33, and in Teotihuacan in general, these burials are tightly flexed and are either placed on their side or seated upright. Perinatals (fetal or neonate in age) were usually placed in a ceramic vessel. There is no evidence of a preferred side or orientation for the body. Interments with offerings were defined by a clear association of purposely placed artifacts with the body. Artifact locations were rigorously scrutinized in the field to distinguish objects that happened to be in the pit fill from placed offerings. A few ambiguous cases were classified as offerings, if the artifact was whole, or else rare and not normally found in nonfeature contexts and thus more likely to be a deliberate offering, rather than a chance inclusion from the fill.

3. Secondary Interment with Offering—8 burials with 8 individuals.
4. Secondary Interment without Offering—8 burials with 11 individuals.

Secondary interments are individuals whose bones were not articulated when placed in a grave, usually because there is no longer much flesh to hold the anatomical position. Nevertheless, these interments are those whose grave and situation show evidence of some care or forethought. Corpses can become disarticulated through deliberate removal of flesh before burial or by being buried for some years, disinterred, and then reburied. There are ethnographic examples of both methods as part of the usual treatment of the dead (see Ubelaker 1989). However, in Tlajinga 33 there are many more primary burials than secondary ones, indicating that bodies, once placed, were generally not expected to be moved. Reburial was not the usual treatment.

Also, there is no evidence on the secondary interments that intentional defleshing, which can leave cut marks on the bones, was practiced. Although defleshing does not necessarily leave clear marks (see Ubelaker 1989), again, the small numbers of secondary interments make it unlikely that this was the usual treatment. Instead, a Tlajinga 33 secondary interment is one defined not just by disarticulation but by deliberate reburial. In all cases, a requirement was evidence of a grave and some care in placing the bones together. In eight cases at least part of the original offerings were also placed with the bones.

5. Refuse Interment—22 burials with 42 individuals.

Refuse interments are all disarticulated, very fragmentary remains that were numbered and excavated as burials only because they formed a concentration of human bone identifiable during general excavation. These remains have no recognizable pit and are never accompanied by offerings. The bones are usually somewhat scattered and often turn out to consist of skeletal fragments from several individuals. They show little evidence of care in placement and are usually found in trash pits or fill layers, mixed up with other artifacts in these secondary contexts. A few also have butchering or cut marks, the significance of which will be discussed in Chapter 5.

The refuse, or secondary-context, interments are instructive because they reveal an interesting dichotomy in the treatment of the dead that has not been previously reported from Teotihuacan apartment compounds. In Tlajinga 33 only 68 individuals (62% of the 110 individuals from numbered burial features) have a grave, that is, some sort of deliberate placing of the body in a prepared location. The 42 refuse individuals, 38% of the sample, indicate that a little more than one-third of the individuals excavated as burials are not truly in graves. Thus, it is apparent at Tlajinga 33 that postmortem treatments of individuals can vary, and not everyone is in a grave.

Although excavated as burials, these secondary-context individuals are found in an archaeological context that is quite different from that of primary and secondary interments; they more closely resemble the faunal bones found in trash pits and middens. Because of this and the fragmentary nature of the skeletal remains, they are combined with the secondary-context human bone from general proveniences, which have a similar context, and are discussed in more detail in Chapter 5. This classification is based on the belief that refuse individuals are probably disturbed primary and secondary interments who were not reburied but who instead were discarded rather unceremoniously. Their ultimate disposition does not reflect their original treatments. In other words, refuse individuals are not in the refuse because that was the treatment necessarily accorded them at death.

A noteworthy characteristic of the Tlajinga 33 burial interment types is that there are no instances of cremated remains, a clear deviation from what has been reported in other Teotihuacan apartment compounds. Although many bones are poorly preserved, there is no evidence of calcined, warped, or cracked bones, as is found in cremated material. It should be noted that much of the faunal remains are burned and calcined, and so the lack of human skeletal material so treated is indeed a clear pattern.

The lack of cremations is really not surprising, as it is in line with the hypothesis that cremation is most likely a treatment for the high-status dead. As Tlajinga 33 may well be the compound of lowest status among those excavated to date, cremations would be unlikely.

Characteristics of the Tlajinga 33 Graves

Mortuary analysis, or the study of the patterns of the treatment of the dead, is relatively recent but growing in importance in the archaeological literature. Many archaeologists believe it is one of the most productive ways for archaeologists to study past social organization. That is because the treatment of the dead reflects something of the relationships of the deceased with family and group. As Binford (1971) put it, the "social persona" of the individual in life is reflected in treatment at death. For Binford, mortuary variations should reflect the social identities of the deceased that are recognized by the society as appropriate for symbolic expression at death. The variations should also reflect the relative rank of the deceased in life, as that determines the level of corporate participation by members of the group in the rituals at death. The varying statuses of the society should thus be reflected in the mortuary practices. Goldstein (1980: 5) and others have called this one of the basic assumptions of mortuary analysis. The other is that the principles organizing the sets of statuses in mortuary practices are the same as those organizing social relations in the group. The higher rank of the deceased should be reflected in the mortuary treatment, and the more complex the ranks and statuses in the society, the more dimensions there should be to mortuary variability.

The challenge has been to develop methods to describe mortuary differentiations in terms of the social systems that produced them. Using the number of status types and their distribution through the population of the skeletal remains, archaeologists believe they can identify ranked versus egalitarian societies (Hatch 1976; Peebles and Kus 1977; Blakely 1977), mainly by looking for evidence of ascribed versus achieved statuses. Achieved statuses are those earned by an individual during life and generally are found with adults. Ascribed statuses are those an individual has regardless of personal characteristics, and they crosscut age and sex differences. For example, the presence of only a few rich child or infant burials within a group's interments is often taken as evidence of ascribed status, as children usually have not lived long enough to achieve high statuses within their group.

Although mortuary analyses are increasing and are yielding more results, some general criticisms of the methodology and assumptions of its study have not been addressed or solved by archaeologists. These criticisms come from the perspective of cultural anthropology (Ucko

1969; Humphreys 1981). For example, although the ethnographic tests of the basic mortuary-pattern assumptions have been positive (e.g., Saxe 1970), Humphreys (1981) believes it is important for archaeologists to remember that ethnographic complications abound. Burial practices can be quite variable and not necessarily closely correlated with many aspects of social structure. Humphreys cautions archaeologists to be aware that there is much in mortuary analysis that really reflects Western attitude toward death, not a truly objective approach. She was referring to the usual mortuary methodology that defines and separates out individual differences between the dead as reflecting differences in status, as Western society thinks in terms of individual differences and characteristics. Humphreys points out ethnographic examples of groups using death to "unindividualize" and of groups where the way one dies can affect mortuary treatment, irrespective of position in life, as in the example of heroes in Western civilization. Archaeologists must look at their data carefully to make sure the pattern does warrant the kind of trait and individual methodology that is usual in mortuary analysis.

No formal mortuary analysis is attempted here on Tlajinga 33. General descriptions of possible status differences among graves are presented to highlight indications of the complexity of internal differences among compound residents, which will help in interpreting their demographic patterns.

Only 68 individuals in Tlajinga 33 were found in formal graves, and this relatively small number is all that can be used for any mortuary analysis. The secondary-context interments are not included here. With that small a sample, which clearly does not represent all the burials that originally took place in Tlajinga 33, there is some question as to whether there is enough information to permit definition of the internal organization and status differences. Since the population to be studied is from one compound within a large urban center, and not from a whole settlement, it is hoped that some internal differences are evident from the 68 examples. However, because Tlajinga 33 is only one small part of Teotihuacan, the sample certainly cannot be taken as representative of wider Teotihuacan statuses or perhaps even of many compounds. Tlajinga 33, and probably most of Teotihuacan in general, is suitable for mortuary analysis. The graves are of a type that can be analyzed individually, as single graves predominate and offerings are placed with certain individuals even in multiple graves. Thus, some assumptions underlying mortuary analysis do seem to apply reasonably well to the compound, and there does not seem to be an undifferentiating ethos pervading the mortuary patterns.

The Nature of the Graves

Three dimensions were isolated for each individual. One dimension was whether the grave had single or multiple bodies (number). Second was whether it was a primary or secondary interment. The third concerned the type of grave: in earth only, inside a ceramic vessel, in a shallow basin scooped up to 15–20 cm into the *tepetate* bedrock, or a deep pit more than 30 cm into the *tepetate*. The first two dimensions reflect variations that may indicate social and/or organizational distinctions, whereas the third is an attempt to do a qualitative scaling of energetic input into the grave, as digging a deep pit into *tepetate* is more work-intensive with stone tools than is digging an earthen pit. It is logical to expect more energy to be invested in higher social persona, as in Tainter's Hawaiian example, where there was a marked contrast between individuals in hand-dug burial caves and those just placed in convenient cracks in the rocks (Tainter 1973).

For the 68 individuals in formal graves, 40 (59%) were alone, but 28 (41%) were in multiple-body graves. Primary interments were distinctly more common, at 49 to 19. As for the type of grave, 15 individuals were buried in ceramic vessels, 24 had an earthen pit, 22 were in the deep *tepetate* pits, whereas only 7 had shallow *tepetate* basins.

Chi-square analysis indicated no statistical significance ($p \rangle$ .05) to the numbers of single versus multiple-body graves. On the other hand, primary versus secondary ($\chi^2 = 13.24$, $p \langle$ .01) and the differences among the four grave types ($\chi^2 = 10.47$, $p \langle$ .01) were statistically significant. At this level of analysis, these results can be interpreted to mean that primary interment was the usual treatment of the dead, with secondary interment probably representing disturbed primary, rather than a normal practice. Also indicated is that grave type may have socially significant variation, as the types cannot be considered to be evenly distributed.

Location

The graves in Tlajinga 33 are in seven locations. These locations were outside the compound walls, under a workshop or large activity area, a courtyard, an apartment patio, or a room, under or in a room wall, and under an altar or shrine. Rooms and walls contain the largest number, 31 (45% of the sample), but activity areas (22%), and altars or shrines (18%) were also common.

However, if one simplifies the location variable to one of interment in domestic space versus interment in public space, the ratio of the public locations—courtyards, large activity areas, and altars—is 28 individuals to 40 from the other locations that are more closely tied to apartment locations. This difference is not statistically significant, and thus location may have status significance only in conjunction with other grave characteristics.

The Nature of Grave Goods

A variety of grave goods, some quite rare, were found with the skeletons and included in the analysis, as they could be crucial to status determinations. For ceramics, the form of each vessel, as well as its frequency, was recorded. Also listed by quantity were obsidian blades and tools, marine shell, shell artifacts, greenstone, figurines, ground-stone tools, worked faunal bones, incensers, mica, bone needles, and slate artifacts. It was expected that the numbers and the types of artifacts present would be important dimensions of the mortuary pattern.

Overall, 48 of the 68 individuals (71%) were accompanied by grave goods, so it was common to place objects with the body. Of these, 39 out of 49 (80%) primary interments had goods, whereas only 8 of 19 (42%) secondary interments did. The obvious drop in grave goods generally found with secondary interments is probably a consequence of their representing disturbed primary burials. Grave goods may not have been placed back with the body in its new location.

Ceramic vessels were the most common grave good, accompanying 43 out of the 48 individuals (89.6%) with grave goods. Of these 43 individuals, 36 (83.7%) had bowls, the single most common grave good. There were wide disparities in the number of bowls placed as offerings. Of those with bowls, only 61% had one or two, but one individual each had 10, 14, 19, and 27 bowls. Other ceramic vessels were found only with two or three individuals and only a couple per individual at most. The importance of these may lie in the variety of different forms found with an individual, rather than in their quantities.

Stone tools were the next most common grave good. Obsidian blades were found with 18 individuals, and as was the case with bowls, there was some disparity in amounts, with one or two blades most common and one burial with five individuals having 30 blades. Other tools were found only one to an individual and include an awl, two obsidian projectile or hafted biface points, and a knife fragment of obsidian plus a ground stone metate fragment and ground stone polisher.

Also present among the Tlajinga 33 grave goods were various exotic goods that would have come into the city as long-distance trade items. Marine shell goods included shell disks (two individuals, one had four of them, and the other, one), shell pendants (six individuals, one had three), shell beads (four individuals of whom two had two and one had circa 4,000), unmodified shells (two individuals, one had three), and pieces of shell (three individuals with one each). Precious greenstone artifacts, made of either serpentine or jadeite, were also found and included beads (six individuals, of which one had two and one had three) and one pendant. Slate was present as one drilled disk and as pieces of painted slate (found with two individuals). Five individuals in one grave were accompanied by a mica disk, and another individual had three small sheets of mica. Mica was otherwise found as small fragments with three individuals. These more valuable grave goods were restricted in their appearance and could be status or wealth indicators.

The other grave goods represent items that cannot be classified in the above categories and were found usually with only up to three individuals and in quantities of one to three. This group includes figurine fragments, bone needles, a sherd disk, a miniature mano and metate, and a piece of worked faunal bone (not obviously a tool). These types of grave goods are likely to be idiosyncratic inclusions but may be useful if they co-occur with many other types. That is, one of the ways grave goods can be used to distinguish mortuary patterns is not only by the quantity of goods that accompany an individual but also by the variety. It may be that the more variety, the wealthier or higher status the individual. This hypothesis is tested below.

Population Characteristics

Knowing the age and sex of the individuals is crucial to understanding and controlling the variations in the other dimensions. Sex was determined only for adults. Age was broken down into categories of infant and perinatal, child (1–9 years), adolescent (10–19), young adult (20–34), middle-aged adult (35–49), and old adult ( ) 50).

As Tlajinga 33 is expected to provide a representative skeletal sample of its residents, there should be all ages present, and both sexes should be evenly represented. The proportions should vary on the basis of mortality and not because of systematic exclusion of certain ages or sex from interment in the compound. For the 68 individuals in formal graves, 47% are subadults and 53% adults, a fairly even split. Male adults outnumber females by a ratio of 19 to 14 (with 3 adults indeterminate), but this difference is not statistically significant. The age breakdown, Table 4-1, reveals that there is at least one individual in every age category. The skeletal ages are analyzed in more depth in Chapter 5, but on a preliminary analysis it is apparent that a few ages are well represented, whereas children, adolescents, and young adults are uncommon. The 6 adults of unknown age can be used to contrast subadult versus adult mortuary patterns but unfortunately cannot aid the finer age analysis. Thus, certain ages are likely to be more informative in any mortuary analysis, and others may be underrepresented. This issue is further investigated below.

Chronological Phase

Also recorded in the analysis were the phase designations of Early Tlamimilolpa, Late Tlamimilolpa, Early Xolalpan, Late Xolalpan, and Early Metepec, corresponding generally to the compound phases discussed in Chapter 3. The phase designations for burials were graciously provided by Dr. Evelyn Rattray of the Universidad Nacional Autónoma de México and the Teotihuacan Mapping Project. It was expected that the mortuary patterns would vary, at least a little, from phase to phase.

If the burials are divided into the three general phases of compound construction (see Chapter 3), then the Early Tlamimilolpa is the smallest with 14 individuals, the Late Tlamimilolpa–Early Xolalpan the largest with 30 and the Late Xolalpan–Early Metepec intermediate with 24. The compound was built during the Early Tlamimilolpa and was smaller than in the later phases. The number of burials should be smaller. For the latter two phases, the compound appears to have been the same size. Chi-square analysis of just these two later phases indicates no statistical significance attributable to the differences in the sample sizes ($\chi^2 = 2.66$, $p \rangle .05$); they can be analytically considered the result of the same size population. Thus, although the number of formal graves is small, the proportions per construction phase and size of compound appear reasonable. Differences in mortuary pattern by phase can be investigated.

Contingency-Table Analysis of Mortuary Variation

By the use of the SPSS-PC+ crosstabs program (SPSS Inc. and Norusis 1986), two-way contingency tables of each variable against every other were obtained so that co-occurrences that might indicate distinct mortuary patterns could be detected. Although statistics were generated, the expected cell frequencies were very often less than 5, as the total sample of 68 is small. When this happens in many cells, the chi-square statistic is questionable (Thomas 1986). Chi square is not actually a measure for strength of association. Instead, the Goodman-Kruskal's *lambda*, which is a statistical measure of the proportional reduction in error when knowledge of one variable is used to predict the classification of another, was used to aid interpretation of any association (SPSS Inc. and Norusis 1986). Goodman-Kruskal *lambda* values are between 0 and 1. A value of 0 means no assocation between the variables, and 1 means

TABLE 4-1
Age Distribution of Individuals
in Formal Graves

Age	Number	Percentage
Perinatals-infants <1 year	24	35.3
Children 1–9 years	7	10.3
Adolescents 10–19 years	1	1.5
Young adults 20–34 years	3	4.4
Middle-aged adults 35–49 years	21	30.9
Old adults 50+ years	6	8.8
Indeterminate adults	6	8.8

perfect association—the value of one variable always indicates the same value of the other variable. A value of .40 to .70 would indicate the presence of a moderate association between the two variables. Each variable is compared in both independent and dependent relation. Thus, the measure of association actually indicates whether the dependent variable clusters in a few values of the independent variable or is almost equally distributed across the latter's categories.

Grave Characteristics

As discussed earlier, the variations of primary versus secondary interment and the four grave-type distinctions were potentially significant, whereas that of multiple versus single bodies was not. When compared for co-occurrence, primary and secondary interments were found to be equally likely to be single or multiple ($\chi^2 = .14$, $p \rangle .70$), so these are independent dimensions. However, when grave type is compared with these variables, patterning of association emerges (Table 4-2). This patterning is especially true of single versus multiple bodies. When an interment is in a ceramic vessel or earthen pit, it is much more likely to be single, whereas a deep *tepetate* pit is multiple. Here the *lambda* measure reveals a moderate 44% association, or reduction in classification error, if grave type is used to predict the number of bodies in the grave. However, number of bodies was much less useful in predicting grave type ($\lambda = .26$), indicating that this variable is distributed fairly equally across all grave types, whereas grave types tended to be associated with single or multiple bodies.

Primary burials are also more likely in ceramic vessels and deep *tepetate* pits, but low *lambda* values reveal no strong predictive value to either

TABLE 4-2
Interment and Grave Type

Grave Type	Total	Number[1]		Interment[2]	
		Single	Multiple	Primary	Secondary
Vessel	15	13	2	15	0
Deep *tepetate* pit	22	5	17	17	5
Shallow *tepetate* basin	7	4	3	5	2
Earth	24	18	6	12	12

[1]λ = .44 with number dependent and .26 with grave type dependent.
[2]λ = .13 with grave type dependent and .00 with interment dependent.

variable, probably because earthen graves were nearly equally divided between primary and secondary interments. Nevertheless, at this point, grave type appears to be an important dimension in the grave descriptions. Patterns evident at this point include the association of ceramic vessel type with primary, single interments, and the association of deep *tepetate* pit graves with primary, multiple interments. Earthen pits were associated with single interments and had the most secondary interments but were just as likely to contain primary ones. The shallow *tepetate* basin type seems to be the least distinguishable here.

Location

One way to look for status differences is to contrast domestic (private) locations with more public ones within the compound. It is expected that the latter will be of higher status or otherwise distinguished from the former. It was seen earlier that there was no statistical significance to the simple numbers of individuals in each type of location. But when these numbers are compared in a contingency table with other variables (Table 4-3), clearer associations stand out. It is evident that domestic locations have single, primary interments in vessels and earthen pits, and only a few in the *tepetate* pits. On the other hand, public locations have multiple, primary interments in deep *tepetate* pits. Secondary interments are more common in the public areas as well. Shallow *tepetate* basins are almost equally divided, and so the pattern here remains unclear. It is possible that there is a status difference between single interments in earth pits in domestic areas and multiple interments in deep *tepetate* pits in public locations. The next step is to see if grave goods further define this difference.

Grave Offerings

It is shown above that there are disparities in the amounts of any one kind of offering placed with an individual and that some kinds of offerings are restricted to a few individuals. A common way to sum up grave goods is to measure and compare their quantity and complexity among individuals (Binford 1971; Sempowski 1987). Tallying the total number of offerings, the number of different types of artifacts (variety), and the number of exotic artifacts are ways to measure quantity and complexity (Sempowski 1987). A three-way score using each measure is calculated for every primary interment at Tlajinga 33 and compared. Secondary interments are not used, since they seem to represent disturbed primary interments, and many may lack all or part of their original offering. Thus, their scores would be misleading.

The 21 individuals (31% of the individuals in formal graves) with no grave goods have not yet been discussed. Obviously, these individuals rate zero in offering. There are 11 secondary and 10 primary interments. Some of the secondary individuals represent those whose offerings were not replaced with them upon reinterment from their primary context, and so they are not considered further here.

The 10 primary interments with no offerings are divided into 4 single and 6 in multiple interments. Seven are in domestic locations, all under rooms. The 3 in public locations were in deep *tepetate* pits with other individuals who had offerings. Thus, domestic locations in earthen pits seem more common in this category.

For those with offerings, the count of actual numbers of artifacts placed with an individual range from 43 to 1. This excludes two burials looted in recent times, whose offerings could not be reconstructed. The average was 7.5 items per individual, but only 15 out of the 37 were above the average. Thus, the bulk of the individuals, 21, have 5 or fewer items, and one has 7. The sample can then be divided into two groups. Of the 15 individuals above the average, 9 are in deep pits, 4 in shallow *tepetate* basins, and 2 in earth. Thus, the higher energy expenditure represented by *tepetate* burial pits correlates with a larger number of offerings, which indicates that these components probably point to higher status. Seven are single interments, and 8 are multiple. Of the latter, 5 are in the same deep pit. As for location, 7 are under altars, 5 under rooms, 2 just outside the compound boundaries, and 1 is in an activity area. This gives an 8-to-7 public-to-domestic location split.

TABLE 4-3
Domestic versus Public
Locations of Burials

	Domestic	Public
Number		
Single	30	10
Multiple	10	18
Interment Type		
Primary	32	17
Secondary	8	11
Grave Type		
Vessel	13	2
Shallow *tepetate* basin	4	3
Deep *tepetate* pit	4	18
Earth	19	5

In contrast, the 21 individuals with 5 or fewer items are divided into 15 in vessels, 1 in a deep *tepetate* pit, 1 in a shallow basin, and 4 in earth interments. Of these, 18 are single interments. Sixteen are in domestic locations, and 5 are in public ones. Thus, although domestic locations are found with high-status burials, they are less common in these locations.

The relative "value" of the offering is investigated by counting the different types of items included. Different ceramic vessels, tool, or ornament types were counted separately. The average here was 2.8 different types of artifacts per offering, ranging from 1 to 9. Of the 15 individuals with above-average numbers of items, 14 also have 3 or more different types of items (see Figure 4-1). Only 4 of the individuals with 5 or fewer items had 3 or 4 different types. Thus, quantity and variety are associated, along with *tepetate* pits in public locations, as higher-status characteristics.

A further measure of the value is to count the number of items made of the exotic materials, which might be thought of as a measure of wealth. The average is 0.9 items per individual, because only 15 individ-

Figure 4-1. The Offering Accompanying the Burial 25 Female. The offering includes ceramic vessels, three greenstone beads, a shell disk, and a toy mano and metate. This is an example of a varied offering, ranking high in number and exotic goods.

uals out of 37 have any of these types of items. However, these 15 individuals are not exactly the same as those with larger-than-average numbers of artifacts; only 12 of the latter have these exotic types of items. Two individuals with less than 5 total items also have exotic items, as well as the individual with a total of 7 items. Three individuals with 8, 13, and 19 total items have none of the exotic materials. Exotic items are associated with large grave good quantities but are not limited to such individuals.

Thus, it is possible to use the association of four mortuary indices: (1) *tepetate* pits with the (2) larger numbers of offerings, (3) greater variety of offerings, and (4) the presence of artifacts made of exotic material, to define a subset of 10 individuals that definitely have all the wealth and energy definitions associated with high status. These individuals are considered the burials of highest status in Tlajinga 33. Below this highest strata are 8 individuals, including those with above-average numbers of grave goods but in an earth pit (2), those with above-average numbers of grave goods but no exotic items (3), and the individuals with less-than-average number of items but at least one of exotic materials (3). This groups the rest of the individuals with deep and shallow *tepetate* pits and offerings, plus a few earthen ones. The 19 individuals with few items and no exotic goods in earth or vessel graves may be the third level. At the bottom are the 10 individuals with no offering. Table 4-4 lists the burials and characteristics in this four-part ranking.

Further analysis could subdivide this general ranking, but for the purposes of the paleodemographic study, it suffices to be able to generally delineate some internal differences in the population. It is evident that the compound has a few individuals whose mortuary characteristics involve more energy and wealth than others. These individuals might be thought of as having high status within the compound. The presence of three other possible subdivisions is an indication that internal status differentiation or other social distinctions reflected in the mortuary characteristics within the compound are likely to be complex. The residents of a Teotihuacan compound are not a socially homogeneous group; the results at Tlajinga 33 have been found at other excavated compounds as well (Sempowski 1987). However, since all of the burials within the compound are likely to be kin-related in some way (Millon 1981), they probably represent a single social strata or class within Teotihuacan society. This assumption suggests that the variable mortuary treatment reflects different wealth accumulation and economic function within the compound, rather than different social classes.

Once several potential status and wealth distinctions on the basis of grave and offering characteristics have been identified, further analysis of the populational characteristics and chronology is needed to further refine the results. It is possible that different segments of the population of the compound fall into different statuses, and there may also be changes through time in mortuary characteristics at Tlajinga 33.

Population Characteristics

Age and sex should be important distinctions in Tlajinga 33, as most societies do define roles and status to different ages and sex. Males were more common among the individuals in formal graves but not significantly so. Sex seems unimportant in whether an individual is primary or secondary or buried singly or with others. Males, for example, are found in a ratio of 16 primary to 3 secondary; females are similarly distributed, with 10 primary and 4 secondary. Males number 9 in single and 10 in multiple interments; females have frequencies of 8 and 6, respectively. *Lambda* is close to zero in both cases, revealing that sex is independent of

TABLE 4-4
Preliminary Ranking of
Tlajinga 33 Primary Interments

Top Level (10 individuals)
High numbers of offerings, including exotic items

Deep *tepetate* pit: Burials 30b, 50a, 50b, 50c, 50d, 50e, 56, 57
Shallow *tepetate* basin: Burials 14, 25

Second Level (8 individuals)
Offerings include exotic items

Deep *tepetate* pit: Burials 6, 42a, 42b
Shallow *tepetate* basin: Burial 11
Earthen pit: Burials 2a, 10, 15, 60a

Third Level (19 individuals)
Five or fewer items, none exotic

Vessel burial: Burials 3, 5, 7, 8, 9, 21d, 32, 33, 39, 55, 64, 65, 66
Earthen pit: Burials 29, 31, 43, 44, 51, 59

Fourth Level (10 individuals)
No offerings

Dee*p tepetate* pit: Burials 21a, 21b, 30a
Earthen pit: Burials 20, 26, 49, 60b, 60c, 60d, 61

these interment types. The distinctions of primary versus secondary and single versus multiple interments have generally been independent in their interactions with other mortuary variables as well.

Grave type, however, has important associations with other variables. Fourteen males have *tepetate* pits but 5 have earth pits; 9 females are buried in *tepetate* pits, 5 in earth. Chi-square analysis reveals a significant difference ($\chi^2 = 5.4$, $p < .05$), which reflects that males are disproportionately more likely to be in *tepetate* pits than in earth pits, whereas grave type in females is more evenly distributed. As for location, females have a breakdown of 10 individuals in domestic and 4 public locations. Males are distributed thus: 11 in public locations and 8 in domestic ones. Males are more common in public locations and much more common under altars, a ritually important location. Although domestic locations have just about equal numbers of males and females, males are more likely to be in public locations and to be in *tepetate* pits.

As for the previously described social divisions (see Table 4-4), 7 of the 10 assigned to the highest status are male, revealing a very definite male bias here. In the next level there are 4 males, 2 females, and 2 infants, making 11 males to 5 females in the highest two statuses of Tlajinga 33. Thus, males dominate in public locations and in the energy and wealth measures of *tepetate* pits and accompanying grave goods. Males, rather than females, predominate in higher statuses.

With respect to age associations, Table 4-5 presents the breakdowns by interment types. Primary interments are quite prominent among perinatals and infants; among the older adults, no secondary interments occur. As for single versus multiple interments, single interments are most common among perinatals and infants, and this is where practically all of the total differential between single and multiple interments lies. Thus, this variable, which has not been well understood, is now explained. Individuals are almost equally likely to be single or multiple interments, except as infants. *Thus, placement in a solo grave and placement with other individuals are both common mortuary patterns in Tlajinga 33, and the difference is determined mostly by whether the grave is in* tepetate *or in earth.*

Infants are also differentiated by grave type (see Table 4-5). All 15 ceramic vessel burials are of perinatals and infants only (see Figure 4-2), and as all are single individuals as well, this pattern accounts for much of the variation in the number in a grave and the grave type measure. It is not uncommon for infants to be afforded special mortuary treatment in many societies (see Ubelaker 1989). Otherwise, adults of known age are much more common in *tepetate* than in earth pits. Of interest is the pattern of mostly deep *tepetate* pits among the middle and older adults, as well as the strong association of middle-aged adults with shallow *tepetate* basins. Many of the earth pits for adults of undetermined age can be explained by the fact that they are secondary, which are more common in earthen pits. Some subadults do have *tepetate* pits but in all cases are in multiple interments. No subadult is interred alone in a *tepetate* pit. The association between age and grave type yields a moderately strong *lambda* of 0.54, when age is used to predict grave type. Thus, adults, except when secondary, predominate in *tepetate* pits, and the energy investment of this type of grave does seem to reflect higher achieved statuses.

When location is investigated, the contrast of domestic versus public locations by age is not as dramatic (Table 4-6). Domestic locations are

Table 4-5
Tlajinga 33 Grave and Interment Types by Age Groups

	Perinatal, Infant	Child	Adoles- cent	Young Adult	Middle- aged Adult	Old Adult	Indeterm. Adult
Interment							
Primary	19	3	0	2	17	6	2
Secondary	5	4	1	1	4	0	4
Number							
Single body	18	2	1	3	12	1	3
Multiple bodies	6	5	0	0	9	5	3
Grave type							
Vessel	15	0	0	0	0	0	0
Deep *tepetate* pit	2	3	0	1	10	4	0
Shallow *tepetate* basin	1	0	0	0	5	0	1
Earth pit	6	4	1	2	6	2	5

more common for all ages except children, young adults, and old adults. As there are very few children and young adults, mortuary patterns for these ages are not likely to be clear. However, the presence of older adults mostly in public locations is exactly what would be expected, if status tended to be achieved through lifetime service. Closer inspection of the location variables indicates that just about all ages are found in rooms and activity areas, the most common locations anyway. Under altars, which might be the most restricted location, there are 5 subadults (under one altar), 1 young adult, 4 middle-aged adults, and 1 older adult. Thus, as is found for other variables, location does not yield the strong association with age that grave type does.

However, as was seen with the variable of sex, the ranking by offer- ing clarifies the situation somewhat. The highest two status categories contain 2 infants, 1 young adult, 10 middle-aged adults, and 5 old

Figure 4-2. A Perinatal Burial in a Vessel. Clearly visible are the ribs, vertebrae, pelvis, right arm, and leg.

adults. Older individuals predominate in the "wealthier" categories, and all but one of the old adults were in these strata. However, the presence of a young adult and two infants indicates that age is not the sole determinant of high social position. Conversely, among the 10 individuals at the bottom of the hierarchy with no offerings, 4 middle-aged adults, 1 old adult, 2 undetermined adults, 2 children, and an infant are present, a wide spread of ages. The middle-aged adult category, especially, seems to be divided between high and low. Although older adults ages tend to have wealthier and higher-status mortuary preparations, other factors than age are present, as not all older individuals are found here, and some younger individuals also appear in the higher statuses.

Chronology

No interment types seem to be affected by differences in phasing. Secondary interments were close to the same proportion in each of the three main chronological divisions: 9 primary to 5 secondary (36%) in

TABLE 4-6
Age Groups of Tlajinga 33
Interments by Location

	Domestic	Public
Perinatals and infants	17	7
Children	2	5
Adolescents	1	0
Young adults	1	2
Middle-aged adults	12	9
Old adults	2	4
Indeterminate adults	5	1

the Early Tlamimilolpa, 21 to 9 (43%) in the Late Tlamimilolpa–Early Xolalpan, and 19 to 5 (26%) in the Late Xolalpan. *Lambda* values were very low, indicating little association of chronology with interment type. Similarly, multiple interments were almost as likely as single in the Early Tlamimilolpa and Late Xolalpan. In Late Tlamimilolpa–Early Xolalpan, only a third were multiple, but the association of number of individuals and chronology still yields lambdas near 0. Thus, as with all other variables except age, number and interment type are independent in action.

Grave type and location are compared by phase in Table 4-7. Vessel burials are rarer in the Early Tlamimilolpa than later. *Tepetate* pits are less common and earth pits more so in the Late Xolalpan. As for location, although the phases have some burials in most locations, a comparison of domestic and public locations is interesting. In the Early Tlamimilolpa public locations are more common, although this may be an artifact of what is preserved from the compound from this phase (see Chapter 3). The other phases have more individuals in domestic locations, 56% in the Late Tlamimilolpa–Early Xolalpan, rising to 75% during the Late Xolalpan. This pattern reinforces the perception of public locations as being more restricted. Altar burials rise from 2 in Early Tlamimilolpa to 5 in both the later phases. Activity area burials are common in the earlier phases but fall to only one during the Late Xolalpan. Thus, there is some shifting in locations through time, and a drop in percentage of public burials through time.

Sex distribution is fairly even through the phases, except for the Late Xolalpan, where there is a ratio of 8 males to 3 females. However, the distribution of sex by phase was not statistically significant. There are

TABLE 4-7
Grave Characteristics of
Tlajinga 33 Burials by Phase

	Early Tlamimilolpa	Late Tlamimlolpa-Early Xolalpan	Late Xolalpan-Early Metepec
Ceramic vessel	1	7	7
Deep *tepetate* pit	9	8	5
Shallow *tepetate* basin	0	7	0
Earth	4	8	12
Domestic locations	5	17	18
Public locations	9	13	6

also minor differences in the age breakdown by phase, but the *lambda* measures indicate only weak association of phase and age. The population by phase characteristics is discussed in more depth in Chapter 5. As for the description of graves, there does not seem to be a serious age or sex bias to the individuals present for any period, as subadults are always 40%–50% of all individuals, and males and females are fairly evenly distributed.

Investigation of the offering rankings (Table 4-4) reveals that of the 10 individuals with no offering, only 2 are from the Early Tlamimilolpa, and they are multiple interments accompanying an individual with a fairly rich offering. There are 4 each in the other two phases, paralleling a pattern of rise of domestic locations. This represents a rise in proportion of burials with no offering from 12%–13% of Early Tlamimilolpa through Early Xolalpan burials to 16% of the Late Xolalpan individuals. For the upper two rankings, 5 are from the Early Tlamimilolpa (36% of that phase's interments), 7 from Late Tlamimilolpa–Early Xolalpan (23% of that phase), and 6 from Late Xolalpan (25% of that phase), so there was a slight diminution through time of wealthy burials, although these differences are not statistically significant.

Although wealth trends could be considered stable across time at Tlajinga 33, this conclusion would be a mistake, as there does seem to be decrease of wealth from the Early Tlamimilolpa through later periods. The measure that best reflects this is the number of exotic items. Greenstone does not occur with any of the Late Xolalpan burials, and the only items present in the Late Xolalpan are mica and one shell pendant. These findings contrast with the wealthy burials of earlier periods, which contained up to 11 (Early Tlamimilolpa) and 4 (Late Tlamimilolpa–Early Xolalpan) different items of greenstone and shell. The highest-ranking individual, Burial 57, is from the Early Tlamimilolpa. This middle-aged male was wrapped or clothed in a garment that had approximately 4,000 olivella shells sewn on it. On the skull was an elaborate headdress consisting of four shell disks (see Figure 4-3). This individual was also accompanied by greenstone beads, shell pendants, and shell fragments. No other individual had such elaborately crafted exotic items. Also, except for the 5 individuals in the shaft tomb during the Late Xolalpan (Burial 50), which had 43 different items in an undoubtedly incomplete recovery of the original offering, no other Late Xolalpan burial had more than 5 items, a wider gulf in offering quantity and complexity than is present in the earlier two phases. There are various individuals with moderate-to-large offerings in the earlier phases. Thus, the Early Tlamimilolpa is probably the wealthiest phase, as more individuals are found in public locations with wealthier offerings of exotic items. Also more individuals have offerings, compared with the last phase, where most individuals are in domestic locations and have few to no offerings, and there is a great gulf between the richest grave and all others of the period (see Figure 4-4).

Summary and Comparison with Other Compounds at Teotihuacan

Sixty-eight individuals in formal graves out of 110 individuals excavated as burial contexts are not a large sample on which to base interpretations of mortuary patterns. Of these, only 49 are primary interments, which appears to be the usual mode of disposal of the dead. Nineteen are secondary burials, which represent disturbed and reburied individuals, sometimes with at least part of their grave goods. Forty-two are secondary-context interments of small concentrations of human bone, usually including pieces of several individuals, found in fill and middens in the compound. These individuals also probably represent mainly disturbed interments (we are ignoring the individuals with cut marks for the moment), but they were obviously reburied with less care than secondary ones and never with any offerings. These individuals are fragmentary and have lost all of their original mortuary characteristics.

However, in spite of these problems, there does seem to be good evidence of internal status differences among the residents of Tlajinga 33, ranging from those in deep graves excavated into *tepetate* bedrock and

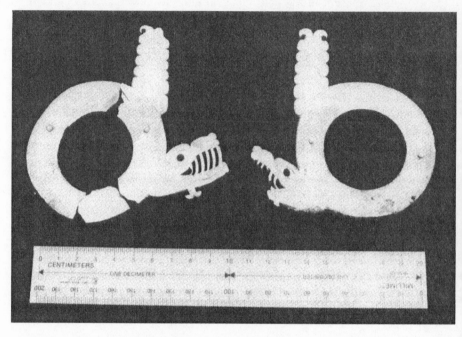

Figure 4-3. Part of the Shell Headdress on the Skull of Burial 57

accompanied by a variety of lavish offerings, including shell and green-stone, to those in simple earth pits dug just large enough to hold a flexed body and otherwise accompanied by no offerings or at most a bowl or other token. Through time, there seems to have been a decrease in the number of individuals of the former type and proportionately more of the latter.

Males are favored with more energy investment in mortuary features and tend to predominate in public locations, although a few females have impressive offerings, one having been buried in an altar. It has been thought that Teotihuacan compounds were lineage-based but probably with patrilineal bias (Millon 1976). Findings in Tlajinga 33 seems to support a possible patrilineal pattern, but the higher-ranking females may also indicate the presence of some cognatic pattern as well. Future analysis of the Tlajinga 33 skeletons may determine if a lineage structure is present. Otherwise, the predominance of middle and older adults in the higher statuses seems to indicate that status within the compound was probably mostly achieved, and that statuses could be defined

Figure 4-4. A Flexed Burial with No Offerings, from the Late Xolalpan

on a compound-wide level. Individuals of ability in the older ages hold positions of social and religious importance within the compound that are reflected in their treatment at death. The fact that children and adolescents lack offerings indicates that they did not live long enough to achieve a position in the compound that would entitle them to wealth indicators at death.

However, there are individuals whose status is possibly ascribed, that is to say, they were born to higher-ranking families. Burial 57 and the infant in Burial 10, both dated to the Early Tlamimilolpa, are examples. Their relative youth at death and the richness of mortuary characteristics seem to indicate that there is some internal social differentiation of families within the compound, with high-status families able to dispose of more wealth. It is, however, more likely that any differential treatment of children simply reflects the achieved status of their parents. These possibly ascribed individuals are always a minority and seem to disappear even by Late Tlamimilolpa times. Thus, the Tlajinga 33 compound seems to have a mostly egalitarian organization, where status differences are affected by age and sex and are primarily achieved. On the other hand, the overall stratification of society in the city may affect the residents by the presence of some individuals with an inherently higher status.

The simpler internal status distinctions and greater poverty of mortuary characteristics in the Late Xolalpan may be due to the shifts in the occupational specialization of the compound and may reflect a shift in the status of the compound in the overall status structure of the city. It may be that during the Early and Late Tlamimilolpa status definitions in the city of Teotihuacan were fluid enough, so that adults could have four or more status types recognizable in mortuary treatment. By Late Xolalpan times, the Teotihuacan structure had become more rigidly defined and institutionalized, and thus the possible adult status types that a craft specialists' compound like Tlajinga 33 could have dropped to two.

It could also be that the shift in craft specialization to stress ceramic production affected the internal status organization. Jewelers and lapidaries could perhaps demonstrate great individual differences in craft skill on the media that was worked that could be reflected in different adult status positions, whereas with ceramic production of a standardized ware like San Martin Orange, there is less opportunity for individual differences. Status can be more simply defined. With a shift of more effort to ceramic production, and perhaps a deemphasis of the lapidary production, the higher status during Late Xolalpan may have been concerned ultimately with compound administrative functions involving the marketing of the ware and the position of the Tlajinga 33 compound in the Tlajinga barrio, rather than with craft skill. Those could have easily been achieved positions that merited burial in the shaft tomb. Whatever the explanation, it is obvious that the burial program of adults of the Late Xolalpan is different from that of the earlier periods.

Although Tlajinga 33 is only one residential compound of a large, complex city and cannot be legitimately generalized to all other Teotihuacan compounds, its internal organization is consistent with a compound of low-status craft specialists living on the edge of the city. In that case one would not expect internal differences among residents to be great, and what differences are present would mostly be the result of individual initiatives and qualities reflected in achieved statuses. And yet Tlajinga 33 also indicates that, as befits a residence composed of multiple families living in proximity and cooperating for their economic support, there are differences among residents that could reflect the nature of the craft specialization and the relation of the compound to the overall social organization of the city.

The mortuary variation observed at Tlajinga 33 is similar to that found in other compounds. Patterns found at Tlajinga 33 are then reinforced as being indicative of the city. Sempowski (1987: 127–128) drew eight conclusions about differential mortuary treatment in the three compounds of Tetitla, Zacuala Patios, and La Ventilla B that she studied: (1) that there was considerable social differentiation within a compound; (2) that adults in general had higher status than subadults; (3) that males had generally higher status than females; (4) that, at least at La Ventilla B, some subgroups (families?) had higher status; (5) that through time there was decreasing social differentiation; (6) that compounds could be ranked in relative status to each other, that is, lower-class compounds can be so identified; (7) that there is change in compound status position through time, and basically there is an increasing gap beween wealthier and poorer compounds and a greater simplification of compound status into high and low; and (8) that there is less appearance of certain artifacts and exotic imported materials at poorer compounds during the latter phases of the city. All these patterns are found in Tlajinga 33 and have been discussed. A general comparison with Sempowski's (1987) ranking of compounds puts Tlajinga 33 very close to La Ventilla B. Thus, although there are some wealthy burials at Tlajinga 33, the overall pattern is of lower-status burials, so that the mortuary analysis reinforces the architectural designation of this compound as of low status within the city of Teotihuacan. Its demographic characteristics should be informative and representative, therefore, as to what it was like to be poor craft specialists in the urban lifestyle of the first city in Mesoamerica.

General Demographic Characteristics of the Tlajinga 33 Population

THE TLAJINGA 33 skeletal population was found in two different contexts. The burials were more carefully and completely excavated, but human material from general provenience contexts was collected from screens and general shoveling and troweling. The burial contexts often contain significant proportions of an individual; the general provenience collections are all skeletal bits, mostly of incomplete elements. A further complication is that 42 of the individuals excavated as burial contexts had no evidence of a formal grave or much care in their deposition but were just a concentration of bones placed together haphazardly. These were called refuse interments and consist of pieces of several individuals placed in midden or fill. Thus, although they were excavated as if they were formal burials, their actual mortuary characteristics do not differ from those of human bone found in midden or fill during screening. In neither case was there evidence of a formal grave. Thus, both the refuse interments and the human bone from general provenience have been analytically combined and classified as secondary-context individuals, representative of human skeletons disturbed by some process or activity during the history of the compound and to whom the living did not feel any strong obligation to provide with formal graves.

The Tlajinga 33 skeletal populaton thus has two sources: (1) skeletons from formal graves, where individuals were fairly easy to distinguish and much of the skeleton could be recovered; and (2) human bones from middens or fill that represent small, incomplete fragments of skeletons. In this second case, individuals can be distinguished only by overlapping elements or obvious age and size differences.

With the refuse burials and the general provenience collections combined together as secondary-context individuals, the Tlajinga 33 skeletal population is mostly composed of incomplete individuals. This problem is compounded by the generally poor preservation of even those individuals in formal graves. Although undisturbed since placement, grave individuals often lacked epiphyses on long bones, and some skeletal elements seemed to have completely disappeared, as they were not recovered even by the careful screening of pit fill. Ribs and vertebrae were often missing, for example, or else were in many fragments. Teotihuacan burials generally have been poorly preserved (for example, La Ventilla B), perhaps because of the chemical effects of the *tepetate* bedrock (a consolidated volcanic ash) on bone, the effect of rodents (quite a few bones had been chewed on), or simply the effect of the alternating dry and wet seasons, with deep pits acting as catch basins for runoff water.

If there is poor preservation anyway, a disturbed burial will then probably suffer a high loss of skeletal elements. It is not surprising that secondary interments generally have fewer elements than primary ones. Individuals that were in trash middens or lacked graves obviously did not reveal careful treatment of the skeleton, and even fewer elements of these individuals are found. Thus, the predominance of fragmentary remains at Tlajinga 33 presented a methodological problem for carrying out a paleodemographic study.

In spite of these problems, this investigation makes the fullest possible use of fragmentary remains in order to use the maximum number of individuals in the paleodemographic study. The Tlajinga 33 apartment compound is appropriate for such research, because the skeletons come from one residence and perhaps were related individuals (Spence 1974; Millon 1976), and as such represent a true population. The Tlajinga 33 compound was occupied only during the Classic period, and thus the population comes from a fairly restricted time period and from one cultural system, the urban center of Teotihuacan at its height.

The length of occupation of the compound is from sometime during the Early Tlamimilolpa period (c. A.D. 200–300) to early in the Metepec period (c. A.D. 650–750), so that the best estimate is between 400–450 years, with a maximum possible span of 500 years. This length of occupation may be slightly too long for an optimum population definition. Much can occur to a population in 400 years, and so attention is given in the analysis to possible time differences. Because of the temporal depth of many archaeological populations, it is not uncommon for skeletal studies to treat individuals as part of one population for more than 400 years. Since there is a continuity in occupation at Tlajinga 33, all the skeletons are lumped together, regardless of phase. Temporal differences should be controlled, but it is reasonable and useful to treat all the Tlajinga 33 skeletons as a group. The two analytical approaches, breaking the population into chronologically distinct units and treating it as a single population, will be used in the analyses to follow. Thus, Tlajinga 33 fulfills the conditions of spatial and temporal integrity necessary to yield reasonable demographic results. It is a valid biological population.

The Tlajinga 33 skeletons themselves constitute the data that are utilized as much as possible to provide the populational standards, patterns, and indices; this study has not just applied standards from other reference skeletal or modern living populations to every skeleton. The more complete remains are used to determine populational standards, after which the fragmentary remains can be investigated to determine which indices and measures might be present, and their values can be compared to the standards. In this way, individuals represented only by fragments can add information to the various aspects of the paleo-demographic study. Although the more fragmentary and incomplete the skeletal remains of an individual, the less the accuracy in determining demographic indicators of age and sex from the bones, it is essential to use all possible individuals to determine the demographic patterns in the Tlajinga 33 compound because of the small sample size involved. Although there are possible errors, whose effects upon the analyses are discussed below, the benefits of using the maximum amount of information available offsets any risks resulting from misclassifying some small proportion of the fragmentary individuals. It is always possible to model the potential effects of misclassification on demographic characteristics to provide a check on the degree of its effect on the paleodemographic analysis.

In this chapter the general demographic characteristics of age and sex of the Tlajinga 33 compound are presented. The purpose is to set the foundation for the paleodemographic study and to further test the skeletal population for its suitability for the study. The age and sex parameters of the skeletons must be representative of a living population if the study is to be valid. The age and sex distributions are first determined from the more complete individuals in formal graves; these establish the populational standards that can then be used for the more fragmentary individuals. Next, the secondary-context human bone is analyzed to determine the number of individuals represented and their determinable age and sex characteristics. The chapter ends with the assembling of the general demographic composition of the total skeletal population available from the apartment compound.

The Sex and Age of Individuals from Formal Graves

Estimates of age and sex from skeletal remains are based on standards derived from twentieth-century skeletons, many from known cadavers. The literature on the subject is still growing, and new techniques often appear (see Black 1978; Iscan et al. 1984). However, application of these techniques to a prehistoric skeletal population is not without risks. These risks are two kinds: (1) there is normal variation among individuals of the same population, which is hard to control for skeletons that provide no individuals of known sex and age, and (2) the differences may be considerable between the modern U.S. white and black populations, which are used as standards, and the prehistoric populations of a different ethnicity that are being studied (Ubelaker 1989). Thus, the estimation of age and sex had to be performed carefully, and any decisions are subject to a certain amount of error. There are preferred techniques for each kind of determination, and the more complete the skeleton, the more accurate the estimation is likely to be. For the Tlajinga 33 skeletal population, the best techniques are used where possible, but the fragmentary specimens, which lack the best diagnostic features, required the use of some alternative methods, which are not as reliable.

Sex

Determination of sex will be discussed first because it is easier to determine skeletally, and the techniques yield more accurate results than do techniques for age. Sex is generally determined only for adults and older adolescents, since it is only in these age classes that secondary sex characteristics are developed enough to allow one to discriminate males from females. Sex is usually not determined for prehistoric subadults. Although methods have been suggested (see Boucher 1957; Weaver 1980), many are for fetal or newborn individuals. Tlajinga 33 has a large collection of fetal and newborn individuals, but sexing methods have not yet been applied to them. For older subadults, the best techniques involve the correlation of differences in the patterns of teeth and postcranial growth per age with sex (Hunt and Gleiser 1955). Prehistoric subadult skeletons are often incomplete, and their chronological age is an estimation based on the maturity of their bones and teeth. Using one estimate, age, to then make another, sex, usually has too great a potential error to make the sexing of subadults worthwhile. Tlajinga 33 subadults, which were highly fragmentary in general, were therefore not sexed, although some methods will be tried in the future.

Most diagnostic secondary sex characteristics are found on the pelvis, which is the preferred single bone. The cranium is next best, although its use poses much more potential error (Meindl et al. 1985a). Although either can be used separately, combining the two has yielded accuracies in sexing of more than 95% on modern specimens (Acsádi and Nemeskéri 1970; Ubelaker 1989). A description of the characteristics from the cranium and pelvis used to distinguish sex can be found in a variety of standard osteological references (see Bass 1987; Steele and Bramblett 1988).

On the pelvis the best criteria for sexing are the characteristics of the pubis (see Phenice 1969) such as the presence of a ventral arc, the subpubic concavity, the nature of the medial ischio-pubic ramus, and the subpubic angle. Next best are characteristics of the ilium, including the width of sciatic notch, the presence of a preauricular sulcus, the elevation of auricular area, and rugosity of the acetabulum. Because pubes were rarely preserved at Tlajinga 33, ilial characteristics had to be employed most often, although they are more variable between the sexes than the pubis.

For the cranium, the sex differences are mostly a result of robusticity and size, males being generally larger than females in human populations (Meindl et al. 1985a; Steele and Bramblett 1988). The size of the mastoids, the ruggedness of the occipital, the size of the supraorbital torus, the shape of the orbits, the strength of the zygomatic process, forehead characters, the shape of the chin, and the degree of gonial angle on the mandible were taken into account. The male cranium usually has more pronounced muscle markings, is larger, and more rugged in its appearance.

However, when descriptive characteristics of pelves and crania on individuals in formal graves were used, only 18 had sufficient pelvis or cranium or both to yield a clear sex determination. Of these, 7 could be sexed by pubic features and other pelvic indicators, usually the sciatic notch and the presence or absence of a preauricular sulcus, and another 8 by other pelvic indicators and the cranium. Only 3 were sexed from just the cranium, and these were judged to be strongly male crania. Of these 18 individuals, 13 were males and 5 were female. This result yields a highly uneven sex ratio, which could be attributable solely to the small size of the sample. However, this explanation does not appear to be the case; instead, the uneven ratio seems to reflect a male-biased mortuary pattern, as discussed in Chapter 4. Males predominated in the higher-status graves, and these graves contained the better-preserved individuals. Thus, additional analysis is needed to determine the sex ratio of the population as a whole.

Although skeletal sexing can be quite accurate, it is subject to some bias, which needs to be kept in mind by a researcher, especially if indices other than the pubis are relied on. In a reanalysis of skeletal sexing, Meindl et al. (1985a) found that mistakes are rarely made on actual female pelves, whereas males are sometimes misclassified by pelvic morphology because of the greater variability allowable by natural selection in male pelves. They also concluded that cranial sexing is less accurate, partly because older age produces a more pronounced male morphology in both sexes. This double effect of age and increased robustness has been noted in other studies. Females increased in certain measures of robustness of bone with increasing age (Pfeiffer 1980; Hamilton 1982). Because much of the cranial sexing and classification of a skeleton as male depends on defining it as more robust than a female one, size indicators may bias the overall skeletal population sexing toward males (Weiss 1972; Hamilton 1982). Both of these biases could be present here, although all females were determined from pelvic indicators that were markedly female. A possible bias may be that some of the individuals are misclassified as males, although again the 18 sexed are the individuals who were sufficiently complete and possessed criteria that could be judged as definitely either male or female. Individuals with more intermediate morphology, even if cranium and some pelvis were available, are not included in the 18.

To be able to check for possible misclassifications and to be able to use more individuals in the sexing study, one must employ a technique that can use more fragmentary remains. One needs more sexed individuals from the population before one can judge whether the Tlajinga 33 population had a representative sex ratio, or if there is a bias that could affect the paleodemographic study.

The best technique to use on the remains that lack good descriptive sex indicators is a discriminant function (Van Vark 1970; Giles 1970). This statistical technique is used when a population is composed of two subpopulations having different means. The technique "discriminates" which individuals belong to which subpopulation and calculates the two means. In human populations, males are generally larger and have more massive bones than females, and thus discriminant-function sexing works on differences in size to define the two subpopulations or sexes.

In a discriminate function, the equation $D_x = k + b_1x_1 + b_2x_2 + b_3x_3 + \ldots b_nx_n$ should be solved so that D_x will tend toward one range of values if male and toward another, lower, range of values if female. Giles (1970: 108–9) provided a series of 49 measurements of the skeleton intended to quantify most sexually distinctive size dimensions in humans.

These measurements are the *x*s of the equation. Each measurement can be combined in various ways and with varying weights, *b*s, with other measures. A particular combination of measures and their weights in the form of the above equation is called a discriminant function. The resulting *D* is then evaluated in terms of the sectioning point of the function—the point that divides the males and females. The sectioning point is chosen as the one that misclassifies the fewest individuals of known sex. Using skeletons of known sex, one calculates functions that are most accurate in discriminating sex in a population, that is, functions that misclassify the fewest individuals. These functions can then be used to classify individuals whose sex is unknown when one uses descriptive criteria.

In humans, the sizes of the sexes overlap, and thus there is always an intermediate area around the sectioning point of any function where sex determination is less accurate because females may fall in the male range, and vice versa. Thus, the error rates of misclassification for discriminant functions average 10%–15% (Giles 1970), although some can be as low as 6%–8% (Hunter and Garn 1972). In spite of these problems, discriminant analysis is a generally accurate method of sexing that can be used to sex material otherwise not usable, although it must be remembered that its accuracy is likely to be less than the descriptive methods on a well-preserved skeleton.

Since the publication of Giles's study, many authors have used the technique and added useful functions. Studies have used the mandible (Hunter and Garn 1972), the foot (Steele 1976), and tooth crowns (Ditch and Rose 1972). A further refinement has been the use of only one bone, like the tibia (Iscan and Miller-Shavitz 1984) or humerus (France 1988). However, there have also been studies that show that although discriminant analysis using multiple sets of variables does have reasonable accuracy, its results are often not much better than those obtainable from the use of certain single measures, for example, the midshaft circumference of the femur (Black 1978) or the diameter of the humeral head or the maximum diameter of the femoral head (Dittrick and Suchey 1986). These latter measures are meant to be more usable with fragmentary remains, as might be present with archaeologically derived skeletons.

For a skeletal population like that of Tlajinga 33, discriminant functions, especially with the use of single bones, and single measures are potentially useful, if not necessary, techniques because of the general fragmentary nature of the remains. A review of the literature indicates that for maximum accuracy, discriminant-function equations and sectioning points have to be uniquely determined for each population.

Thus, if the Tlajinga 33 individuals sexed by pelvis and cranium are to be used as the basis for discrimination, functions could be calculated for the Tlajinga population that would allow a determination of unsexed individuals, although with some potential error.

A total of 87 measures could be taken on the Tlajinga 33 bones and teeth when those measures used by Giles (1970) were incorporated with various others found in the literature (see the Appendix for a description of all measures employed). Ideally, discriminant functions should be performed on complete data sets, where there are no missing measurements. The Tlajinga 33 material certainly does not provide such an ideal data set. The number of measures available per individual varied greatly, ranging from only 2 to 76 for the 33 grave-context individuals used in this analysis. The average was 28 measures, but 24% of the sample had 6 or less. Fortunately, those with the most measures tended to be the individuals sexed by pelvis and cranium (the average number of measures for these individuals was 39), so they could be used in many of the combinations of measures needed to calculate discriminant functions for this skeletal population (see Table 5-1). Because of the few measures usually available per individual and the fact that relatively few of these overlapped among the unsexed individuals, many different discriminant-function calculations, using various combinations of measures, had to be run to assign a sex to a previously unsexed individual. It was not uncommon to run a particular combination of measures only to be able to classify one of the unknown individuals, and many combinations failed to assign any unknown individual to a sex.

Discriminant functions were calculated on the basis of one bone and often by the use of only one measure, which were the most successful strategies as identified by Dittrick and Suchey (1986). The final sex determinations, made after all the runs, were based on results of all bones available for an individual. The procedure DSCRIMINANT of the SPSS PC+ statistical package (SPSS Inc. and Norusis 1986) was used to calculate the linear discriminant functions. The only drawback to the Tlajinga analysis is that with such small samples, it was not possible to test for violations of assumptions of the statistics, that is, that the measures are from multivariate normal distributions and the covariance matrices for both sexes are equal (SPSS Inc. and Norusis 1986). In tests on larger, known sex samples, it has been found that human populations do meet these assumptions (see Van Vark 1970), and it is assumed here that Tlajinga also meets these assumptions and only the small samples available prevented the direct proof. Another possible complication was that since the sexed sample was heavily biased toward males, so would the discriminant functions calculated on the basis of that sample. Whether this was happening would be evaluated by the results on the unsexed individuals.

So that the potential problems might be minimized and as accurate results as possible achieved, given all the inadequacies of the sample for this type of analysis, very strict classification accuracy standards were used. In order to use a discriminant function to sex an unknown individual, one needs a 90% (and mostly 100%) correct classification of the known sex sample. In some cases a discriminant function was used if the classification accuracy was less but the unsexed individual very definitely was in male or female range.

An example illustrates the analysis and results obtained. Six measurements were taken on the tibia (see Appendix). Seven sexed individuals (unfortunately only one female) had all six measures. The direct-entry method, rather than the step-wise, was used, and one measurement (the tibial anterior-posterior diameter at the level of the nutrient foramen) failed the tolerance test and so was not used in calculating the discriminant function. Tolerance is a check of whether a variable is almost totally just a linear combination of the other variables; such variables create computational difficulties and violate assumptions of the procedure (SPSS Inc. and Norusis 1986). In this case, with the other particular five measures, this measure was a linear combination, although in further runs with other combinations this variable passed the tolerance test and could be used in calculating a function. With so small a sample, it was not possible to test for the violation of the other assumptions, as discussed above.

The resulting function may be judged as successful, with an eigenvalue of 2.07 (the ratio of variability, the between-groups to within-groups sums of squares) and a correlation coefficient of 0.82 of discriminant scores to the groups. These measures indicate that two groups could be discriminated. Also, when known cases were classified by the function, no misclassifications occurred (100% accuracy). Thus, in spite of there being only the solitary female, there is enough distance in her measures from the males to define a reasonable sectioning point, although the male range and potential overlap area are greater. Because the classification results were 100% accurate by the function, the discriminant score for the one unsexed individual (Burial 50b) also with all five measures was felt to be reasonable. This individual fell well above the male group mean (his probability of belonging to the male group given his discriminant score was 1.00), and thus on the basis of the tibia, this individual was classified as male. This classification was compared with results from other bones available for this individual to make the final sex determination for Burial 50b.

The procedure on the tibia was run again with another combination of five measures, then one with four measures, several with different combinations of three measures, and so forth, until all individuals with tibial measures were used. Generally, the more measures, the higher the classification accuracy. The discriminant functions based on one or two measures often were only moderately successful and yielded unacceptably low classification results (70%–79% accuracy). For example, the tibial shaft measures at the nutrient foramen yielded a discriminant function based on 11 males and 3 females, which misclassified 4 of these individuals (71% accuracy). These 4 individuals fell around the sectioning point. In this case, 4 unsexed individuals also had these measures, but fortunately in all cases their discriminant scores fell definitely within the range of one or the other sex (all probabilities of belonging to that group were 1.00), with 3 of these individuals clearly falling in the female range and 1 in the male (Figure 5-1). Thus, some confidence as to their classification is warranted and was used. However, for these unknown individuals, the evidence of the tibia is weighted less in the final determination than evidence for other bones for which the discriminant function was more successful. Where unsexed individuals fell around the sectioning point of a function, the classification was ignored.

The main drawback of this analysis was the large number of discriminant-function runs necessary to classify unsexed individuals with a few measures on several different bones. However, if the Tlajinga 33 population was to be used as fully as possible, this had to be done. The results were worth it, as all unsexed individuals with measures could be sexed (Table 5-1), and the number of individuals that could be analyzed by sex in mortuary characters (see Chapter 4) and in demographic and health indicators was expanded. Thus, in spite of the fragmentary remains, discriminant functions based on the Tlajinga material could be calculated to yield reasonable determinations for all individuals entered. The Tlajinga results are also heartening in that, although there was a male bias in the input cases, the unsexed individuals were determined to be 9 females and 5 males, thereby providing a more even sex ratio of 18 males to 14 females. The sex ratio of the individuals in formal graves is still biased toward males, but the difference in the numbers of males and females in formal graves is not statistically significant ($\chi^2 = .5, p \rangle .05$).

Table 5-1 shows the results of the discriminant-function classifications, so that it can be seen exactly how they performed and how the individuals with previously unknown sex were sexed. It can be seen that the individuals sexed from pelvis and cranium were generally consistently sexed correctly. There are mistakes, but in no case would the individual have been incorrectly sexed when all bone results were

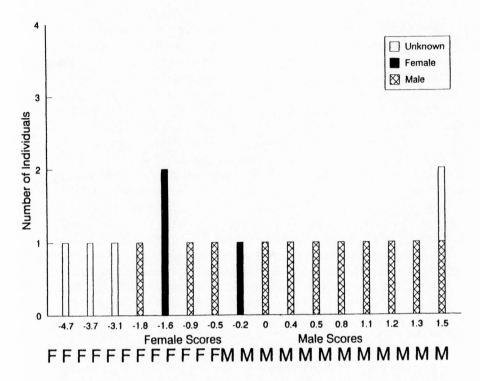

F F F F F F F F F F F FM M M M M M M M M M M M

Figure 5-1. Sex Classifications Based on Discriminant-Function Scores of Two Tibial Measures

compared. Fortunately, in most cases of the unknown individuals, the results of the functions were also consistent, and sex could be assigned easily. In four cases, Burials 14, 15, 18, and 61, only three bones had measures, and the classifications were split two to one. Before a sex for these burials was decided, the functions and classifications were re-checked to determine whether the result was from a successful discrimination run and whether the probability of sex membership based on the individual's function score was 0.80 or better. In the cases of Burials 15, 18, and 61, the odd classification was judged weaker on either or both of these grounds. Only Burial 14 was strongly male on mandible and cranium and strongly female on the femur. The femur is often judged a strong bone for discriminant sexing (Black 1978; Dittrick and Suchey 1986), whereas the mandible and cranium may reflect environmental and aging variability rather than just sex (Meindl et al. 1985a). In Tlajinga the femur discriminations were not strong, and for three females sexed by pelvic characters (Burials 6, 50e, and 60c), the discrimination error in classification as a male came from the femur, but as these were older females, such results might have been expected. Thus, all three runs might be considered equally ambiguous in this case. Burial 14 was the most difficult to sex by far. It was finally decided to sex this individual as a female, in essence because a strongly female classification based on the femur seemed more convincing than the more environmentally labile cranial measurements, although this individual was not particularly elderly.

Of course, skeletal sexing always involves error. In discriminant functions this error averages 10%–15%, although descriptive pelvis measures tend to be more accurate (Phenice 1969; but see Lovell 1989). Thus, it is possible that an already male-biased sample is more so. If true, this bias would probably indicate that mortuary behavior in Tlajinga 33, and probably Teotihuacan as a whole, was highly sexed-biased. Such bias was not found to be true of La Ventilla B (Spence 1974) and also does not seem to be true of other New World skeletal populations. The original sex determinations were made mostly from pelvis. One error here could be that one or more of these pelvises was actually female, although the chances of such a mistake are low. Archaeological populations also tend to be more sexually dimorphic (Meindl et al. 1985a), so that males and females definitely differ in robustness and size. Tlajinga 33 seems to support this conclusion, for although males predominated in setting up the discriminant functions, females were clearly distinguishable and smaller, and many of the unsexed individuals clearly fell into female ranges. Thus, with perhaps the exception of Burial 14, the sexes determined for the individuals with formal graves seem secure and reasonable. The worst-case scenario would be as much as a 20% misclassification of males as females, which would mean that there were actually 11 females to 21 males. However, even this sex ratio is not statistically significant, although close ($\chi^2 = 3.12$, $p \rangle .05$). Thus, the Tlajinga 33 population does seem to include burials of both sexes at close-to-even numbers. This result is reevaluated in light of the sexing of the secondary-context individuals.

Age

The aging of the individuals in formal graves used a variety of techniques, the choice of which depended on the age and completeness of the skeletons, but the aging generally was based on the seriation technique of Dr. C. Owen Lovejoy (Lovejoy et al. 1977; Lovejoy et al. 1985a). Age can be determined from a skeleton fairly accurately, and it is relatively easy in the case of a child or adolescent, because the growing process in humans leaves many chronological markers in teeth and the

TABLE 5-1
Sex Classifications of Tlajinga 33
Burials from Discriminant Functions

		Discriminant Result by Bone											
Burial	Known Sex	Ulna	Tibia	Mandible	Radius	Skull	Femur	Humerus	Scapula	Clavicle	Teeth	Sex Decision	Number of Measures
6	F	NA	F	F	F	NA	SP-M	F	NA	NA	F	F	51
11	M	NA	NA	NA	SP-M	NA	M	M	NA	NA	M	M	10
13	M	SP-F	NA	M	NA	M	M	NA	NA	NA	M	M	15
14	U	NA	NA	F	NA	NA	F	NA	NA	NA	NA	F	5
15	U	NA	NA	NA	F	NA	NA	NA	F	NA	M	F	21
17b	U	NA	NA	NA	NA	NA	F	NA	F	NA	NA	F	4
18	U	NA	NA	NA	NA	NA	F	NA	F	NA	M	F	13
20	U	NA	NA	NA	NA	M	F	NA	F	NA	F	F	14
23	U	NA	NA	M	NA	NA	NA	NA	NA	NA	M	M	12
24	U	NA	M	NA	NA	M	M	NA	NA	NA	NA	M	6
25	F	F	NA	F	NA	F	F	F	NA	SP-F	F	F	35
26	M	NA	NA	NA	NA	M	M	NA	NA	NA	M	M	25
30a	U	NA	F	F	NA	NA	NA	NA	F	NA	SP-F	F	23
30b	M	M	M	NA	M	NA	M	NA	M	NA	M	M	37
41c	F	F	F	F	F	NA	F	NA	F	F	F	F	60
42a	M	F	M	M	F	M	M	M	F	NA	M	M	43

42b	M	M	M	M	M	M	SP-M	M	M	F	M	M	76
43	M	M	M	M	M	M	M	NA	NA	NA	M	M	61
44	M	SP-F	M	M	M	M	M	M	SP-M	NA	NA	M	45
45a	U	NA	NA	NA	NA	NA	NA	M	NA	F	SP-M	M	4
45b	U	NA	NA	F	NA	NA	NA	NA	NA	NA	F	F	22
49	U	NA	F	NA	NA	NA	NA	NA	NA	M	NA	F	2
50a	M	M	M	NA	M	SP-F	M	M	M	NA	M	M	33
50b	U	M	M	SP-M	F	NA	M	M	F	NA	F	M	41
50c	M	NA	M	NA	M	M	M	NA	M	M	M	M	28
50d	M	M	M	M	M	F	M	M	NA	NA	M	M	37
50e	F	F	F	NA	NA	NA	SP-M	NA	NA	M	NA	F	14
56	M	M	M	M	SP-M	M	M	M	NA	NA	M	M	64
57	M	M	M	M	NA	M	M	M	NA	NA	M	M	54
58	U	NA	NA	NA	NA	NA	F	NA	NA	NA	F	F	6
60a	U	NA	NA	NA	NA	NA	M	NA	NA	NA	NA	M	2
60c	F	NA	NA	NA	NA	NA	SP-M	NA	NA	NA	NA	F	5
61	U	NA	NA	M	NA	M	NA	NA	NA	NA	SP-F	M	61

Note: NA indicates that no measures for bone were available. SP-M indicates value was at the sectioning point for the discriminant function and on the male side. SP-F means the same for females.

union of bones that can pinpoint age at death. After growth ends in late adolescence, a few belated unions of bones can indicate age during the twenties, but fairly complete skeletons are needed. After that, the aging of adults is difficult, and osteologists and forensic anthropologists are always searching for new techniques and greater reliability. Adult aging techniques are based on degenerative changes, which do have chronological correlates, but they are not as regular as the growth standards. Thus, estimates of adult age are inherently less accurate than estimates of the ages of children, and it is hard to be more accurate than within five and even ten years. Also, many of the aging standards presently used lose accuracy after age 50, so most skeletal populations have individuals above that age lumped together.

The individuals in formal graves consisted of 23 perinatals (34.3% of the sample), 9 children and adolescents (13.4%), and 35 adults (52.2%). So that more specific ages could be obtained, different techniques were used for each general age group.

For perinatals, the important age indicators are long-bone lengths, teeth-calcification standards, and the appearance of certain bones that ossify only during the last two months *in utero*. The teeth of growing individuals are considered the most accurate age indicator, as they are fairly uniform in their development across human populations and less subject to environmental factors (see Ubelaker 1989: 46). The teeth in perinatals have not erupted and, in fact, are quite incomplete. However, the amount of calcification of the crowns, especially of molars, indicates the number of weeks *in utero*. Because of the fortunate preservation and fine-screen recovery of perinatal molars, it was possible to age 9 perinatals by using the calcification standards of Kraus and Jordon (1965). For other individuals, long-bone lengths and ossification standards were used. If complete long-bone diaphyses were present, the crown-rump length, an indication of age (Krogman 1962), could be estimated by the use of the formulae of Scheuer et al. (1980). From these techniques came the most securely aged individuals.

All perinatal individuals, some fairly fragmentary, were then seriated by size of various skeletal elements, from smallest to largest. These elements include all long bones, ilia, the basilar of the occipital, and the mandible. All perinatal individuals were aged by their relation to the standards set by the securely aged individuals. Thus, the use of the populational method of seriation allowed many more perinatals to be aged than could have been done on the basis of individual features. Of the grave-context perinatals, 2 were aged as six months *in utero*, 2 as seven months *in utero*, 10 as eight months *in utero*, and 8 as full-term or non-premature newborns. The accuracy of the age determinations is felt to be good, as calcification and size are sensitive chronological indicators.

For infants and children tooth eruption was the main standard; Ubelaker's (1989) standards for indigenous North American populations compiled and adjusted from existing dental standards were used. Most dental standards available have been determined on the basis of North American white children (Moorees et al. 1963; Lunt and Law 1974), although the timing of dental formation and eruption does vary by ethnic group. Thus, there is likely to be disagreement between the usual standards and the dental ages of various teeth of an American Indian sub-adult (Owsley and Jantz 1983). This problem was recognized for Tlajinga and was controlled by the use of two methods: averaging the ages of the teeth available for an individual and checking where the individual fell in the seriation of long bones. Also employed were long-bone lengths based on standards from indigenous North American populations compiled by Ubelaker (1989). For adolescents, long-bone lengths, from Ubelaker, and more importantly, the presence and amount of epiphyseal union of bones, determined by standards from Krogman (1962), were utilized. As for the perinatals, the individuals with teeth and clear states of bone union were used as standards, and all children and adolescents were seriated by size and related to the standards, although this procedure assumes relatively little size variablility per age, which did seem to be justified on the basis of the standards for the same age. Again, it is felt that the results are accurate, given the populational method of determination and the general relationship of size and age in childhood.

There were only 10 infant and subadult individuals among the grave-context sample from Tlajinga, fewer than the number of perinatals. These were aged as 2 infants (beyond the perinatal period but less than one year old), 2 one-year-olds, 1 two-year-old, 2 three-year-olds, 1 eight-to-nine-year-old, 1 ten-year-old, and 1 thirteen-year-old. (See Table 5-4 for the complete age breakdown for Tlajinga 33).

The aging of adults, on the other hand, is a more difficult and contentious process. Several different age indicators have been identified by various researchers. All, however, are ultimately based on aspects of degeneration or remodeling processes of bone through time that are subject to much more individual variability than are the standards for subadults. Although individual indicators are often used to assess age, there has been a trend toward the use of more than one indicator as a means of increasing accuracy (Acsádi and Nemeskéri 1970; Lovejoy et al. 1985a).

The pelvis has become the focus of attention in adult aging, as it is the place considered generally to record most accurately chronological changes. Most osteologists have focused on the standards developed for degenerative changes in the face of the pubic symphysis by Todd (1920 and 1921), McKern and Stewart (1957) for males, and Gilbert and Mc-Kern (1973) for females. Pubic-symphysis standards have been recently updated, mainly because of unreliability and bias in the age standards used in those original studies. There is a modified system of six age phases for male symphyses (Katz and Suchey 1986), and a revised Todd system to correct an underaging bias (Meindl et al. 1985b). One of the underlying questions that forensic specialists have wrestled with is that even with Gilbert and McKern's (1973) work, the female pubis shows more variability because of childbirth effects that render it less accurate than the male pubis (Suchey 1979). The Todd system with revisions is felt to be applicable to both sexes with accuracy, with certain adjustments to female pubes as necessary (Meindl et al. 1985b).

Because of the somewhat fragmentary nature of even the Tlajinga 33 grave adults, the pubic standards were not very useful; only six were recovered. However, there is another similar surface on the pelvis that goes through similar chronological, degenerative changes—the auricular surface. Recently, published standards for the auricular surface have been developed (Lovejoy et al. 1985b). These are useful because this part of the pelvis is much more often preserved archaeologically than is the pubis. The method has been tested for both accuracy and interobserver reliability (Lovejoy et al. 1985b). It has been criticized for being based on a mixed sex-race sample with possibly suspect known ages (Iscan 1988). However, Lovejoy et al. (1985b) found generally little sex effect in their standards, and that which is present can be recognized and corrected. They also found that the indicator performs well in accuracy tests and in relation to other indicators. The virtue of the auricular-surface technique and the revised pubic standards (Meindl et al. 1985b) is that they are designed to be used in a populational seriation, which helps to improve consistency of judgment and accuracy of placement within the age ranges represented by the skeletal population. For an archaeological skeletal population like that of Tlajinga 33, the auricular surface used in seriation is an important part of the age determination.

Also used for adult aging are the closure and obliteration stages, seen both endocranially and ectocranially, of cranial sutures (see Krogman 1962). However, these have been generally judged to be unreliable because of the extreme variability in the rates of closure and obliteration. Most researchers have advocated the use of this method only in conjunction with other indicators (Acsádi and Nemeskéri 1970). Although the endocranial closure sequence was considered more accurate, as lapsed or arrested union is common on the ectocranial surface (Krogman 1962),

Meindl and Lovejoy (1985) have presented a new method that scores small, 1-cm sections of ectocranial sutures. They found that what was called the lateral-anterior system—the mid-coronal, pterion, spheno-frontal, inferior, and superior sphenotemporal sutures—was the best, especially for the older ages (over 50), where more aging indicators are needed for adults. They also have developed a system for the vault sutures—lambdoid, sagittal, and coronal. These systems were applied to some of the Tlajinga crania. Meindl and Lovejoy's system has been criticized for the same reasons that the use of the auricular surface has been questioned (Iscan 1988), but again, the investigators detected no sex-race effects in use on known-age individuals, and it is meant to be used only with other indicators in a multifactorial age determination.

Dental attrition is also a potential aging indicator in adults, especially in prehistoric populations where wear is much more drastic than among modern populations. Dental attrition is, however, variable in relation to age (Ubelaker 1989). Standards can be developed to apply only within a population, where one can assume dietary patterns are likely to be sim-ilar for all individuals. Especially in prehistoric populations, where life-style regularities lead to regularities in attrition amounts, dental wear can be an accurate indicator of age at death (Lovejoy 1985; Lovejoy et al. 1985a).

One methodological problem has been the development of a simple scale by which to judge the amount of dental attrition. Similar scales that rate all teeth from one to eight in degree of attrition have been developed by Molnar (1977) and Smith (1984). Scott (1978) uses only molars, divides each tooth into quadrants, and scores each quadrant from one to ten in the degree of wear. All quadrants are summed to score attrition for each tooth.

There are two general methods, it seems, to determine age by dental wear. One is to use one or more of the rating scales, assign age at death where possible on pelvic or cranium indicators or both, use linear regres-sion to determine wear by age, and interpolate other crania with teeth (see Costa 1986). The second method is to use Miles's method (1963), without a corresponding rating scale, and seriate the dentitions (Lovejoy 1985). Miles's method uses aged subadult dentitions to determine func-tional gradients of wear for the molars by summing the years between eruption plus the years of occlusal function of each successive molar from M1 to M3. This method can also be extended to premolars and anterior teeth (see Lovejoy 1985). For Tlajinga 33, Miles's method with seriation of the dentitions was performed, although there were few sub-adult dentitions available for determination of functional wear gradients, so these may be less accurate than is desirable. However, the use of seria-

tion makes the relative aging of dentitions accurate, and the multifactorial method allows one to check if the wear gradients are grossly
inaccurate in relation to other indicators. These controls on dental aging
make this indicator reasonable to use for the Tlajinga population.

Other aging methods that can be applied to adults include radiographic standards for proximal femur and clavicle (Walker and Lovejoy
1985) and changes in the sternal extremity of the fourth rib (Iscan et al.
1984). The latter provides a very promising technique that is easily
learned but hampered for archaeological populations like Tlajinga 33 because of the fragmentary nature of the skeletons, as well as the difficulty
of identifying the fourth rib from an already excavated skeleton, or even
from many still *in situ*! The researchers also stress using sex and race-
specific standards (Iscan et al. 1987; Loth and Iscan 1987), which do not
include Native Americans at this point. Thus, this technique was not
applied to Tlajinga. Four individuals had X-rayed proximal femurs, and
though they were few, these were used.

All of these aging methods depend on macroscopic assessments, but
microscopic methods are also available, methods based on the total
number and ratio of four microstructural components of cortical bone in
long bones (Kerley 1965; Kerley and Ubelaker 1978). Recent improve-
ments have included the extension of its use to cross-sections of rib
(Stout 1986), but the technique has problems because of the actual aging
processes of the microstructures and the complex ways biomechanical
processes affect them (Frost 1987). However, this method will probably
be used more in the future, as these processes become better understood
and controlled.

The final age of the adult skeletons of Tlajinga 33 at death was determined by the use of the multifactorial method (Lovejoy et al. 1985a). This
method requires one to use as many age indicators as possible, seriating
each individual with an indicator in the population from youngest to
oldest, and assigning each an age in years for every indicator. A correlation matrix is generated and subjected to principal-components analysis.
The first component, which explains the most variability, determines the
weighting of each age indicator, according to the correlation of each indicator with the component. On the basis of a weighted mean of all
available indicators, a summary age is calculated for each individual. The
summary age is the best estimate, and the age distribution thus obtainable from all ageable adults should not differ significantly from the
actual distribution of the population (Lovejoy et al. 1985a: 12).

Recently, the age determination of adult skeletons was severely criticized as inherently inaccurate (Bocquet-Appel and Masset 1982). The
two main criticisms were that age standards cause skeletal populations to

reflect only the age structure of the control population that the standards were determined from and that no indicator or combination of indicators is accurate enough to allow a good estimation of the age distribution of deaths of the skeletal populations. These criticisms were refuted strongly by both Van Gerven and Armelagos (1983) and Buikstra and Konigsberg (1985). Van Gerven and Armelagos showed that the skeletal age distributions from the Sudan, the example used by Bocquet-Appel and Masset (1982), are different from the Todd reference population that was used to determine the pubic standards that aged the Sudan population and that the adult ages determined were not random. The latter point was very much the concern of Lovejoy et al. (1985a). They found that skeletal age indicators do have bias and inaccuracy but that these are affected by particular ages. The multifactorial method is the best way to control for these problems. Skeletal age indicators do correlate with aging processes (Mensforth and Lovejoy 1985) and do not make just random assignments or errors. The same point is made by Buikstra and Konigsberg (1985) in an article that is discussed in more detail in Chapter 6. Lovejoy et al. (1985a) also show that, using various indicators and their method, they were able to closely replicate the actual age distribution of deaths. Thus, although the aging of adult skeletons can be difficult, it is possible to obtain satisfactory results.

The small sample provided by the Tlajinga 33 population poses problems for doing the complete multifactorial method, as was the case with sexing. Data were collected on five age indicators (see Table 5-2), but so few radiographs of proximal femurs, four, were available, that this indicator could not be used. In fact, of the 33 adult individuals from grave contexts, only 1 had all five indicators. Thus, efforts were concentrated on the pelvic auricular surface, pubic symphyseal surfaces, tooth attrition, and suture closure indicators. Unfortunately, only 4 individuals had all four indicators, and even with a pair-wise treatment of missing values to increase the numbers of individuals used in calculating the correlation matrix, the matrix for a four-indicator sample was not suitable for principal-components analysis.

The problem is probably a combination of small sample sizes in the co-occurrences between indicators and the fact that a few individuals have disparate agings on one indicator as compared with the others. For example, pubis age and suture age co-occur on only 3 individuals, and in two cases the pubis is estimated to be older and in one, younger. In larger samples the pattern of correlation can be clearer, and the impact of one deviant observation is less drastic. Thus, here the variables did not show strong enough correlations to produce a valid principal component.

TABLE 5-2
Age of Tlajinga 33 Burials
Determined for Each Age Indicator

Burial No.	Sex	Auricular Symphysis	Pubic Symphysis	Dental Attrition	Suture Closure	Femur Radiograph
6	F	61	-	50	40	44
11	M	-	-	43	51	-
13	M	38	36	32	-	-
14	F	42	-	40	-	-
15	F	32	-	36	-	-
17b	F	No age indicators preserved				
18	F	42	-	45	-	-
20	F	-	-	40	-	-
23	M	-	-	24	22	-
24	M	No age indicators preserved				
25	F	34	-	48	35	-
26	M	47	-	48	42	-
30a	F	-	-	44	30	-
30b	M	46	39	47	44	-
35	U	-	-	42	43	-
41c	F	36	40	44	-	29
42a	M	44	-	57	45	35
42b	M	55	42	57	40	37
43	M	41	-	50	37	-
44	M	-	-	46	43	-

Only three-indicator component analysis was possible for the Tla-jinga 33 individuals. Although this means that the multifactorial method cannot be used to its full potential, it can still be applied to Tlajinga. A study by Reeves and Mensforth (1986) revealed that the summary age technique is still robust even when based on a differential sampling of age indicators, as here. For Tlajinga, four different combinations using three indicators were possible, but only two yielded adequate analyses. The two combinations that included both pubis and suture indicators do not yield suitable correlation matrices, probably for the reason indicated above. Both auricular-pubis-teeth and auricular-suture-teeth had suitable matrices and yielded first components with 78% and 77.5% of the total variance explained, respectively. Correlations of indicators with the factor were 0.96 for auricular, 0.87 for teeth, and 0.80 for pubis in the first

Burial No.	Sex	Auricular Symphysis	Pubic Symphysis	Dental Attrition	Suture Closure	Femur Radiograph
45a	M	-	-	42	-	-
45b	F	No age indicators preserved				
49	F	No age indicators preserved				
50a	M	63	61	53	-	-
50b	M	38	-	33	41	-
50c	M	33	45	34	40	-
50d	M	52	53	47	-	-
50e	F	-	-	39	-	-
56	M	-	-	36	30	-
57	M	40	43	42	-	-
58	F	-	-	43	-	-
60a	M	64	-	-	-	-
60c	F	-	55	-	-	-
61	M	-	-	44	40	-

Secondary-context individuals

12	M	18	-	-	18	-
38b	U	36	28	-	-	-
Lot 432	F	24	-	20	-	-

combination, and 0.94 for auricular surface, 0.86 for teeth, and 0.84 for sutures in the second. These analyses were felt to be robust enough to extract summary ages (Table 5-3).

As seen from the age matrix and summary age tables (Tables 5-2 and 5-3), 39% of the individuals only have two indicators and 18% have only one. That means that only 43% could be used in the principal-component analysis. This type of analysis does not work well with only two indicators, as each variable will load equally on the first component. It was done anyway on each two-age-indicator combination for two reasons: (1) to check whether the correlations between the indicators are suitable for a multifactorial method, so that both can be averaged to calculate a summary age; and (2) to see whether high amounts of total variance are accounted for by the first component. The combinations

TABLE 5-3
Summary Ages of Adult Individuals Among Tlajinga 33 Burials

Burial	Sole Indicator	Auric./Pubis/ Dental	Auric./Suture/ Dental	Dental/ Suture	Auric./ Pubis	Auric./ Dental	Auric./ Suture	Final Age
6	-	-	51	45	-	56	51	51
			Mean of all summary ages = 50.75	SD = 4.5 years				
11	-	-	-	47	-	-	-	47
13	-	35	-	-	37	35	-	35
			Mean of all summary ages = 35.67	SD = 1.15 years				
14	-	-	-	-	-	41	-	41
15	-	-	-	-	-	34	-	34
18	-	-	-	-	-	44	-	44
20	40	-	-	-	-	-	-	40
23	-	-	-	23	-	-	-	23
25	-	-	39	42	-	41	35	39
			Mean of all summary ages = 39.25	SD = 3.09 years				
26	-	-	46	45	-	48	45	46
			Mean of all summary ages = 46	SD = 1.41 years				
30a	-	-	-	37	-	-	-	37
30b	-	44	46	46	43	47	45	45
			Mean of all summary ages = 45.2	SD = 1.64 years				
35	-	-	-	43	-	-	-	43
41c	-	40	-	-	38	40	-	40
			Mean of all summary ages = 39.33	SD = 1.15 years				
42a	-	-	49	51	-	51	45	49
			Mean of all summary ages = 49	SD = 2.82 years				

42b	-	52	51	49	49	56	48	51
			Mean of all summary ages = 50.83		*SD = 2.92 years*			
43	-	-	43	44	-	46	39	43
			Mean of all summary ages = 43		*SD = 2.94 years*			
44	-	-	-	45	-	-	-	45
45a	42	-	-	-	-	-	-	42
50a	-	59	-	-	62	58	-	59
			Mean of all summary ages = 59.67		*SD = 2.08 years*			
50b	-	-	37	37	-	36	40	37
			Mean of all summary ages = 37.50		*SD = 1.73 years*			
50c	-	37	36	37	39	34	37	37
			Mean of all summary ages = 36.67		*SD = 1.63 years*			
50d	-	51	-	-	53	50	-	51
			Mean of all summary ages = 51.33		*SD = 1.52 years*			
50e	39	-	-	-	-	-	-	39
56	-	-	-	33	-	-	-	33
57	-	42	-	42	42	41	-	42
58	43	-	-	-	-	-	-	43
60a	64	-	-	-	-	-	-	64
60c	55	-	-	-	-	-	-	55
61	-	-	-	42	-	-	-	42

Secondary-context individuals

Lot 432	-	-	-	-	22	-	-	22
12	-	-	-	-	-	-	18	18
38b	-	-	-	-	32	-	-	32

given in Table 5-3 all produced statistically valid correlations, accounted-for 75% to 88% of the total variance on the first component, and had 0.87 to 0.94 correlations of each indicator on the component. Thus, these indicators were averaged to make a summary age when appropriate. The pubis-teeth and pubis-suture combinations did not produce valid correlations, and so were not used. No individual, fortunately, had only those particular combinations.

As can be seen from Table 5-3, the summary ages calculated from the two three-indicator analyses are very close in the few individuals for whom both can be calculated. The 14 individuals who could be included in the principal-component analysis are considered to be the most securely aged. Each two-indicator combination is given for these 14 individuals as well, so that the possible variability in age estimates from between three to eight years can be seen. Thus, the aging from two or only one indicator has to be considered to be prone to a larger possible estimation error. However, as variation in age indicators falls within a ten years' range for one individual, the potential error using one or two indicators is not so great as to totally distort the age distribution of the population. Thus, all age estimations were used to increase the sample.

Although many Tlajinga 33 adult individuals from formal graves are fragmentary, it was possible to determine reasonable ages for all but four individuals. When one looks at the final age determinations in Table 5-3, it is obvious that the bulk of adults are aged 35 on up. There are few young adults. This lack jeopardizes the use of the Tlajinga 33 skeletons as a representative sample of the residents, because although young adults should be expected to die in lower proportions than older individuals, they are quite underrepresented here. The reason for their relative absence probably has to do with the nature of the formal graves recovered from the compound.

It is established that adults predominated in *tepetate* pits and that in such a pit one was more likely to have an elaborate grave offering as well (see Chapter 4). Thus, an achievement-based status system was generally indicated for Tlajinga 33, where older ages were more likely to have significant energy and wealth expended on their graves. The adults in formal graves should then be expected to be older. Where, then, are the young adults?

It was found that the Tlajinga 33 stratigraphy was shallow and prone to extensive reconstruction, with horizontal movement of the compound through time (see Chapter 3). Burials in earthen graves within the compound would therefore be prone to disturbance, whereas those in *tepetate* pits would likely be untouched. The large number of human bones recovered from refuse contexts is probably the result of the disturbance of graves during reconstruction. The Tlajinga 33 skeletal study must take these human bones from this alternate context into account.

Secondary-Context Individuals

Formal graves were not the only source of human bone in Tlajinga 33. Twenty-two contexts were excavated and numbered as burials (with 42 individuals), but the context of these burials was general midden. These 22 refuse-context burials were not included in the mortuary analysis, or in the aging and sexing. Because their context and that of the human bone separated out from general excavation proveniences is the same, they can be combined with it.

An important source of human material to add to a demographic study, if it is common, is the human bone found and collected from general proveniences much as faunal bone is collected. The Tlajinga 33 excavation systematically collected and studied this human material. There was a striking amount of human bone available from general proveniences: of 736 nonburial lots, 265 or 36% had human bone. Of these, 39 lots had at least two or more individuals readily identifiable even from a few bones. Screening was also important in the collection of this material, because more was recovered from screened lots. However, many unscreened lots also yielded human bone. Thus, human bone was a significant part of the artifacts collected.

The problem with the secondary-context human bone (which includes the 22 refuse-context burials because they have a similar context) is that the fragments may or may not belong to one individual. The refuse burials and the 39 lots mentioned above indicate that often more than one individual is present and is represented by only one or two bones. The problem was to try to identify as accurately as possible the number of individuals present in this secondary-context bone.

All secondary-context bone was identified as to skeletal part, where possible, and inventoried. Pieces that were diagnostic for sex, age, and paleopathological conditions were further studied, and all possible measurements and observations were made. Even from a few fragments, perinatals and children could often be distinguished by differences in size and development of teeth. Bones of different sizes corresponding to those ages in the same provenience are from different individuals. Adolescents could be distinguished by differences in stages of bone union. All these young individuals could then be aged by placing them in the seriations with the grave individuals.

It is much harder to distinguish individual adults, because there are no growth clues and often there is just not enough bone available to tell differences in size, which would also distinguish individuals. One way to tell the number of individuals present is by the number of the same bones recovered. That is, if there are seven left proximal humeri, there have to be at least seven different individuals. This is a conservative way to estimate the number of individuals. At Tlajinga 33 this method yielded a minimum of 8 adult individuals from repeated mandible parts, for the general-provenience bone only. However, with the amount of secondary-context bone present, it is highly probable that more than 8 adults are represented. Also, since it was evident from the refuse burials and the general-provenience perinatals and children that individuals are represented by only a few skeletal elements, the use of only the minimum number would seriously underestimate the number of adults present.

Three methods were used to estimate the number of adults in all of the secondary-context bone. First, all proveniences with human bone were divided into those from the Early Period (Early or Late Tlamimilolpa–Early Xolalpan) and the Late Period (Late Xolalpan–Metepec), divisions that reflect the difference in craft specialization among the residents and a temporal difference in construction techniques and reorganization of the compound. These designations must be considered tentative and may be changed as the chronology of the compound is refined. There were 126 proveniences tentatively dated to the Early Period and 139 to the Late Period. The Early Period contexts were well sealed from later contamination. Individuals in the Late Period contexts, however, do not necessarily come from only Late-Period disturbed interments. It is possible that some have been disturbed from earlier contexts. Although the number of earlier individuals cannot be estimated, the Late Period deposits were made up overwhelmingly of Late Xolalpan artifacts and thus more probably consist of disturbed Late-Period interments. This possibility is a source of potential error, but it is assumed that the number of earlier individuals mixed in Late Period deposits are few.

As the second step, the context within each period could be used to decide whether different individuals are involved. Thus, fragments from two different rooms in different parts of the compound are likely to be from two different individuals, even if no overlapping skeletal parts are involved. If fragments came from the same area of the compound, only one individual was counted, unless the skeletal parts themselves indicated that more than one individual was involved.

Third, all skeletal elements that could be aged or sexed were separated out and compared with standards from formal-grave individuals to make age and sex determinations. Different sexes and different ages indicated different individuals. For ages, pelvis and teeth were compared with grave-context individuals and, where possible, seriated with them. Of course, as secondary-context bone was more fragmentary, ages were determined on the basis of only one or two indicators. Thus, although it is valuable to get as many aged individuals as possible for the paleodemographic study, these secondary-context individuals are more likely to be under- or over-aged than they would be if at least three indicators were available. Sexing was done in a few instances by morphological criteria but most often by comparing any measures—often only one was available—with the grave-context individuals' values. Most fit clearly into the male and female ranges, and there were only a few measures near the sectioning points determined in the discriminant-function sexing. These may be subject to some error in sex determination.

Once context was controlled for and any same-sex or -age bones found in the same area were collapsed into one individual, the aged and sexed individuals were compiled for both periods of the compound. A total of 151 individuals were found in the secondary-context bone. These, plus the grave individuals, gives a total Tlajinga 33 skeletal population of 219. The secondary-context bone significantly added to the number of individuals available for the paleodemographic study.

Before the total Tlajinga 33 population is assembled from the secondary-context and grave-context individuals, one group of secondary-context bone needs to be discussed, because its unique characteristics affect its further use in the paleodemographic study. A small percentage of the bones in middens have cut marks or some sort of deliberate modification for decoration or use. There is no evidence on any of the formal-grave individuals that defleshing, which would produce cut marks, was a specialized burial treatment at Tlajinga 33. Cut marks are found on a few adult or late adolescent bones. These bones apparently represent pieces of humans that were deliberately dismembered and then ultimately discarded with little care.

It seems likely that these bones and their treatment can best be explained as pieces of human sacrifices. There is evidence for human sacrifice at Teotihuacan in the form of skeletal finds (see, e.g., Batres 1906; Cabrera et al. 1982; Sugiyama 1989) and in painted murals that have been interpreted as human hearts (Miller 1973), resembling later Central Mexican sacrifices of hearts. However, most of these skeletal finds consist of just heads or whole skeletons whose context indicates they were sacrificed. At Tlajinga 33 the cut marks are mostly on femurs, humeri, and ribs and do not appear to make up one, or most of one, dismembered skeleton. When any possible overlaps in provenience are counted and checked a maximum of only 13 individuals are involved, and these consist of small pieces spread throughout the compound. Of these, 8 were sexable and 5 ageable. Interestingly, 5 were female and 3 male, and the ages were 16–30 years. It is probable that only pieces of a victim would be present in the compound and that perhaps several compounds would have parts of the same individual. Although this treatment resembles the later Aztec practice of dismemberment, partitioning, and eating of sacrificial victims (e.g., Durán 1964), none of the bones with cut marks at Tlajinga appear to have been burned or boiled. Why there were pieces of humans and what was done with them is unknown. Because these individuals were probably outsiders, they cannot be treated as part of the compound population. Thus, the 219 figure for all skeletal individuals must be revised; the Tlajinga 33 compound residents recovered from skeletal remains numbered 206.

General Demographic Characteristics of the Tlajinga 33 Population

With the complete population available for study now inventoried and identified, the overall suitability of Tlajinga 33 for more detailed paleodemographic study can be evaluated. The main question is whether the population is representative of both sexes and all ages, or whether it has biases that might preclude certain kinds of analyses.

The preponderance of grave individuals were male, which translated into an uneven sex ratio of 139 males to 100 females. The secondary-context individuals had the reverse pattern, 13 males and 22 females, a sex ratio of 59 males to 100 females. The totals from all contexts were 31 males and 32 females, almost even. Thus, Tlajinga 33 does not seem to have a sex bias in individuals present in the compound, although there is no doubt that females are more casually treated, more fragmentary, and more likely to be recovered from midden contexts.

As for ages, see Table 5-4 for the totals for the secondary-context individuals, the grave-context individuals, and the compound as a whole. Of the 151 individuals identified in the general provenience, 114 could be aged, a sizable addition to what was available from grave-context individuals.

Table 5-4 also provides the age breakdowns for the two chronological periods and the sacrificed individuals separated out for study. It can be seen that the age distributions among the periods are generally similar. The differences between the Early and Late Periods are that there are more adults in the Early and slightly more children through young adults in the Late Period. In all breakdowns the Tlajinga 33 population follows the general human mortality curve (Weiss 1973), with high infant numbers dropping down through the childhood years to a low point in early adolescence, then rising gradually through the young adult years and rising more quickly in middle and older adults. If the general mortality curve is not present in the population of deaths, as it is here, the usefulness of a population for paleodemographic study should be questioned. The complete Tlajinga 33 age distribution seems to have a reasonable number of deaths in each five-year interval.

The general age breakdown of Tlajinga 33 is compared in Table 5-5 with other well-known skeletal samples having fairly large numbers of skeletons. These populations have been judged as representative, except for La Ventilla B, which is put in only for purposes of comparison with Tlajinga 33. Tlajinga 33 is generally similar to these other samples.

A problem that has bothered paleodemography has been the underrepresentation of infants and subadults (Ubelaker 1989), which means that adults are more generally found to be a larger proportion of the deaths. Tlajinga 33 appears to be free of this problem, as adults are not in the majority and younger ages are much in evidence. For example, it is obvious that the Tlajinga 33 perinatals and infants form a higher percentage than they do in other populations, except for Hiwassee/Dallas. This high percentage could indicate a different demographic pattern from the other populations, which is investigated in greater depth in later chapters. As Tlajinga 33 does fit within the general variation seen in the other populations, it appears to be an acceptable skeletal population for further paleodemographic analysis.

The Importance of Secondary-Context Remains to the Tlajinga 33 Study

The use of individuals recovered from refuse-context burials and general-provenience collections dramatically increased the number of individuals available for a paleodemographic study. Other generalizations could also be made about the Tlajinga 33 population because the individuals recovered from secondary deposits were included. The main effect was to change slightly the conclusions about mortuary patterns at Tlajinga 33, and perhaps for much of Teotihuacan. These secondary deposits yielded 151 individuals. Even if the 13 potential human sacrifices are removed, the 138 individuals with no grave constitute a clear majority over the 68 with a grave. In other words, 67% of the individuals in the Tlajinga 33 population were not recovered from careful excavation of graves, as is the usual case, but from the systematic recovery of human bone from all kinds of contexts within the compound.

A main question is why there are so many individuals literally in the trash. It could be that some individuals were just thrown into the trash

TABLE 5-4
Complete Age Breakdown
for Tlajinga 33 Skeletons

Age	Secondary Context		Grave Context		Cut Marks	Early Period	Late Period	Total
	Early Period	Late Period	Early Period	Late Period				
7th mo. or less gestational age	3	5	2	2	0	5	7	12
8th mo. gestational age	3	6	5	5	0	8	11	19
Term newborn	7	5	6	2	0	13	7	20
Undetermined perinatal	3	1	0	0	0	3	1	4
Infant (<1 yr.)	1	5	1	1	0	2	6	8
1–4 yrs.	6	4	5	0	0	11	4	15
5–9 yrs.	2	6	0	2	0	2	8	10
10–14 yrs.	6	3	0	1	0	6	4	10
15–19 yrs.	5	6	0	0	2	3	6	9
20–24 yrs.	4	7	0	1	1	3	8	11
25–29 yrs.	4	1	0	0	0	4	1	5

30–34 yrs.	0	3	2	0	0	2	3	5
35–39 yrs.	2	0	3	3	0	5	3	8
40–44 yrs.	3	1	8	2	0	11	3	14
45–49 yrs.	1	2	4	1	1	5	2	7
50–54 yrs.	5	0	2	1	1	6	1	7
55+ yrs.	1	1	2	1	0	3	2	5
Undetermined juvenile	4	0	0	0	0	4	0	4
Undetermined adult male	6	2	1	1	2	5	3	8
Undetermined adult female	10	3	2	1	3	10	3	13
Undetermined adult	11	3	1	0	3	10	2	12
Totals	87	64	44	24	13	121	85	206

TABLE 5-5
General Age Composition of Tlajinga 33
and Other Skeletal Populations

Population	Number	Perinatals/ Infants %	Children %	Adolescents %	Adults
		%	%	%	%
Tlajinga 33					
Overall	206	31.0	14.0	9.0	46.0
Early Period	121	26.0	14.0	7.0	53.0
Late Period	85	38.0	14.0	12.0	36.0
Pecos Pueblo[1]	1722	18.7	14.0	8.0	59.0
La Ventilla B[2]	174	20.0	13.0	5.0	62.0
Libben[3]	1289	18.0	22.0	14.0	46.0
Hiwassee/Dallas[4]					
(Mississippian)	437	38.0	20.0	12.0	29.0
Arroyo Hondo[5]	120	26.9	23.1	12.7	37.3
Casas Grandes[6]	612	10.0	22.0	14.0	54.0
Dickson Mounds[7]					
(Mississippian)	221	21.7	23.5	14.9	39.9

[1]Mobley 1980.
[2]Serrano and Lagunas 1974.
[3]Lovejoy et al. 1977.
[4]Lewis and Kneberg 1946.

[5]Palkovich 1980.
[6]Benfer 1968.
[7]Goodman et al. 1984a.

upon death, but ethnographically and logically, that behavior should be rare. Actual burial in the trash would have yielded primary burials anyway, not just a few scraps. Instead, as indicated earlier, these individuals probably represent disturbed primary burials. With all the major reconstruction and remodeling done at the compound during its occupation, it would not be surprising if burials were often disturbed, as was discussed in Chapter 3. Some individuals were reburied, as the secondary interments attest, but others were probably just put into the current midden area. Why the different treatments? Perhaps the difference can be explained by how soon after burial the disturbance took place. It may be that, if the individual was recognized or remembered, the burial was moved with some care, becoming a secondary interment. But, and this would have occurred more often, if the original burial had taken place too far in the past for the individual to be clearly remembered, the remains would just be thrown out, where later disturbances and poor pro-

TABLE 5-6
Secondary-Context Versus
Grave-Context Individuals by Age

Age	Secondary Context	Grave Context
Perinatals and infants	39	24
Children (1–9 yrs.)	22	7
Adolescents (10–19 yrs.)	20	1
Young adults (20–34 yrs.)	19	3
Middle-aged adults (35–49 yrs.)	9	21
Old adults (50+ yrs.)	7	6
Totals	116	62

tective conditions would quickly reduce most individuals to a few recoverable fragments.

Some support for such a hypothesis is found in a comparison of the age breakdowns by grave and secondary contexts in Table 5-6. Here it can be seen that for all ages up to middle-aged adults, secondary-context individuals predominate. The Tlajinga 33 compound organization was mostly egalitarian, with achieved status differences (see Chapter 4). Younger ages were not accorded many offerings and had mostly earthen pits, because they simply died too young to have achieved a status that merited a better mortuary treatment. They were likely to have been forgotten as individuals fairly quickly, to have been disturbed in their earthen pits during construction, and when disturbed, very likely to have ended up in the middens. The middle-aged and older adults, especially males, were often able to achieve a status that would give them a *tepetate* grave that would have been deep enough to protect them from later disturbance and to be remembered, if disturbed not too long after death.

Thus, the age and sex distribution of secondary-context individuals provides further support for the mortuary pattern analyzed in Chapter 4: the highest statuses seem to be accorded to older male adults. Because these were the burials least likely to be disturbed by later construction, they probably are represented in a higher proportion in the formal-grave skeletons than they actually had in the overall mortuary customs for the residents. Thus, it is hypothesized that earthen pits with few or no offerings were the most common mortuary type at Tlajinga 33, but many of these would not be recoverable *in situ* because of later disturbance.

Table 5-6 also reveals how important the secondary-context individuals are to the demographic profile of Tlajinga 33. Children, juveniles, adolescents, and young adults especially were underrepresented in the formal graves. Perinatals, however, were well represented in both contexts. As burial was most common in a vessel in an earthen pit, perinatals would be easily disturbed, thrown in middens, and the vessels perhaps reused. It was also easy to just move a burial vessel, if need be. Perinatals, a large proportion of the sample anyway, might then be expected in either context. With the addition of individuals from secondary contexts, the Tlajinga 33 population is suitable for further study. Without them, it had a serious underrepresentation of adolescents and young adults. If this pattern is common at other Teotihuacan apartment compounds, it will be imperative for future excavations to recover bone systematically from general proveniences. The lack of study of such human bone probably explains why La Ventilla B had an underrepresentation of children and adolescents (see Table 5-5).

CHAPTER 6

Paleodemographic Analysis of the Tlajinga 33 Skeletons

The Validity of the Paleodemographic Method

Paleodemography, the use of demographic methods on skeletal populations to characterize demographic processes and determine the vital rates of past populations, has always been a somewhat controversial enterprise. It has been characterized as

> a subject which is simultaneously intensely interesting and devilishly difficult. It is intensely interesting because its subject matter is the life and deaths of our ancestors. We cannot have a clear idea of the history of our species without knowing quite a lot about the risks of mortality to which they were subject and about their ability to bear children to keep the groups alive. The subject is difficult because of the nearly complete loss of the data needed for the analysis. (Howell 1976: 25)

The skeletons used in paleodemography are the most direct evidence available of what occurred in the past, and certainly the best evidence available for those cultures and populations who left no written records. Thus, there is a need to try to learn as much as possible from skeletons about their past, about their health, lifestyle, and, if possible, the vital rates that characterized their living populations. The balance of fertility, mortality, and migration played a large role in whether they were simple or complex societies, whether they prospered and evolved, and for how long the society and culture were able to endure. The use of anthropological populations in the twentieth century to model the past needs to be checked against the past populations available, to under-

stand how valid is the analogy. Also, the widespread effects of acculturation and modern medicine may have changed the demographic
characteristics of even fairly isolated groups studied by anthropologists,
so that past populations are different in some way from even the recent
past. Only in the past population themselves will one find the evidence
of human population patterns that are no longer extant. Anthropological
demography is interested in the full range of demographic characteristics of humans, and this knowledge is important, as discussed in
Chapter 1, for understanding how culture and population have inter-
acted in cultural evolution (see Hammel and Howell 1987).

Nevertheless, it is difficult to extract demographic information on
vital rates from skeletons. They have to be recovered in an unbiased
manner, and they must represent all ages and sexes that would have
been present in the living population. In addition, even if the skeletons
have been accurately sexed and aged, they represent only an age distribution of deaths. The controversies in paleodemography, which have
waxed and waned, have all concerned what it is possible to learn about
vital rates from an age distribution of deaths that is based on skeletal
estimates. Skeletons are accepted as giving information on health,
trauma, and biomechanics, but is it possible to learn about mortality and
fertility from them? The main question concerning the validity of paleodemographic methods is whether it is truly possible to use skeletal populations to create life tables containing vital rates.

A life table is a parsimonious way to represent the mortality experience of a population. As an actual model of mortality, a life table calculates the probability of dying and the proportion of survivors at each age
in a lifespan. The calculation can be done in two ways. A cohort life table
records the mortality experience of individuals born in the same year, or
other interval, and continues until all have died. The more commonly
calculated current life table, the kind to be used here, looks at a population at a given time, such as a year or five years, and records the mortality pattern seen for all ages; it does not follow the same cohort
through time. Anthropological demographers can use longer periods to
smooth out any sampling fluctuations, and paleodemographers construct current life tables that can cover several hundred years. Thus, a
life table allows the researcher to quickly sum up the mortality pattern of
the population. The life table also provides a series of mortality and fertility characteristics underlying its values that can be used to investigate
many different demographic aspects of a population and to compare it
with other populations.

However, the calculating of life tables with any descriptive validity
for the demographic reality of a population depends on a population's

meeting certain assumptions. These include the ones already discussed—the legitimate classification as a population in time and space, a representative sample of the deaths of the population, and an adequate accuracy in estimating sex and age at death. Acsádi and Nemeskéri (1970) were among the first to create life tables for skeletal samples and also to list the most important assumptions needed to use life tables: that the population does not violate stable-population-theory characteristics and that there is no migration. If all these assumptions are not met, the life table is not demographically representative of that population.

Stable-population theory consists of the traditional set of models and simplifying assumptions used by demographers to study the relation of vital statistics to demographic characteristics, like age structure. A stable population is defined as one that, if fertility and mortality rates are constant for 100 years, has an age and sex structure, the proportions of the total population in each age class, that approaches stability. That is, the population pyramid does not change its shape from generation to generation. Stable-population theory is a simplifying model, because implicit in stable-population assumptions is the idea of underlying vital rates that characterize populations for some time. The rates do not change every generation. The no-migration assumption is also a simplifying one, because the life table is meant to follow cohorts from birth to death, and rates calculated for certain ages would be biased by the inclusion of individuals who were suddenly "born" in the population at age twenty, for example.

It has long been recognized that stable-population assumptions and characteristics are unrealistic for many populations. Many modern populations have shown rapid shifts in fertility and mortality rates in the past fifty years, shifts that indicate that they are not technically stable populations. Also, migration, whether incoming or outgoing, is practically universal in human populations; humans do not live in closed societies but move often, for mating and economic purposes. However, assumptions of stability underlie the mathematical models used for the formulae for the calculations for the life table, and thus, although most populations are not necessarily stable, they are often studied in demography and anthropological demography by the use of stable-population methods.

The advantage of the stable-population mathematics is that all vital rates of a population are clearly related to one another and to the population structure visible at a moment in time. Given the census of a population to create its population pyramid and with a little other data on fertility, mortality, or growth rates, it is possible to calculate other measures. The advantages of these methods to anthropological demography are obvious. One of the easier pieces of information to gather in a small population is its census and age structure. Thus, the observed age structure could be assumed to be the stable one, and other demographic rates could then be calculated.

For anthropological populations in particular, as opposed to large nation-states, the assumptions were thought to be more realistic. When people live in traditional societies using traditional cultural patterns of interaction with the environment and other groups, it is likely that fertility and mortality characteristics are stable for generations, and a stable population is present. Also, mobility in these societies is usually within the culture, for marriage or kinship purposes, and the individuals who leave, and more importantly, who enter the study area are members of the population and often near the same ages as those who left. The small anthropological populations very often could be treated as, in fact, closed ones. Thus, the small populations of anthropological demography, and by extension, the skeletal remains of anthropological populations, have been considered suitable for analysis by stable-population methods.

The pioneering study in paleodemography using stable-population theory and calculating life tables from skeletal populations was that of Acsádi and Nemeskéri (1970). Their detailed monograph on paleodemographic method studied the way that the average lifespan of human beings has varied, from Paleolithic times until the Industrial Revolution brought about a "demographic revolution" (p. 7). During that revolution, mortality has fallen and life expectancy at birth has dramatically increased, to the seventies enjoyed by people in developed countries today. For all of the time under investigation, skeletons were the main source of demographic information. The challenge was to be able to use them for information on mortality and life expectancy. For this, the authors forwarded the best method to determine age from adult skeletons as one based on multiple factors, rather than on one "best" indicator, a break with previous practice. Information from all possible indicators was averaged to come up with an estimated age. From the estimated ages, a life table for the skeletal population could be calculated by the use of formulae for stable-population life tables that would transform the age distribution of deaths into survivorship measures, which could in turn be used to calculate life expectancies at all ages (see below).

For these formulae to work, the assumption is that the skeletal population is both stable and stationary, neither growing nor declining. From a series of skeletal populations, mostly European in origin, Acsádi and Nemeskéri calculated many life tables showing that Paleolithic lifespans were very short, and that since the advent of agriculture there has been a gradual increase in the average lifespan, from less than 20 to between 30 and 40. These European results were compared with North American skeletal populations, where possible. Thus, for most of human history, there has been a gradual rise in life expectancy, although mortality can also be shown to increase with epidemics, and the like, that followed upon the Neolithic and the "antique empires" (Acsádi and Nemeskéri 1970: Chapter 5).

Although these authors' paleodemographic methods have been largely superseded by recent innovations in paleodemography, the importance of the work of Acsádi and Nemeskéri in influencing the methodology of researchers dealing with skeletal populations cannot be overstated. Their influence is partly the result of their having discussed much more than just life tables; they discussed fertility implications, differences in patterns of mortality by sex, cultural patterns that may affect skeletal recovery, and possible disease effects in their survey. Although the methods used here are somewhat different, the outline of this paleodemographic study and its concerns are influenced by what Acsádi and Nemeskéri included in their study. Moreover, criticisms of paleodemographic methods and changes all hark back to the base that these researchers provided.

Questions about the validity of the methods of paleodemography have been present since just before Acsádi and Nemeskéri, but so also for some time have there been questions about the suitability of stable-population methods in general. However, it is only recently that alternatives to stable-population methods have appeared. During the 1980s demographers have developed mathematical models for nonstable populations, which are actually just more general equations for the relationships described for stable populations (Preston and Coale 1982). The importance of these more generally applicable equations for the purposes of anthropological demography is that the age structure still contains the information on vital rates but now is no longer dependent on the stability of those rates for accurate demographic estimation (Gage 1985). These methods depend on age-specific growth and mortality rates, so the focus is on the different age groups, not the whole population at once.

The development of nonstable-population methods may remove one of the more enduring objections to the paleodemographic method: that stable-population assumptions are not suitable for use with skeletal populations. Because skeletal populations come from small populations, it is often felt that the large yearly fluctuations in vital rates usually characteristic of these communities preclude any attainment of the stable-population conditions necessary for life-table construction (Angel 1969;

Bennett 1973). Also hindering life-table construction is the poor preservation of infant's and children's bones, which results in subadult underrepresentation and a nonrepresentative population. It is also practically impossible to control for migration on the basis of the evidence of skeletons. Thus, Acsádi and Nemeskéri's (1970) pioneering effort was subject to immediate criticism.

However, some researchers performed experiments to meet the objections of critics and support the validity of a paleodemography that uses life-table analysis, a paleodemography that could then be allied to other demographic analysis and not shunted aside in its own world of inference. For example, the problem of infant and child underrepresentation has long plagued the use of many skeletal populations. This lack is a result of poor preservation, but also of poor archaeological recovery techniques that can find adult burials but not the smaller bones of young children and infants. There are also cultural biases, which can mean that infants and young children may be buried somewhere separate from most of the population, or in a way that means not all are recoverable. Moore et al. (1975) demonstrated that subadult underrepresentation does not affect many calculations of the life table for the older ages that are felt to be representative. Survivorship is directly affected, but life expectancy is not. Thus, much of the life table can still be considered valid for the population and can thus be useful, even with significant subadult underrepresentation.

As for the problem of small-population fluctuations and stability, simulations by Weiss (1975) and Weiss and Smouse (1976) revealed that even small populations rebound to stable-population characteristics quickly from stochastic demographic disturbances, and that skeletons collected from a period of one hundred years would reflect the stable mortality rates and not be grossly distorted by the very short-term fluctuations that might have occurred. They also demonstrated that populations have to be stable for as little as fifty years to have a stable age distribution. Given that migration in past societies was almost always within the culture, thus technically within the population, so that a closed-population assumption is possible, skeletal populations have the potential to fulfill the stable-population assumptions and thus are suitable for life-table analysis.

Another test of skeletal populations and life tables was undertaken by Hall (1978). Here, the sex and age at death were obtained from cemetery headstones, an analogue to such determinations from skeletons, and then compared with federal census data for a central Indiana township from 1830 to 1972. Life tables constructed from the headstones yield life expectancy figures nearly identical to those from censuses, and the reconstructed age structure, though not the same, was similar to the census and really represented a smoothed version of the census-derived age structure. Thus, since the work of Bourgeois-Pichat (1966) showing that stable populations could be derived from an age distribution of deaths alone, through the work of various researchers who countered the various criticisms that could be made about the suitability of skeletal populations for stable-population analyses, paleodemographic methods seemed by the end of the 1970s to have achieved respectability and to be ready to make more breakthroughs based on life-table analysis of suitable skeletal populations.

Then, starting in 1982, a new round of ferment and criticism began in the discussion of paleodemographic methods. The debate continues, and solutions have not yet been found for all the problems raised. The focus of criticism has shifted from questions whether skeletal populations can be analyzed by life tables to questions about exactly what the life tables of skeletal populations tell us about the demographic characteristics of their past populations. A good example of this type of criticism is one of the earliest of the new critical articles. Howell (1982) investigated what the living population would be like using the life table constructed for the Libben population (Lovejoy et al. 1977). Libben is an Ohio Late Woodland skeletal population numbering 1,327 that has gained prominence in paleodemographic studies because of the care used in its recovery and the aging techniques used as the basis for the life table. The skeletal population has 18% of the deaths as infants; survivorship of the individuals ever born in the stationary-population table is 52% to the age of 15, and only 13% to age 40, which drops to 2.5% to age 50. None of the individuals lived past the age of 60. The life table for Libben (Lovejoy et al. 1977) resembles many other constructed from skeletal populations in its low life expectancy at birth of 19.88 years; its short adult lifespan, with most adults dying during their thirties and forties; and its few individuals who lived past the age of 50.

Howell's (1982) point is that because of the high adult mortality, higher than any historically known population, marriages would be short and many children would be left as orphans. The result would be a population with very high work loads from high dependency ratios and in which there were only two generations alive at any time, patterns that imply difficulties for successful child raising and enculturation. She only implies this, but such a society may be highly unstable and prone to change, as traditions may not get handed down very successfully from generation to generation because of high losses of parents by the time offspring are teenagers. Thus, a life table like the Libben one seems to imply an impossibly hard and short life for human populations in the past or is in grave error when taken literally (Howell 1982).

One of the underlying criticisms of Howell's article, and recognized by Lovejoy et al. (1977) when they published the Libben life table, concerns the pattern common to paleodemographic life tables of low life expectancy coupled with high young and middle-aged adult mortality. This pattern was evident in the work of Acsádi and Nemeskéri (1970), where it is present in many of the life tables. The distinctiveness of the paleodemographic pattern was that the low life expectancy was not due just to high infant and child mortality, which is usually the cause in historical and contemporary populations, but also to the adult mortality mentioned above, which means that very few people live to the age of 60 and virtually none to age 80. This pattern contrasts to all historically known patterns (Howell 1982), where at least a few lived to their eighties and mortality is more gradual throughout the adult years.

The difference between the paleodemographic pattern and historical and ethnographically known populations is not in the life expectancy at birth, which is also in the upper twenties and thirties in many pre-modern populations (see Hassan 1981), but in a more moderate child and infant mortality and higher young- and middle-aged adult mortality than in the historical pattern. Lovejoy et al. (1977) recognized this pattern in Libben and suggested that prehistoric life in the New World had a distinctive age-specific mortality pattern because of the difference in the types and number of diseases present (see Chapter 2, above). Their hypothesis postulates that the endemic diseases of the New World promoted moderate mortality throughout the lifespan, whereas the Old World epidemic disease pattern, which characterizes all known historical populations, is especially hard on young children. Survivors in the Old World pattern would gain "immunological competence," which promotes better adult survivorship. It should also be noted that the idea of infectious epidemics that affect childhood mortality and the resulting adult longevity, characteristic of the Old World disease pattern, is an idea of epidemiology (Burnet and White 1972) with some support in U.S. historical demography (Meindl and Swedlund 1977). The Meindl and Swedlund study found that cohorts in the historic middle Connecticut Valley of Massachusetts that were "stressed" by epidemics as children had longer average length of life than those that were not. Thus, it is quite possible that there is an "immunological competence" that makes many prehistoric populations, especially from the pre-Columbian New World, subject to a different mortality profile than that seen in contemporary and historical mortality. This extremely important question is discussed in more detail below.

A more general criticism, not only of the distinctive mortality pattern often seen in skeletal populations but of paleodemography in general, is that skeletal aging techniques are not accurate enough to allow valid life-table construction. This criticism has been most recently raised by Bocquet-Appel and Masset (1982). The authors question the potential for accurately aging an adult skeleton and then recreating the age structure of the population. They find the potential error of estimation unacceptably high for the biological age indicators used by researchers to estimate individual age, because the correlation of age indicators and actual age is often less than 0.9. Thus, the manipulation of skeletal ages into age classes for life-table calculations of the probability of dying during an age just compounds the errors, so that nothing can be learned, as the age structure calculated is really just a mélange of random error. Thus, paleodemography ought not to exist; the best that can be known about past preindustrial populations comes from historical demography. Whether prehistoric populations are truly different will never be known. The implication of the article is that the problem of subadult underrepresentation and lack of old adults is the problem of skeletal aging and is essentially unsolvable.

The Bocquet-Appel and Masset article prompted rebuttals by Van Gerven and Armelagos (1983) and a more detailed point-by-point critique by Buikstra and Konigsberg (1985). Both rebuttals focused on the same points in the Bocquet-Appel and Masset article. Although the correlations of skeletal aging indicators with true age is usually between 0.80 and 0.90 for adults, this does not mean that the potential for error is equal across the lifespan, as Bocquet-Appel and Masset assume. Children are easier to age, and so are young adults. The problems and errors occur with the aging of older individuals, where the processes of biological aging are more variable, as is the relation to chronological age. Adulthood is a time when the correlations are lower and bring down the overall correlation (see Buikstra and Konigsberg 1985). Thus, Bocquet-Appel and Masset are correct in their criticisms of the effect of possible age misassignment on the calculation of valid probability-of-dying figures, but the rebuttals stress that their being correct does not mean that the total age distributions generated have no information. Both rebuttals discuss the information that has been gained from paleodemography, in spite of the weaknesses of aging methods and their use by different observers. Both believe that problems identified by Bocquet-Appel and Masset are not insurmountable; neither concludes that what has already been accomplished should be dismissed out of hand. Paleodemography has revealed differences by subsistence type (Buikstra and Konigsberg 1985), and the relations between paleopathological indicators and skeletal ages resembles those in modern populations (Van Gerven and Armelagos 1983). Paleodemography seems to make sense; the key is to keep refining it, not to reject it as useless and problem-prone.

There has always been criticism of paleodemography, with objections stressing that there is too much potential for error in its methods (Bennett 1973; Corrucini et al. 1989). Paleodemography is certainly not for those who prefer more certainty in life, but then neither is anthropological demography. Such study always involves potential error in estimates and inference from indirect evidence. However, many critics do not seem to be aware that many of the problems of paleodemography also affect anthropological demography on living populations, and it is not at all certain that the potential errors are really any less critical in the demographic conclusions made on these anthropological populations. In many of these living populations people are not aware of their chronological age, and the researcher must very often make estimates, even for children. In situations where people do have an idea of their age, how can the researcher be certain that individuals are not under- or over-aging themselves? Both cases have certainly been found in ethnographic field situations. In skeletal aging estimates, researchers actually have independent and multiple indicators of age and probably control and know the potential error and bias of their populations better than do researchers working on living peoples who have no written records to prove age. In a case similar to the subadult underrepresentation of many archaeologically derived skeletal populations, living peoples do not necessarily remember, or tell the researcher, about all the children who have been born and do not necessarily recall the age at which they died. It is routine in anthropology and demography to compensate for the underestimation of children (see Howell 1986) in fertility and childhood mortality rates. Thus, any kind of demography in situations where good registry of vital events is lacking, which is to say, for most populations that are and that have ever been, must deal with significant potential errors in estimates and age structure. Yet, no one seems to be attacking the Yanomamö study (Neel and Weiss 1975) or the Dobe San (Howell 1979) as not worth doing and yielding invalid demographic results.

Paleodemography is not easy to do, nor is it done by straightforward counting and entering into an equation for simple answers. Paleodemography, like any and all of anthropological demography, must question its data, check and recheck, try various methods to smooth it out, calculate the effects of potential error, and always put it up to the models available from demography and other paleodemographic studies for comparison. It is an enterprise involving demographic inference from indirect evidence and is validated by comparison with the uniformitarian potential characteristics of human populations, that is to say, whether humans can exist with such vital rates; it is validated by suitability to the cultural characteristics of the past populations, whether such demographic characteristics are likely for a complex, stratified society, for example; it is validated by comparison with anthropological theory concerning the relationships of demography with culture in general. It is an enterprise that works by building up a corpus of paleodemographic studies that will provide researchers with a better idea of what past populations may have been like in fertility and mortality rates, and by continually refining its methods and assumptions to yield more accurate demographic information.

A second type of critique of paleodemography has not focused on the possible problems of accurate skeletal aging and whether underenumeration occurs in various ages, but instead on what the age distribution of deaths, the base data of paleodemographic analysis, actually indicates. Paleodemography, since the time of Acsádi and Nemeskéri (1970), has been based upon life-table analysis of the stationary-population case. That is, the life tables have been calculated on the assumption that births are equal to deaths, so that the population is not growing and—as is necessary in stable-population theory—there is no migration. This assumption of stationarity has always been a first and simplifying method in demography for constructing life tables.

Paleodemography, however, has generally been satisfied with discussing and analyzing only the stationary case. The reason probably has been that most prehistoric populations were not growing, or else were growing slowly, so that an assumption of a stationary condition is more justified for the past than for contemporary populations. If human populations had not been nearly stationary for most of the past and thus regulating their numbers in a variety of ways, then the numbers of humans that would have been alive in an area in just a few thousand years would have been staggering (Hassan 1981). Thus, an assumption of stationarity is not unjustified, although it was recognized that populations could have short-term fluctuations of growth and decline, as is very characteristic of demographic events in small populations, that averaged to stationary over a long period. Most paleodemographic populations were therefore thought to fulfill the assumption of a stationary case. Thus, that assumption and analysis is ubiquitous in paleodemography.

However, recently, paleodemography has come to realize that its age distribution of deaths can have quite a complex relationship to the living population that produced it, and that the stationary population is likely to be rare. Regions, through time, may not grow quickly, but the individual skeletal populations, caught at various points in time, are likely to be from populations that were either growing or declining at the time the skeletons were deposited. The stationary case, where births exactly balance deaths for the several generations necessary to have a stable population, is unlikely (Johansson and Horowitz 1986).

Paleodemography has begun to realize that the age distribution of death has a complex, and perhaps counterintuitive, relation to the living population that produced the skeletons. One of the first articles to question the assumption of stationarity was by Sattenspiel and Harpending (1983). They demonstrated that what had been calculated for skeletal populations as life expectancy at birth is actually the mean age of death of the age distribution of deaths available. They then went on to demonstrate that if the growth rate is nonzero, mean age of death and life expectancy at birth are not the same, and in fact, increasingly diverge as the nonzero rate increases. Thus, the age distribution of deaths of the skeletons is related to mortality in an unknown way, *if* growth rate is unknown. This is because the death rates of a life table are calculated on the basis of the proportion of survivors to deaths in an age class, that is, they are based on the size of cohorts. If you do not know the size of the cohorts to calculate survivorship, you cannot calculate expectation of life at birth, except in the rare stationary case (Sattenspiel and Harpending 1983: 492). On the other hand, the mean age at death is closely related to the reciprocal of the birth rate. Thus, the usual paleodemographic assumption that a decrease in the mean age of death indicates higher mortality actually should be revised to an understanding that it actually indicates an increase in fertility. Thus, mean age of death in paleodemography does not tell anything about mortality, but instead provides good information about fertility. This counterintuitive conclusion works because with a positive growth rate, the size of each birth cohort grows over the previous one. A growing population will have an increasing proportion of deaths in the younger ages, the situation that causes a decrease in the mean age of death, just because there are ever-larger numbers in the young cohorts to die, no matter what mortality rates are present. Thus, when you compare two skeletal populations through time, the increase or decrease in mean age at death is much more easily attributed to changes in birth rate than to mortality, because of the clearer relation of mean age at death to fertility (Sattenspiel and Harpending 1983; Johansson and Horowitz 1986).

Paleodemographers have been slow to use this insight partly because of its profound challenge to the assumption of the stationary condition, although this assumption has actually been criticized for some time (e.g., Bennett 1973; Ammerman et al. 1976). The assumption makes demographic estimation easy, but it also yields great inaccuracies when the population is not stationary. Also difficult for paleodemography has been the realization that what had been thought were mortality indicators might actually be fertility ones, although the reasonable implications of the fertility information were demonstrated by Sattenspiel and Harpending (1983). They pointed out, on the basis of Old World skeletal studies, that indications of growing and declining populations are supported by other historical sources. Also, they questioned the widespread assumption that population growth rates increased dramatically in the Neolithic, with the advent of agriculture and sedentism, over the Paleolithic, pointing out that not all contemporary information supports a population increase with sedentism (e.g., Harpending and Wandsnider 1982). Similarly, the accompaniment of the transition to agriculture by a decrease in mean age at death, in the skeletons available from several points in time from the New World Dickson Mounds population (see Goodman et al. 1984a), is best explained as revealing an increase in fertility with the subsistence change, rather than an increase in mortality (Johansson and Horowitz 1986).

One paleodemographic study that has taken Sattenspiel and Harpending into account focuses on the skeletal populations from west-central Illinois (Buikstra et al. 1986). The authors point out that problems with underenumeration of the numbers of infants and the aging of older skeletons make the calculation of an accurate mean age at death difficult for many paleodemographic situations. Thus, they suggest using the proportions of individuals 30 and over to individuals 5 years and over to estimate relative fertility rates, rather than the more exact rates generated from mean age at death. This proportion was tested and found to have an inverse relation with birth rate. Thus, the decrease in this proportion through time among the skeletal populations indicates a rise in fertility that matches the archaeological evidence for increasing population in the region paralleling the greater reliance on maize agriculture. The authors feel that their method has great promise for the use with skeletal populations to obtain their fertility information while avoiding pitfalls of aging estimations.

Although the discovery of the relation of the mean age of death and the fertility rate of the population is important and certainly not to be ignored, important criticisms can and have been made about its basis. A recent article has shown that the relation of the mean age of death and the birth rate is true only in special circumstances, especially when death rates are uniform or minimal (Horowitz and Armelagos 1988). In fact, one of the underlying problems with the Sattenspiel and Harpending (1983) relation is that it dismisses too cavalierly the possible effects of mortality upon the skeletal population. The fact that it is hard to estimate mortality from skeletal populations does not mean that it cannot be affecting the age distribution at death. Johansson and Horowitz (1986) point out that because of the clearer relation of mean age of death to fertility, the basic assumption should be that differences between skeletal populations are due to fertility, rather than mortality, when there is no other evidence. However, assuming a minimum death rate or unchanging mortality profile is also not realistic (Horowitz and Armelagos 1988), and often there is other evidence that should be taken into account.

Perhaps the best recent article on what paleodemography should do to improve its demographic validity is that of Johansson and Horowitz (1986). They model the process of paleodemographic estimation as a four-phase operation. First is the careful archaeological analysis of the site's cultural patterns that may affect burial patterns and vital rates, and its possible growth rates, followed (second) by careful age and sex determination of the skeletons. Then, in the third and fourth phases, the calculation of reasonable mortality and fertility rates is followed by the use of these estimates in theoretical reconstruction of demographic characteristics for the society from which the skeletons were derived and for more general purposes, if appropriate. These last two phases constitute the heart, and most difficult, part of the study. This four-phase model is the one being followed in this study.

Johansson and Horowitz (1986) also point out that paleodemography must always be methodologically separate from modern demography, because it is dependent on the age distributions of deaths, not on the proportions dying out of a living population. This point reiterates the earlier insight of Sattenspiel and Harpending (1983) that since the age structure of the living population cannot be directly recovered archaeologically, mortality estimation is not possible. For Johansson and Horowitz, however, mortality must be taken into account for good paleodemographic estimation, and this can be done if an *independent, usually archaeologically derived, estimate of the growth or decline rate of the population can be made. With such an estimate, stable-population model tables can be used with the mean age at death to estimate approximate life expectancy and analyze what kinds of mortality rates could have produced the pattern found.* Fertility can be estimated from mean age at death, and thus, the most probable demographic characteristics of the skeletal population can be discussed. The authors stress that the suitability of the skeletal population for stable-population analysis must be tested, including for the effects of migration.

The recommendations of Johansson and Horowitz are that paleodemography should not just assume stationarity and then construct life tables, but instead should use the untransformed or unsmoothed age distribution of deaths from skeletons in conjunction with growth rate estimates to match to the best-fitting model stable-population characteristics using model life tables (such as those of Coale and Demeny 1983). From the investigation of the model tables plus knowledge of the archaeological context will come the best estimates of the demographic characteristics of the past population represented by the skeletal series. Johansson and Horowitz's article is a strong condemnation of paleodemography as it has been practiced, but it also holds out hope for better paleodemography in the future.

Two recent articles have tried to incorporate some of the Johansson and Horowitz suggestions about using the untransformed age distribution of deaths from skeletal populations, although both articles still deal better with the possible fertility implications than with mortality. Milner et al. (1989) fit an Oneota skeletal sample from the North America Midwest to age-at-death distributions modeled from two well-known anthropological populations, the San and the Yanomamö. When the skeletal sample's distribution was similar to that of the Yanomamö reference model, the skeletal series was determined as likely to be the result of a stable population, and more importantly perhaps, to be similar demographically to the warlike, horticultural Yanomamö, a reasonable cultural reconstruction for the prehistoric Oneota. A similar article by Paine (1989) generated model age distributions at death from the first edition (1966) of Coale and Demeny's West model life tables. Paine used maximum likelihood estimation to determine the best fit between three skeletal age-at-death distributions and the model distributions. From this, he was able to determine some demographic parameters that might have characterized the living populations and judge how reasonable they are. In two of the three skeletal examples the reconstructed demographic parameters or age distributions did not fit closely to the model distributions, so that demographic estimates are tentative. In these cases Paine concludes that the skeletal series may have some serious sampling biases in them, hindering present reconstructions. Both the Milner et al. (1989) and Paine (1989) articles present some important new, useful methods for the use of stable-population methods in paleodemography that should help in building up a database of demographic comparisons among skeletal populations for understanding past fertility behavior. However, both articles are still based on an assumption of uniform or minimal mortality underlying the distribution and depending on the larger effects that fertility has upon stable-population reconstructions in such a case.

Already universally held to be difficult, paleodemography has undergone a revolution in the 1980s, during which it has questioned its methods, sometimes its very existence, and reformulated what needs to be done to yield valid demographic results. The revisions in methods, and the potential solutions, seem to fall into two general, but related, areas. First, there are the characteristics of the skeletal populations themselves: the potential for subadult underrepresentation, for misestimation of skeletal ages, and for underenumeration or underaging of very old individuals. Paleodemography has to face the potential for errors in the use of skeletal evidence, as skeletal characters are often what make paleodemographic analyses yield somewhat different demographic results than historically known or contemporary populations. The question must be posed whether the difference is due to still inadequate skeletal aging techniques and inadequate archaeological recovery of all ages, or is indicative of an actual pattern that has been extinct for centuries. Second, paleodemography has to consider what it can deduce from the age distribution of deaths, the only demographic measure one can possibly derive directly from skeletons, but a measure only indirectly related to fertility and mortality. The paleodemographic method must concentrate on attempts to reconstruct the living population that produced the skeletons, using evidence from archaeology, ethnographic analogy, and model tables to make correct inferences about the influence of mortality and fertility on the population. Paleodemography can no longer depend on the assumption of stationarity, but must justify its use on archaeological grounds. Paleodemography must also remember to fulfill the uniformitarian assumption and must always consider whether it is reasonable to conclude that the characteristics of the living population implied by any analysis of its skeletons actually existed (Howell 1976, 1982). The recent criticisms have been very salutary for paleodemography; the challenge is to be able to use methods that have been suggested and to develop new ones so that valid statements about vital rates in past populations can be made.

The Tlajinga 33 Age Distribution of Deaths

The age distribution of deaths in the Tlajinga 33 population is presented at the end of Chapter 5 (see Table 5-6). The population contains all ages and also has both sexes in just about equal numbers. Judging by the archaeological context of the Tlajinga 33 population, a representative sample of deaths of the residents could have been recovered, as burial was apparently within or just outside the apartment compound walls. Burial around or within residences was a common pattern in pre-Columbian Mesoamerica, and the Teotihuacan Mapping Project was not able to locate clear extra-compound cemeteries of residents. Certainly, not all the deaths at Tlajinga 33 are represented by the recovered skeletal series. Residents not buried at Tlajinga 33, for whatever reason, can never be recovered, but it does not appear that any age or sex is obviously excluded from burial within the compound. Also, the compound was not completely excavated, but it is felt that both public and domestic locations within the compound were adequately sampled to control for the differences in ages and sex buried in different locations (see Chapter 4).

Thus, the skeletons recovered from Tlajinga 33 do not show any obvious exclusion biases that would prejudice paleodemographic analysis, and the archaeological contexts of human skeletons and recovery techniques used would allow recovery of a representative cross-section of the deaths that occurred in the compound. Actually, almost all skeletons present in the excavated portion should have been recovered, although some secondary-context individuals may have been lost to poor preservation. Some of these latter individuals may also have been lost because middens may have been cleared of refuse sometimes, so not all skeletal material would have remained in the compound. However, this process, if present, would impact all middens and the skeletal material within them equally. It should not be the source of any bias.

The age distribution was divided generally into the five-year age classes used in demography. For skeletons, it is harder to do finer age determinations for many adults. Below the age of five, the age determinations were broken into finer categories, because it is often instructive to look at the age distribution of deaths here, instead of just lumping them together in one five-year cohort (see Mensforth et al. 1978). Because in most populations the first year is often one of the most perilous for an individual, and the data are available for Tlajinga 33, perinatals are separated out from infants, two months to one year. Perinatals are also enumerated by fetal age. Then, one- and two-year-old children are separated from three- and four-year-olds, because of the possible effects in many anthropological populations of weaning stress and higher mortality in these younger ages. This breakdown will enable diagnosis of mortality problems here, if present.

One feature of the Tlajinga 33 age distribution of deaths, in contrast to many other skeletal series, is the large number of subadults present, and especially the high proportion of perinatals and infants to children. At Teotihuacan the mortuary practices seem to have provided a very favorable situation for their preservation, so that even prematurely born fetuses were accorded burial. Individuals the size of fetuses in the last trimester of gestation were recovered. Thus, instead of presenting the more usual problem of infant underrepresentation, Tlajinga 33 actually provides information not usually available in skeletal samples regarding fetal loss in the last trimester of pregnancy. It is interesting that individuals only six or seven months *in utero* would be interred in formal graves at Teotihuacan, and interred in ways resembling those of term-age perinatals, that is, in vessels. This finding, of course, raises the question of whether such individuals represent deliberate abortions, as suggested by Serrano and Lagunas (1974), stillbirths, or just premature live births where the perinatal soon died. Although a few perinatals were interred under an altar, it seems unlikely that ritual abortion or infanticide is involved. Abortion in late pregnancy is risky for the mother, and it is hard to believe that societies would risk many young women for such a ritual purpose. Also, on a cross-cultural basis, cultures generally do not inter stillbirths or abortions. Thus, *a priori*, it is most likely that the perinatals, whether premature or term-age, were live births. Though a few may have been ritual infanticides, there is really no physical evidence for or against. Also, the ritual inference is solely from the context of three perinatals under an altar. Most perinatals recovered at Tlajinga 33 were buried much as other residents of the compound were and probably died from natural causes. It is more probable that the few perinatals under an altar merited such interment because of their cause of natural death, or more likely, because of their families' importance within the compound hierarchy. Adults are also buried under altars, and these are clearly not sacrifices but instead interments awarded on the basis of their ages, as discussed above.

Possible sources of error in the Tlajinga 33 age distribution of deaths include the 33 adults (16% of the total) who could not be aged into any finer age categories other than simply "adult." Most of these individuals were in secondary context and thus were generally too fragmentary to offer preserved age indicators. Although these were determined to be separate individuals on the basis of context and chronology, it is quite possible that the number is over- or underestimated. How to treat these individuals analytically has to be decided. It is common in paleodemography to apportion unageable adults into five-year age categories according to the proportions of deaths already determined from ageable individuals in those categories (e.g., Lallo 1973; Milner et al. 1989). This method is used here for both the undetermined adults and subadults present. As for the potential error in estimating the number of these individuals, it is felt that the estimate of the numbers of all secondary-context individuals is a conservative one, because individual skeletons were represented by a few pieces and there was a large amount of bone that could not definitely be separated out as distinct individuals. Thus, the chance of overestimation is low. Of course, this approach does not rule out the possibility of some underenumeration. If so, the proportion of adults would likely be about equal or slightly more than those under age 15. This situation would raise the mean age at death somewhat. Therefore, it should be remembered throughout the following analysis that the mean age of the Tlajinga 33 distribution could be higher than that given, although the effect of that difference would be only to reinforce the demographic trends that are found in Chapter 8. The numbers used here are based on the best information presently available for context and chronology and are felt to be a reasonable and realistic estimation.

Other potential sources of error in the age distribution are: (1) errors in the aging of adults, especially those based on the most fragmentary skeletons, which may indicate that perhaps 10%–20% of the adults might be an age class too old or too young; (2) that the Late Period individuals include some proportion of individuals that actually belong to the Early Period; (3) that there is systematic underaging of the adults, so that there are too few aged 50 or older; and (4) that some part of the population, for example, very old adults, are buried elsewhere and not recovered in the excavation. Although attempts were made to evaluate these and minimize their potential effect upon the study, their possible effects must be discussed. All are addressed as the study is discussed.

Traditionally, the first step in paleodemographic analysis has been the construction of a life table based upon an assumption of stationarity for the population. In many ways, this is a simplifying assumption, actually better used as a starting point for analysis than as the conclusion. The problem with much paleodemography is that such an assumption was too often the end point as well. However, as Johansson and Horowitz (1986) have pointed out, this assumption does need to be justified by preferably independent archaeological evidence. In Teotihuacan, *for all the period during which the Tlajinga 33 compound was occupied, the city appears to have been stable in size and population* (Cowgill 1979). Also, the Tlajinga 33 compound seems to have been stable in size from the Late Tlamimilolpa until the Early Metepec, a period of about 400 years, after which it was abandoned by the entire group at one time, as best as can be presently reconstructed. Thus, for much of the time of the skeletal series, an assumption of a stationary condition seems warranted, and it does seem to be a valid starting point for investigating the Tlajinga 33 age-at-death distribution.

Table 6-1 presents the stationary-population life table constructed on the untransformed age distribution for the total population of Tlajinga 33, except for the 13 individuals with cut marks, which have been excluded. The method for calculating a stationary paleodemographic life table has been well described by Acsádi and Nemeskéri (1970) and Weiss (1973), although there are some differences between the equations they use. Because Acsádi and Nemeskéri are concerned only with skeletal populations, their method is used here.

Each column of the life table can be described as follows: (1) the D_x is the actual number of deaths in each age class; (2) the d_x is the proportion of the overall deaths that occurred in the age class; (3) l_x, survivorship, based on a radix of 1,000, is interpreted as the proportion of those ever born surviving to the beginning of the age class; (4) q_x is the proportion of those reaching the age class who die before reaching the next age class; (5) L_x is the total years lived in age class x by all individuals who enter the class and is calculated on the assumption of even yearly deaths within the age class, such that at the halfway point of the age class, half the deaths will have occurred; (6) T_x is the total years left to be lived by individuals entering the age class until all have died and is part of the basis for calculating life expectancy; (7) e_x is the life expectancy at age x, the average number of years left to be lived by those who reach the age class (e_0 is the measure of life expectancy at birth).

The last age class was set at 60 +, because this was near the upper limit of good discrimination of the aging methods used. However, the length of this last class was set as 25 years, so that all individuals in the population would have been dead by age 85. Although only 2.5% of the total skeletal sample was aged to this cohort, the number of years given to this cohort does have some effect upon all the life expectancies of the life table. If the last cohort is treated as having only five years, the life expectancy values in the life table would drop one to three years for each age class from birth to age 40. After age 40, the effect is more dramatic, as life expectancy drops by five to seven years for each age class. Spreading out the last cohort to a more realistic maximum human lifespan of 80–85 years does seem reasonable and makes the life table more comparable to model tables as well. However, the erratic pattern of deaths from age 40 on and the small percentage of deaths over age 60 do raise the perennial question of the problem of underaging older skeletal individuals, given current techniques.

Researchers have explored the effects of older adult underaging and

TABLE 6-1
Stationary-Population Life Table
for All Residents of Tlajinga 33

Age	D_x	d_x	l_x	q_x	L_x	T_x	e_x
Perinatal	55	.27	1,000	.27	144	20,492	20.49
Infant	8	.04	730	.05	592	20,348	27.87
1	18	.09	690	.13	2,580	19,756	28.63
5	11	.05	600	.08	2,875	17,176	28.63
10	10	.05	550	.09	2,625	14,301	26.00
15	9	.04	500	.08	2,400	11,676	23.35
20	16	.08	460	.17	2,100	9,276	20.17
25	8	.04	380	.11	1,800	7,126	18.88
30	7	.03	340	.09	1,625	5,376	15.81
35	12	.06	310	.19	1,400	3,751	12.10
40	22	.11	250	.44	975	2,351	9.40
45	11	.05	140	.36	575	1,376	9.83
50	11	.05	90	.56	325	801	8.90
55	3	.02	40	.38	163	476	11.90
60+	5	.02	25	1.00	313	313	12.50
Totals	206	1.00					

Note: Skeletons with cut marks are excluded.

underenumeration in skeletal populations (Willey and Mann 1986; Buikstra and Konigsberg 1985). Both studies found that older adult underenumeration has a more drastic and deleterious effect upon demographic reconstructions because the effect of the missing numbers is the overestimation of mortality, q_x, through all the age classes of the population. On the other hand, the underaging of adults distorts mortality and life expectancy primarily for the older ages (Willey and Mann 1986), in a form similar to that of truncating the last age class. There is no clear *a priori* evidence that older adults would not have been interred in Tlajinga 33, although it is possible that very old individuals could have been buried in special locations in their *barrio*, for example. However, the mortuary analysis (Chapter 4) indicated a common pattern of older male individuals in the richer graves, which points to the likelihood that old, respected individuals were interred within the compound, not elsewhere, and thus recovered by the excavation. Also, 25% of the sample is aged as 40 years or older, a sizable proportion, compared with that of many paleodemographic samples, such as Libben (Lovejoy et al. 1977). Thus, underenumeration is not considered a problem here.

However, underaging may be. Although the best methodology was used to age the population, one that should not be biased against older ages (Lovejoy et al. 1985a), the small numbers and fragmentary nature of many individual skeletons may have caused the underaging of older individuals and some lumping into the 40–45 and 50–55 cohorts. The older individuals were identified primarily by auricular surface standards and the dental wear seriation (see Chapter 5), which should identify older individuals. Mensforth and Lovejoy (1985) evaluated the summary age technique according to some independent correlates of the skeletal aging process, because of general criticisms of skeletal underaging. They found that their paleodemographic sample accorded well with many of the correlates and lacked those found in modern populations in individuals of very advanced age. Thus, they feel that their summary age techniques are valid over the whole lifespan, and if many skeletal samples have relatively few older adults, that is because few people lived to such ages. The implication is that very few individuals reached their seventies and eighties in past societies, and paleodemographic samples reflect this truth. In the small populations recovered as skeletal samples, it is possible that no or only one very old individual would have been present, because of the low probabilities of reaching such an age. It should also be remembered that the Tlajinga population is from the poorest social and economic strata of Teotihuacan, and so its members, even those with high status within the compound, did not have the same standards of living and access to health, nutrition, and resources as populations from higher strata. These facts may explain why very old ages are not found. This situation continues to be true in modern and preindustrial cities as well, and so the lack of very old individuals is not unexpected.

Although the summary age technique is the best one for aging skeletal populations, the Tlajinga 33 sample could not make full use of it. Thus, although a reasonable case could be made for each individual age assigned by either the use of the summary age technique or by seriation of individuals in relation to those aged by the summary technique, it is possible that not enough skeleton was available from some adults to avoid age misestimation or systematic underaging of older adults by 10 or 15 years. That is, had more of the skeleton been available, these individuals would have been aged differently, or more accurately, than they were. The adults aged 40 or less, because of the greater accuracy of aging standards for these ages and less individual variability than for older ages, are likely to be accurately aged to within five years. This means practically that as many as one or two individuals in those younger age classes should be in the preceding or succeeding age class. In practical terms, making such shifts would have little effect on the age distributions in these ages. Mensforth and Lovejoy (1985) did find that there may be a small bias toward overaging of individuals in the early twenties. However, this bias is usually a year or less and would minimally affect the age cohorts of the life table. In general, a skeleton with young indicators is young, and the potential for misclassification is low. The younger adults will be left as determined by the aging seriation. Thus, if there is a weakness in the Tlajinga 33 age distribution of deaths, it may be in the underaging of some of the older adults, although not all would be affected. This potential error is corrected through modeling below.

Also characteristic of the stationary-population life table is the effect of the large numbers of perinatals in the sample. Life expectancy at birth is about 20.5 years but rises dramatically to more than 28 years if an individual just survived infancy. This effect is, of course, a direct result of the extraordinary preservation of perinatals at Tlajinga 33. Although some of the individuals are late fetal in age and thus not usually included in many mortality statistics, these perinatals are all likely to have been live born, since they have been treated like those known to have lived and died, and thus are legitimately used as examples of neonate and infant mortality.

Other measures visible in the life table include the finding that only 50% of the individuals ever born survive to the age of 15 (l_{15}). At age 20 an adult had an average life expectancy of 20 more years, indicating that the average age of death of the Tlajinga 33 adults is 40. From the reciprocal of life expectancy at birth, the crude birth rate can be calculated, and it is equal to the crude death rate in a stationary population (Acsádi and Nemeskéri 1970). Here, 49 per 1,000 people per year are born. This figure is high for many modern nations, but not for the fastest-growing nations, although the comparable crude death rate would be higher than that in contemporary nations (Shyrock and Siegel 1976). This life table is quite similar in pattern and measures to many of the stationary-population tables that have been constructed for paleodemographic purposes (e.g., Buikstra and Konigsberg 1985; Hassan 1981).

This stationary-population life table is different from the previous stationary-population table calculated and published for the Tlajinga 33 population (Storey 1985, 1986). In that table life expectancy at birth was 17 years, 34% of all individuals ever born survived to the age of 15, and the average adult lifespan was 37 years. Also, only 13% of the population survived to the age of 40, and the crude birth rate for such a demographic regime was 59/1,000 per year. Table 6-1, in contrast, does not look as severe in mortality and does not imply a population dying at such young ages, as in the original table. There are two underlying differences between the Tlajinga 33 sample presented here and the one available when the other table was calculated. One is that the estimated number of individuals in the population is now greater. This increase was a result of a recalculation of the individuals in secondary contexts, aided by better chronological control than was possible earlier. With more control of chronological differences, more individuals could be defined with more confidence, even if no sexing or aging was possible for them. These individuals, mostly unageable, were then prorated with the aged individuals to increase the sample size. Thus, the effects of underenumeration of adults from secondary contexts are clearly visible in the differences between the two stationary-population life tables. The calculation used here is felt to be accurate, but if it is still an underenumeration, the effect would, however, be the same, to increase life expectancy over the entire life table.

A second factor responsible for the differences seen between the old and new life tables is the reseriation of the Tlajinga 33 adults on the basis of the indicators and techniques suggested by Lovejoy et al. (1985a). When the original seriation was done in 1981–82, the standards for the auricular surface available were slightly different from the final published ones. Use of the earlier ones by the author quite definitely tended to underage adults in the sample, and this affected the final age determination. The effect is seen by comparing the 25–39-year-olds in the two tables. In the original table 20% of the total sample fell in this group, but only 13% were 40 or over. In Table 6-1 the 25–39-year-olds constitute 13% of the total sample, whereas those over 40 total 25%. The effect of the newer Lovejoy et al. standards was to correct an earlier bias and more accurately identify older individuals, especially when the skeletal completeness is not the best. Thus, Mensforth and Lovejoy's (1985) support for the summary age technique as yielding accurate skeletal ages, even for older individuals, seems to be borne out by this study. This revised Tlajinga 33 skeletal age distribution now contains more older individuals, which would be expected and desirable for social continuity and success (Howell 1982). The revised stationary-population life table for Tlajinga 33 still indicates high infant and child mortality, but the probability of dying as an infant is slightly less, and the life expectancy in the adult years is higher, making the adult lifespan longer than was implied by the previous life table.

Though the stationary-population life table has some justification as a possible demographic model for Tlajinga 33 on archaeological grounds, it is also likely not to be the best model. Tlajinga 33 was an apartment compound of poor artisans in a densely populated center. For one thing, it is not likely to have been a closed population. All known urban centers are characterized by at least some migration, which means they are not closed populations as required by the stable, stationary methods. There is no reason to assume that Teotihuacan would have been different, and it certainly reached its large size early in its history as a result of migration (e.g., Sanders et al. 1979). Although migration to the city during the period of occupation of the Tlajinga 33 compound has never been clearly demonstrated archaeologically, it almost certainly happened and must be addressed in the Tlajinga 33 paleodemographic analysis.

Also, although Teotihuacan may have been stable overall in population, the individual apartment compounds may not have been. Another possible complication of the Tlajinga 33 situation is the possible effect of a high-population-density environment on health and thus fertility and mortality. These two complications are not unrelated (see Chapter 2). Often, dense concentrations of people, as in preindustrial cities, brought with it mortality that exceeded fertility; migration often made up the shortfall. Thus, it is possible that Tlajinga 33, especially as a lower-class compound, would have had the mortality that exceeded its natural fertility. It could have been a declining population. Thus, a stationary-population model is perhaps not suitable for the skeletal series.

Several alternatives to the untransformed age distribution that assumed stationarity should be investigated, for they might control for possible migration and compensate for possible older adult underaging. There is no real evidence that the other potential sources of error in the Tlajinga 33 age distribution are distorting the age distribution or that it is necessary to model for them. The study also focuses on the characteristics of these alternatives to Table 6-1.

Other Demographic Models for Tlajinga 33

In any investigation of alternatives to the stationary-population life table, paleodemographic analysis enters the center of the controversy that has dominated the 1980s, that is, exactly what does an age distribution of deaths reveal about the demographic characteristics of the living population that created it? As one of the tasks of the "New Paleodemography" is to build up a series of studies upon which good inference about past populations may be made (see Hammel and Howell 1987), it behooves each paleodemographic analysis to build upon what is already accomplished, and not just suggest new methods. In this study methods that have already been suggested and tried are used. What is new, it is hoped, is the synthesis of methods and inference available to paleodemography that can add to knowledge of the past. This synthesis consists of the use of fertility inferences plus mortality methods of reconstruction. However, the pertinent anthropological and archaeological knowledge is always used as the final arbitrator in judgments of the reasonableness of the demographic reconstructions, a procedure that is not always followed. It is expected that if the best methods that have been forwarded for paleodemographic analysis are combined with good, sound archaeological and anthropological inference, the Tlajinga 33 skeletal sample will reveal important factual information about the demography of Teotihuacan.

Migration

The first adjustment to the Tlajinga 33 series concerns the issue of migration. A decision must be made as to whether migration would have affected the age distribution of deaths available and what its impact would be. The Tlajinga 33 compound, like most of the Teotihuacan apartment compounds, was probably a kin-based residence group organized by occupational specialty (see Chapters 2 and 3). Thus, one would not expect wholesale replacement of residents by migrants, but a few people were probably added now and then. Modern anthropological and demographic theories of migration are, naturally, heavily affected by modern world realities and economics. However, for preindustrial cities, and even more so for a pre-Columbian urban center like Teotihuacan, modern economic reasons for migration such as moving closer to place of work, education, health, housing would not be relevant (see Rogers and Castro 1984a). However, certain causes for migration identified in the modern world would also be present in pre-Columbian Mexico. These include marriage and change in employment. The consideration of migration thus forces the creation of hypotheses that explain how recruitment would have worked for individual compounds in the city.

The movement of individuals into and out of the compound because of marriage would have been a continuous feature of Teotihuacan life, especially if the residents were linked by kinship. Exogamy would have required most individuals to look outside the compound for suitable mates. Of course, many of these would have probably come from the city and most probably from surrounding compounds. The nearly equal replacement of individuals marrying out by individuals marrying in from the city proper would not violate the assumption of a closed population. The question is really how migrants would have entered the compound: were a few husbands and wives brought in from outside the city, or were young families of migrants adopted into the compound?

The standard model migration schedule has a very definite age-specific pattern (Rogers and Castro 1984b) (see Figure 6-1). The age of highest rate of migration is either the early or late twenties, depending on the reason for migrating. Children reflect the migration rates of the parents, with the highest peak in infancy and dropping quickly to a low in the early teens. Then, through the late teens, it rises sharply to the peak. After that, it falls more gradually and often there is little migration after the age of 50. The age-specific pattern does vary slightly depending on the reason for migrating (see Rogers and Castro 1984a: 99–104). If marriage is the reason, then there is primarily a peak from the late teens through twenties, with negligible migration rates at other ages. If change in employment is the reason, the pattern is more like the standard model, for obvious reasons, as entire families are more likely to be involved in this type of migration than the other. Thus, the age pattern of the migrants expected in Teotihuacan depends on the nature of the migration.

Unfortunately, there is no independent archaeological information that would allow estimation of the migration rate into Teotihuacan during the Middle Horizon period of occupation of a compound like Tlajinga 33. Information from European preindustrial cities would be only marginally useful here, as cultural differences are likely to be quite influential in determining the nature and amount of migration. The difference is particularly important, given that there were no draft animals available for transportation in pre-Columbian Mesoamerica. For example, the British population was actually quite mobile, although most of it for relatively short distances during the seventeenth and eighteenth centuries (Clark and Souden 1987). Investigation of the British pattern reveals that the largest stream of migration to towns and cities would have been lower class, and generally consisting of unskilled young men and women (Clark and Souden 1987). The movement of skilled artisans was present but not as important in quantity, although they often moved long distances. Long-distance migration for subsistence purposes was common, especially during poor years in the rural countryside, although this kind of migration was usually discouraged by towns and cities (Clark and Souden 1987). Of interest is that sources indicate that occupational specialization, kinship, and regional ties were important mechanisms for integrating migrants into the city, although the poorer the migrant, the harder these were to exploit (Clark 1987). One sample of female migrants in London had more than 20% living with kin, and 37%

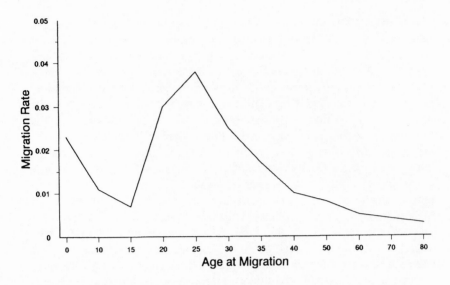

Figure 6-1. Model Migration Curve by Age of Migrant (adapted from Rogers and Castro 1984b: Figure 12)

with kin residing in the capital, although they did not live with them (Clark 1987: 272–273). Again, the general impression of researchers is that migrants were composed mostly of young people and young families.

Potential differences between the London and the Teotihuacan cases include the probably generally higher mobility of British populations, higher than that of many European countries at the same time, for example (Clark and Souden 1987), and perhaps the greater importance of kinship in linking migrants and compounds in Teotihuacan. As the size of Teotihuacan appears to have been stable over the period of the Tlajinga 33 occupation, migrants would then have been just absorbed into existing compounds. Similarities include a probable dominance of lower-class migrants and a preponderance of young people.

If most migration into Teotihuacan was of single, mostly male, individuals looking for marriage partners and, at the same time, entering into occupational specialization, the effects upon a compound like Tlajinga 33 would probably have been minimal. Only a few individuals would have entered that way and would not have been distinguishable from other marriage partners. Their effect demographically would also have been minimal and could be modeled just as other marriage partners, as balancing individuals leaving the compound for marriage. Of course, migrants in the modern world, and also in preindustrial London (Clark and Souden 1987), are also young women and young families. Young female migrants were very common in London and mostly were used as various kinds of domestics. Such might also be the case at Teotihuacan, but a lower-class compound like Tlajinga 33 would not likely have needed domestics, but would have accepted young women as marriage partners. The main effect migration would have had demographically on a compound like Tlajinga 33 would have occurred if there were a number of migrant families just taking up residence in the compound. These families would have added new adults and young children to the resident population, "new births" that are not the result of the intrinsic rates of growth of the compound residents. These individuals are not part of the closed population of Teotihuacan and the result of its demographic characteristics. There is no clear archaeological evidence at Tlajinga 33 of the presence of migrant families, as culturally the compound appears very uniform in artifacts and burial patterns across time. This is to be expected, if the migrants to Tlajinga are primarily from Teotihuacan's immediate hinterland. There is, of course, evidence that ethnic groups from other parts of Mesoamerica were residents of some compounds in the city (see Millon 1973), but these do seem to be in the minority. It does seem likely that the residents of Tlajinga 33, and probably many other artisanal compounds, periodically needed to recruit new labor and residents for the compound. Recruitment would have been most easily done by bringing in males in marriage. However, it is likely that there was an agnatic bias to the kin grouping of a Teotihuacan compound (see Spence 1974), and thus, most males would have tended to stay in their compound and bring in brides. It is possible that one of the reasons that cognatic descent grouping might have been the primary Teotihuacan compound organization is that females of the family could remain in their natal compound and bring in migrant males as partners. The compound apartment suite organization would have fostered the potential for new families to move in and just take up residence. It was probably necessary for Tlajinga 33 to recruit labor sometimes in just this way. Thus, there is not likely to be one simple way to model migration in a Teotihuacan compound like Tlajinga 33.

Because they are thought to be kin aggregations with long-term stability, apartment compounds were probably little affected by migration in the short term. Over the 500-year occupation of Tlajinga 33 there was probably some percentage of migrants among the residents. The question is, how do these affect the age distribution of deaths? If migration was primarily of marriage partners, there would be no demographic effect different from the closed population, because the new partners would just take the place of another local individual and would probably have been about the same age. Marriage exchanges are accepted as part of the population in small-scale demography. Thus, the effect of migration upon the assumption of a closed population would be negligible and the population could be treated as a closed one. However, the presence of new families or migrants, especially if they did not live long after migrating, could have an effect on the deaths recovered from the compound. Young child and adult deaths would be present that are extraneous to the internal demographics of the compound. Of course, if migrants lived for any time in the compound, their deaths would be the result of the mortality rates affecting that population, that is, they would be expected to die in the same proportions per age class as those born in Teotihuacan. Thus, longer-term migrants should not be distinguishable. Controlling for migrants presents a methodological dilemma, especially since there is no good estimate available from other data as to the migration rate.

Deciding that, for example, 20% of the deaths in the total compound population may be of migrants and removing them would just reduce the population numbers without changing the proportions in each age class. Such an adjustment would have no real effect on the stationary-population life table or any demographic modeling. The problem is to control for the potential distorting effects that migrants would have on the age distribution.

There are two possible solutions. One that has been used by historical demographers working with preindustrial urban populations (e.g., Finlay 1981) is to use only children under the age of 15, as the great majority of these would have been born and died in the compound, for example. A few possible migrants are not likely to distort this part of the demographic profile very much. But in such a small sample as Tlajinga such an approach would mean ignoring half the data and therefore is not considered a good solution. The second solution is to look critically at the Tlajinga 33 age distribution of death to see if any effects of migration might be visible or where they are most likely to be. For example, the addition of unknown numbers of adult migrants would lead to sudden increases in the proportions of young-adult age classes and could lead to sudden jumps in the numbers of deaths, as these cohorts are bigger. If any distorted age classes can be identified, then a range of possible corrections can be applied to control for possible migration distortions.

In the stationary-population life table, Table 6–1, the numbers per age cohort do follow a standard curve for mortality that typifies humans.

A high proportion of infant and perinatal deaths decreases to a low in the teen years and then rises generally through the adult years. There are some jumps in this pattern that are probably mostly due to the fluctuations expected from small samples. However, two age cohorts that might be of interest to the study of migration stand out. One is, of course, the large proportion of perinatals. The other is a dramatic increase in the numbers of 20–25-year-olds over the surrounding age cohorts, a probable age of peak migration. It is possible that an increase in the proportion of young adults leads to proportionately more deaths among them and also inflates the perinatal numbers, as there are more childbearing individuals present. However, the numbers of subsequent juveniles are not similarly inflated. The jump at age 40 is probably not due to migration effects, as migration is rare at this age. If it is not just an artifact of the sample size, it may be the result of an underaging of fragmentary older individuals and is discussed below.

Table 6–2 details the age distribution by sex and chronological period. The numbers of individual adults both sexed and aged are small but seem to be about equal in each age. Thus, migration does not seem to be distorting sex and age ratios. The chronological breakdowns are more informative, though again fluctuations due to small samples are present. Here, it can be seen that high proportions of perinatals are present in both periods, although the proportion of the total sample is higher in the Late Period. However, the jump in 20-year-olds is seen to be an artifact of the Late Period only and includes late teens as well, where proportions of 7% (15–19) and 15% (20–24) of the sample are in these ages in the Late Period, whereas only 2% and 4% are during the Early Period. It is possible that these might be inflated by migrants. Why? One hypothesis suggests that although migration is important to the continuance and stability of a city, migrants often have high mortality (de Vries 1984) and thus help fuel the urban decline. One explanation might be that migrants are likely to die soon after arriving in a city, because of the sudden exposure to the infections and other effects of high-density populations. Thus, 15–25-year-olds were probably the most common migrants at Teotihuacan, and it is possible that their presence at Tlajinga 33 is indicated by the deaths of recent migrants in those age groups. It is interesting that these possible migrants are dramatically indicated only during the Late Period, as if perhaps Teotihuacan required significant numbers of migrants only toward the end of its florescence. Another interesting feature of the individuals in these ages is that all but one were found in secondary deposits, indicating that not much care was given to the bones when they were disturbed, certainly a possibility if the individual had lived in the compound very briefly and had been quickly

TABLE 6-2
Age Distribution of Tlajinga 33
Individuals by Sex and Period

Age	Male	Female	Early Period	Late Period
Perinatals and Infants			29	26
15	4	2	3	6
20	4	2	5	11
25	0	1	7	1
30	1	1	3	4
35	4	4	8	4
40	5	6	18	4
45	4	1	8	3
50+	5	6	15	4
Totals	27	23	96	63

forgotten. However, the other young adult age group (25–29) is not inflated, so these "jumps" may be the result of sampling only.

The possibility of migrants is not clearly indicated by either the age-at-death distribution or other archaeological evidence. As a functioning corporate group, Tlajinga 33 quite possibly had only a minimal number of migrants during its history, at the periods when there were labor shortages, because of excess mortality, loss of young men in warfare, or a myriad of possible reasons. It is probable that both individual migrants and young families were added.

Therefore, as possible controls for migration, it seems reasonable to look at two different scenarios, which should span the range of possible situations at Tlajinga 33. One is to assume that migration was minimal and mostly of marriage partners. Under this scenario there are no adjustments to the age distribution, as removing a few individuals from all adult ages would have little effect on the proportions present. The other, worst-case scenario is to assume that there may have been as much as a 20% influx of migrants during the occupation of Tlajinga 33, which is reflected in only certain ages and impacts only the age distributions there, and perhaps was concentrated primarily during the Late Period.

To model the worst-case scenario, we may need to adjust two different parts of the age distribution of deaths to correct for migration distortions. If the effects of a possible 20% influx of migrants are modeled, these effects must be concentrated in a few age cohorts only. Thus, a total of 41 individuals (20% of 206) were removed proportionately from ages 0–4 and 15–39, the ages where migration rates are highest in the model migration schedule. The number of perinatals in the un-transformed age distribution is high, partly because of the recovery of actual premature individuals. However, as these are born in the compound and most probably represent live births, they are legitimate members of the skeletal population. Perinatals were born and died quickly within the compound and so are part of the actual compound population, no matter where their parents originated. However, as some of these would not have been born in the compound if their parents had not migrated, the perinatals have to be adjusted as well.

Thus, the influx of young families, who might have died soon after arrival, is modeled in Table 6–3. The added adults and the young children brought with them or born to them soon after migrating are removed from the age distribution. When this table is compared with the untransformed life table, it can be seen that the life expectancy at birth rises about two and one-half years, which partly reflects the reduction in the proportion of perinatals with this correction. The overall effect is to raise the mean age of death and increase the proportion of older individuals; 31% rather than 25% of the individuals are over 40, for example. In the migration correction, as opposed to the old-age correction to be modeled later, the effect is felt through all ages over 15, and not just in a restricted number of age classes.

This migration correction is not the only one that could have been done with this population. It is meant only to highlight migration effects from none to significant, so as to allow demographic modeling of the actual residential population of Tlajinga 33 without possible migration distortions. A migration of more than 20% is possible but is considered unlikely beause of the compound organization, which could accept only small numbers of migrants at a time. The true situation at Tlajinga 33 is likely to lie somewhere between none and 20% migration, between Table 6–1 and 6–3.

The Underaging of Old Adults

A second question about the untransformed age distribution that requires adjustment concerns the older ages and whether there is any underaging. The difference between treating the last age cohort as ending at 70 years (the likely age of the oldest individual) or 85 years, without doing any other adjustment, is a half-year in the life expectancy at birth, under an assumption of stationary population size. The main effect is in the life expectancies at the older ages. But if systematic underaging has occurred, one solution is to take all the individuals aged as 40

TABLE 6-3
Stationary-Population Life Table
for Tlajinga 33, Adjusted for Migration

Age	D_x	d_x	l_x	q_x	L_x	T_x	e_x
Perinatal	36	.22	1,000	.22	149	23,898	23.90
Infant	5	.03	780	.04	637	23,749	30.45
1	12	.07	750	.09	2,860	23,112	30.82
5	11	.07	680	.10	3,238	20,252	29.78
10	10	.06	615	.10	2,925	17,014	27.66
15	7	.04	555	.07	2,675	14,089	25.39
20	8	.05	515	.10	2,450	11,414	22.16
25	6	.04	465	.09	2,225	8,964	19.28
30	6	.04	425	.09	2,025	6,739	15.86
35	12	.07	385	.18	1,725	4,714	12.24
40	22	.14	315	.43	1,238	2,964	9.41
45	11	.06	180	.36	738	1,726	9.59
50	11	.06	115	.57	413	988	8.59
55	3	.02	50	.40	200	575	11.50
60+	5	.03	30	1.00	375	375	12.50
Totals	165	1.00					

Note: Skeletons with cut marks are excluded.

or older and distribute them more evenly through the lifespan to age 85. The effect, as Willey and Mann (1986) demonstrated, is to raise life expectancy at all ages, but again most of the effect is on the probability of dying and life expectancy from ages 40 on. What was done to apportion the individuals was that since there were about 25% of the deaths at age 40 or older in the untransformed age distribution, the West Male Level 2 model life table (Coale and Demeny 1983), which also has about 25% of the deaths in that age range, was used to determine the new d_xs. Table 6-4 shows the result. The life expectancy at birth does rise two years, and this increase is up to three more years by age 5 and rises up through the lifespan until age 55, where it is the same as in the untransformed stationary-population life table. The effect is also visible in the q_x column as well, where the rise in probability of dying is more gradual. The main difference between this old-age correction table and the untransformed with lifespan modeled to 85 years is in the more moderate mortality

TABLE 6-4
Old-Age Corrected Stationary-Population
Table for Tlajinga 33

Age	D_x	d_x	l_x	q_x	L_x	T_x	e_x
Perinatal	55	.27	1,000	.27	144	22,515	22.52
Infant	8	.04	730	.05	592	22,371	30.65
1	18	.09	690	.13	2,580	21,780	31.57
5	11	.05	600	.08	2,875	19,200	32.00
10	10	.05	550	.09	2,625	16,325	29.68
15	9	.04	500	.08	2,400	13,700	27.40
20	16	.08	460	.17	2,100	11,300	24.57
25	8	.04	380	.11	1,800	9,200	24.21
30	7	.03	340	.09	1,625	7,400	21.76
35	12	.06	310	.19	1,400	5,775	18.63
40	9	.04	250	.16	1,150	4,375	17.50
45	8	.04	210	.19	950	3,225	15.36
50	8	.04	170	.24	750	2,275	13.38
55	7	.03	130	.23	575	1,525	11.73
60	7	.03	100	.30	425	950	9.50
65	6	.03	70	.43	275	525	7.50
70	4	.02	40	.50	150	250	6.25
75	2	.01	20	.50	75	100	5.00
80	1	.01	10	1.00	25	25	2.50
Totals	206	1.00					

Note: Skeletons with cut marks are excluded.

figures in the young and middle-aged adult range, rather than in its effect over 50 years. Willey and Mann (1986) found the same effect and believed that it was perhaps more realistic because it makes the adult years look less stressed than is usual in many paleodemographic studies and provides for better social stability and continuity, in line with Howell's (1982) criticism.

As was found by Mensforth and Lovejoy (1985) in their Libben skeletal population, the individuals at Tlajinga 33 do not appear to have been extremely aged, and thus although the correction may be more realistic in terms of modern demographic models, it is not necessarily more realistic for Tlajinga 33. Most older individuals were believed to have been accurately aged, although there is some chance of underaging because of the fragmentary remains. For that reason, the older-age correction will be used for comparison with the untransformed age distribution.

The untransformed age distribution was felt to be reasonable in terms of representativeness, completeness of archaeological recovery, aging, and sexing estimates. The stationary-population life table revealed a population with high mortality, especially of juveniles. It had a relatively low mean age at death, the same as life expectancy at birth in a stationary-population table, of 20.5 years. Two corrected age distributions were created to compensate for possible complications. One was an old-age correction for underaging of older adults, although it is believed that the potential underaging was minor and largely controlled by just running the oldest age class to age 85. The other correction was for migration and needs to be considered for the urban center of Teotihuacan, although there was no real clear *a priori* evidence for the presence or an amount of migration in the Tlajinga 33 compound. The migration correction was intended to model the greatest impact that migration might have had upon the age distribution of deaths of Tlajinga 33, affecting 20% of the individuals in the young adult and the infant and young child ages. Figures 6-2 and 6-3 compare the survivorships and probabilities of dying for the three stationary-population life tables.

The graphs show the differences discussed above. In survivorship, the steep descent through childhood is visible, followed by a more gradual descent until old age. The migration-corrected survivorship is better at all ages, until it, too, drops precipitously at age 50. The old-age correction smooths out the survivorship decline only from age 40 until the end. In Figure 6-3 the effects of the small-sample fluctuations from one age class to another in the untransformed age distribution are clear. These kinds of jumps are often mitigated by smoothing the age distribution (e.g., Weiss 1973), which was not done here. The two corrected age distributions clearly smooth out these jumps, the migration one up to age 35 and the old-age one past age 35. This figure hints that perhaps the best age distribution for Tlajinga, the one that produces a J-shaped curve most similar to general demographic models, is to combine the migration-correction to age 40 with the old-age one after that to make a new composite. This possibility is considered in Chapter 8.

These three age distributions, the untransformed together with the two corrected ones, form the basis of further investigation of the Tlajinga 33 demographic profile. Again, these are not the only models that could be applied to Tlajinga. Paleodemography is very much an enterprise of developing various models for the skeletal population. A main concern is to provide a range of demographic models that might be realistic for a

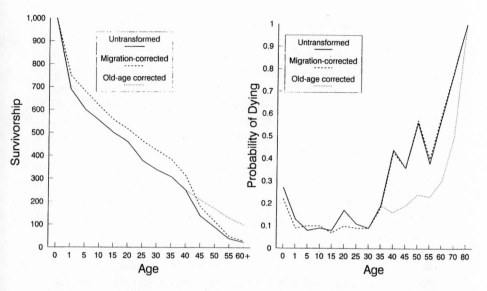

Figure 6-2. Survivorship (l_x) of the Three Stationary-Population Life Tables for Tlajinga 33

Figure 6-3. Probability of Dying (d_x) for the Three Stationary-Population Life Tables for Tlajinga 33

past population (e.g., Bennett 1973; Johansson and Horowitz 1986). Often, it is not possible to narrow investigation down to just one, best model. Thus, here in the Tlajinga 33 study, models to correct possible errors that distort the age distribution are developed, and so that a large number of possible models need not be created, only those that embody the most extreme effects are used. These will show the range of demographic conditions that actually were present in the compound. The objective is to see what effects different models have and what similarities might be present. In this study it is hoped that one or two best models can be identified, not only on demographic grounds, but because these are also compatible with all the archaeological and paleopathological evidence available for these skeletons.

Demographic Modeling of Fertility in Tlajinga 33

Since the publication of the work of Sattenspiel and Harpending (1983), most paleodemographic analyses have focused on the study of fertility obtainable from an age distribution of deaths (see Buikstra et al. 1986; Milner et al. 1989). Although it seems counterintuitive that fertility should be obtainable from skeletal deaths, fertility, and more directly, the growing size of cohorts of a growing population, can have a dramatic effect on the ages of skeletons deposited in a site. Sattenspiel and Harpending's (1983) contention that the mean age of death of a skeletal population is a direct measure of fertility has been shown to be true only under certain very limited assumptions and to be characteristic of stationary populations (Horowitz and Armelagos 1988). In spite of this, researchers have been using the insight and a variety of methods to look at what skeletal populations can reveal about fertility.

Buikstra et al. (1986), studying long-term trends in west-central Illinois, suggested that one look at a ratio of deaths over 30 to deaths over age 5, instead of the mean age of death, as the latter can be easily biased by various kinds of skeletal age misestimations. They found that this ratio was highly correlated with birth rate in the Coale and Demeny (1966) model stable populations. This ratio yields a value that can be compared only relatively with that of other populations. Although Buikstra et al.'s method is best for a chronological series of skeletons, as was the Illinois situation, the ratio for Tlajinga 33 can be instructive when it is compared with their results. The ratio of D_{30}/D_{5+} for the untransformed Tlajinga 33 age distribution is 71/125 or .568; slightly over half of the deaths are over 30, in other words. With 95% comparison intervals calculated as suggested by Buikstra et al. (1986: 534), Tlajinga is compared with three of the west-central Illinois samples, including the one closest in value to Tlajinga, and the two with the lowest ratios (Figure 6-4). The comparison intervals are calculated on the basis of four sample comparisons in a multiple comparison test and so differ from the intervals calculated by Buisktra et al. for eight samples.

There is slight overlap in the figure between the Schild Mississippian value and Tlajinga, an indication that there is no statistically significant difference at the .05 level between the two samples. Tlajinga would be among the upper values in the west-central Illinois samples, but the value of the ratio really indicates only relative differences in possible fertility and is not necessarily indicative of a particular birth rate. The ratio has a generally inverse relationship with birth rate, so the Tlajinga ratio indicates possible moderate fertility in relation to the high-fertility Mississippian sample. Through time in Illinois, the decreasing trend in the ratio probably indicates an increase in fertility (Buikstra et al. 1986). If one compares the ratio for the migration-corrected Tlajinga distribution (the ratio for the old-age-corrected is exactly the same as the untransformed), it is .625, 70/112. Its comparison interval would be from .7258 to .5242 and does not overlap with the Schild Mississippian population. Thus, the migration-corrected ratio could indicate statistically sig-

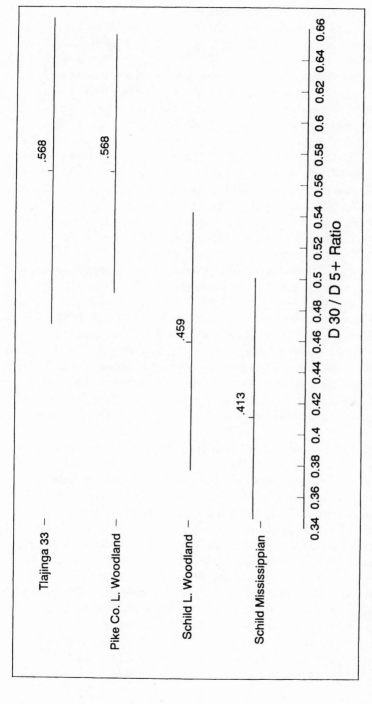

Figure 6-4. Fertility Ratios of Tlajinga 33 and Three Illinois Skeletal Populations (95% comparison intervals; Illinois populations from Buikstra et al. 1986)

nificant lower fertility than the Schild population has and again supports the notion that Tlajinga has a moderate fertility in comparison.

Another comparison made by Buikstra et al. (1986) is of the ratio of deaths in ages 1–5 over deaths in ages 1–10. This ratio may indicate child mortality by allowing one to see whether possible weaning deaths, in ages 1–5, are the majority of the childhood deaths. As death rates are generally higher for groups under age 5 than for older groups in contemporary populations, the more weaning deaths in proportion to all childhood deaths, the more likely it is that there is significant childhood mortality in the population. The ratio for the Tlajinga untransformed distribution is .620, 18/29, which indicates more deaths in the weaning years. However, when these results are compared with three of the Illinois samples (Buikstra et al. 1986), Figure 6-5, it is apparent that the small sample size of Tlajinga yields such large comparison intervals that it easily overlaps with all the others. The migration-corrected ratio is .520, 12/23, and its comparison intervals also overlap. The effect of the migration correction is, of course, to remove some individuals under 5 years of age as migrants, and thus to lower the ratio. Thus, Tlajinga does not show any child-death ratios that are statistically different from those of the Illinois paleodemographic samples. Buikstra et al. (1986) see no real evidence in their chronological series that maize agriculture brought with it higher subadult mortality, as the ratio actually declined and deaths are more equally distributed over the childhood years. The Tlajinga untransformed ratio does indicate proportionately more weaning deaths. As the sample in these ages is good, even though it cannot be shown to be statistically significant here, this ratio should be kept in mind.

Looking for fertility trends by comparing Tlajinga 33 with other samples and using the ratios of Buikstra et al. (1986) puts Tlajinga in the middle of an Illinois sample, but the results are not statistically significant, except in one case, from either end of the range of samples. Thus, this comparison reveals only general similarities of Tlajinga 33 with some other pre-Columbian skeletal samples. What is needed is a look at any chronological trend in Tlajinga; this is done below. Chronological analysis may be more useful. Although the method at Buikstra et al. (1986) can be useful, for a series like Tlajinga where infant underenumeration is not a problem and where the bulk of the subadult skeletons fall under one year of age, this ratio loses much of the information available and may not represent Tlajinga 33 accurately.

In a recent article Milner et al. (1989) also wanted to characterize skeletal samples by comparing them to reference age distributions of death affected by high versus moderately low fertility. As references they

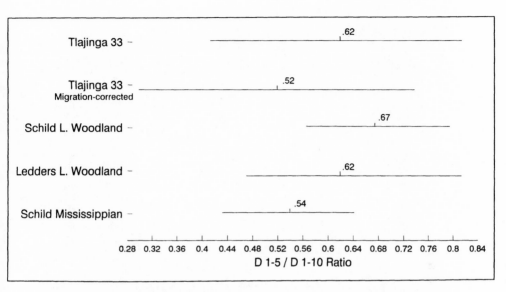

Figure 6-5. Juvenile Mortality Ratios of Tlajinga 33 and Three Illinois Skeletal Populations (95% comparison intervals; Illinois populations from Buikstra et al. 1986)

chose two of the best-known anthropological populations, the Yanomamö (for high fertility) and the !Kung San (for low). They especially use the ratio of skeletons less than 5 years of age to those over 45 to assess fertility, as those with a high ratio represent high fertility populations, whereas those with a low ratio have a much lower fertility. Although this ratio is fairly high for the untransformed Tlajinga distribution, 2.7 times the number under 5 as over 45, the age distribution of Tlajinga is otherwise somewhat different from any of the reference populations Milner et al. (1989: Figure 1) used. This is graphically evident in Figure 6-6, where the proportions 0–5 are closer to the San, but in the proportion 45+, Tlajinga is closer to the Yanomamö. In the middle age categories Tlajinga has different proportions than either reference population, usually higher except for age category 25–35. The overall similarity, however, is more to the high-fertility profiles than to the low. Among the Tlajinga age distributions, the effect of the migration correction is to lower the ratio of deaths under 5 to those over 45. But this correction raises the proportions 5–15 and 35–45, ages that were not affected by any adjustments, to make them quite different from the reference populations. The overall effect is that Tlajinga has more deaths distributed across the middle categories and less heaping in the first and last one, as the reference populations do.

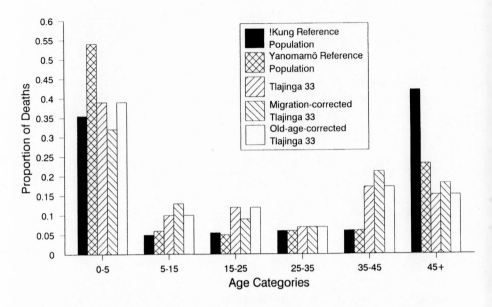

Figure 6-6. Proportions of Deaths in Six Age Categories in Tlajinga 33 and Two Reference Anthropological Populations (reference populations from Milner et al. 1989: Figure 1)

Figure 6-7 expands this comparison to the Oneota and Libben skeletal samples discussed by Milner et al. (1989). The Tlajinga sample seems to fall generally between those two, although it is generally more similar to these skeletal populations than to the reference ones in Figure 6-6. Again, the Tlajinga pattern is closer to Oneota in some categories and to Libben in others. It does not show quite the profile of the Libben population, criticized by Milner et al. (1989) as not exemplifying a known stable population, but like Libben, it seems to show a more even profile across the age distribution than do the reference or Oneota populations. The differences are not surprising, in that Tlajinga is the result of a lower-class urban population and should not necessarily be expected to be like either of those nonurban populations.

In fact, the main effect of using the comparison of Milner et al. (1989) is that Tlajinga seems to show a more moderate fertility than the reference population of the Yanomamö and the Oneota skeletal series. On the other hand, Tlajinga differs in the ratio of young to very old individuals from the moderately low-fertility San. The fact that it is not quite like the reference populations discussed by Milner et al. (1989) may be due to its distinctly different cultural background, as an urban population. It was

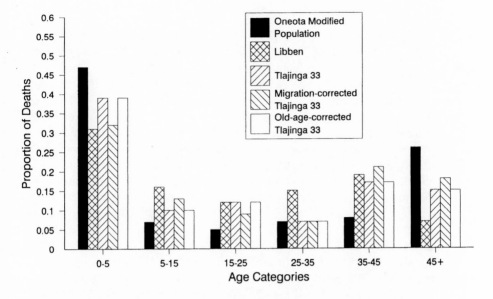

Figure 6-7. Proportions of Deaths in Six Age Categories in Tlajinga 33, the Oneota Skeletal Population (Milner et al. 1989), and Libben (Lovejoy et al. 1977)

useful, though, to see how Tlajinga 33 and its corrected versions compared with other paleodemographic samples; definite differences between it and all other populations compared with it were revealed in some categories. The categories with higher proportions of death should be kept in mind for further analysis in Chapter 8.

A third possible method for investigating fertility patterns in Tlajinga 33 is to use Henneberg's (1976) model of fertility and his method for measuring the reproductive potential of a past population by use of its stationary-population life table. Although the age distribution of death is now known to be a complex reflection of the living population that produced it and the assumption of stationarity must be justified, Henneberg's method is useful in that it is a way to check the internal consistency of an assumption of the stationary condition. His approach is that the most reasonable way to estimate reproduction in a past population is to measure the impact of mortality on its reproductive capacity, which tests if the stationary-population table truly seems to indicate that fertility and mortality were likely to balance each other.

Henneberg constructed a model of the regularities in fertility in noncontracepting populations, which are what prehistoric populations should be. This method is thus based on a uniformitarian assumption. He determined an "archetype of fertility," which details the proportion of fertility left to complete, s_x, during a five-year period in the reproductive span of a woman from ages 15 to 45. This archetype is based on fertility from populations known by records of vital events and includes some that could be called anthropological. He noticed the regularity of the distribution of births, which is affected by biological changes in fecundity, which are correlated with age. That is, a woman's ability to conceive is not greatest at menarche but rises in the teen years to a peak during the twenties and then declines, usually precipitously, after age 35–40. Thus, the relative cumulative proportion of a woman's total births that have occurred by a certain age class is fairly constant across non-contracepting populations. Thus, Henneberg's (1976: 43) proportions for s_x are .95 (for ages 15–19), .77 (ages 20–24), .55 (ages 25–29), .35 (ages 30–34), .17 (ages 35–39), .05 (ages 40–45). Therefore, for example, females aged 30–34 have completed about 65% of their total births and have about 35% left to complete, and so on.

The importance of the archetype is that it allows the calculation of the reproductive potential, or potential gross reproductive rate. This is basically the sum of the reproductive potential remaining after the premenopausal deaths of adults. Thus, the calculation tells what proportion of the total reproductive potential of both sexes, although it is modeled on females, will be realized under the given adult mortality conditions revealed in the life table. If no one died before age 50, the reproductive potential would be 1.0, and the total fertility possible would have been realized. The equation is $R_{pot} = 1 - \Sigma d_x s_x$, where d_x is the proportion of those dying in age class x among all persons beginning the reproductive period, and s_x, the proportion of completed fertility left to those in the age class.

But, if one is to make a more accurate assessment of reproductive success, one has to take the mortality of subadults into account. Henneberg came up with what he named the net reproductive rate, which calculates the success of a parental generation in replacing itself, given its reproductive potential and the mortality before age 15. (This reproductive rate is not comparable to the general demographic index of that name, which is calculated differently and only for females.) Thus, if this rate equals 1.0, the generation of parents and their adult descendants of both sexes are of equal size and age structure. If it is less than one, the population is declining, as the population is not replacing itself. If it is greater than one, the population is increasing. The equation for this net reproductive rate is $R_0 = R_{pot} (0.5) U_c (100 - d_j/100)$, where 0.5 corrects for the sex ratio at birth, U_c is the completed family size, and d_j, the proportion of those ever born who die before reaching 15 years. The accuracy of the R_0 estimates depends on reliable subadult mortality data. When Henneberg calculated the R_0 for various skeletal populations, he found that most of the stationary-population models had a value above 1.0, and he concluded that many of these populations were capable of at least moderate natural increase. Actually, all Henneberg's method allows is to look at the real implications of the assumptions of a stationary case, as Howell (1982) has urged, and it does allow one to compare relative measures between populations. The only key to Henneberg's method is the determination of the completed fertility, the U_c, as this figure must be reasonably selected by the researcher, and the size of the family, of course, affects the magnitude of the R_0. The bigger the family at completion of fertility, the easier for a population to reproduce itself, and the smaller the family, the harder. Thus, it all comes down to whether the population was a high- or low-fertility one.

When one applies these equations to the Tlajinga 33 stationary-population life table, the untransformed one, Table 6–1, produces a reproductive potential of 0.70, indicating that adult mortality in the population is high enough that 30% of the maximum reproduction is lost. A decision must then be made as to the average completed family size, U_c, of women in Tlajinga. The pattern for sedentary, contemporary non-contracepting populations is between seven and eight children (e.g., Hassan 1981; Howell 1976). The comparison with the ratio of Milner et al. (1989) indicated that Tlajinga's was not a low-fertility age distribution, so that seven is a reasonable figure, although perhaps six, for a more moderate fertility, is also reasonable. In this stationary-population table, 50% of those born are dead by age 15, so the R_0 is equal to 1.23 if the completed fertility is seven, and 1.05 if the completed fertility is six. Thus, in this case the population could just about be holding even or have the capacity for some moderate increase, depending on the fertility of the population. If completed fertility was below six, then the population would have been declining.

When Henneberg's (1976) method is applied to the corrected Tlajinga age distributions of deaths, only the migration correction will show any differences from the untransformed. The old-age correction changes only from age 40 on, and the adjustment has very little effect on the reproductive potential measure, 0.705 instead of 0.70, with about the same R_0 measures as the untransformed. The migration correction, on the other hand, removes some juveniles and some young adults from the original age distribution and thus affects the Henneberg measures. The reproductive potential is 0.76, and the R_0 is 1.5 if completed fertility is seven, and 1.3 if it is only six. Thus, under the migration correction by this method, the Tlajinga population appears to be capable of definite increase.

All these paleodemographic methods of analysis have revealed that the Tlajinga 33 age distribution at death is one of at least moderately high fertility. That finding is not a surprising one, considering the cultural context of the skeletal population. This was a sedentary population living in a complex society dependent on intensive agriculture (see Sanders et al. 1979), living in a society where human labor was the main form of energy (Sanders and Santley 1983). As occupational specialists dependent on their production for subsistence, the compound residents undoubtedly valued human labor and would have been pronatalist. Fertility was probably encouraged but would have been affected by other cultural and environmental factors (see Handwerker 1983), such as age at marriage and health factors. It is reasonable to conclude that this would have been a moderately high- to high-fertility population. However, if this is all that can be concluded, not much has been learned about the demographic characteristics of Tlajinga 33, and by extension, Teotihuacan. A first step toward further investigation is to see if there are sex differences that might be significant, and to apply the above methods to chronological information, to investigate the possibility of changes through time that might be significant at Tlajinga 33.

Sex-Specific Differences

For skeletal prehistoric populations sex cannot be determined with reasonable certainty for subadults, so only adult differences by sex can be studied. For modern populations there is a difference in adult mortality patterns by sex, in that females tend to have higher survivorship and longer average life expectancy than males in most nations (Hassan 1981). However, researchers have found in paleodemographic stationary-population tables that males generally have better adult survivorship (Acsádi and Nemeskéri 1970). The explanation generally forwarded for this difference is that, before modern times, the mortality and general toll taken by childbearing on women in their twenties and thirties seemed to have shortened their average lifespan.

The Tlajinga 33 data consisted of only 50 individuals fairly evenly divided between males and females that could also be aged. The age distribution is given in Table 6–2. A small sample is involved, but not much difference in life expectancies is visible. The proportion over 40, a rough indication of survivorship, is 52% for males and 56% for females, which certainly reveals no evidence of excessive young female mortality. This result is interesting, because the large proportion of perinatals might be thought to indicate that more women were also dying as a result of childbearing. Although the numbers of males and females have not been shown to be significantly different (see Chapter 5), it is possible that not all young female deaths would be recovered. Ethnohistoric sources for the later Aztec Period indicate that women who died in childbirth were accorded special mortuary status and buried in a temple dedicated to a goddess in charge of childbirth (Soustelle 1961). If this custom went back to Teotihuacan times, it is possible that such women would be missing from the recovered skeletal sample. Thus, the age distribution of deaths would lack young females that should be there. There is no evidence from Teotihuacan of such specialized burial samples in temples, but, frankly, not enough excavation has been done to be able to judge whether this custom was present. Therefore, the possibility of underrepresentation of young females cannot be confirmed or denied but should be kept in mind. The sex differences in Tlajinga cannot really be further investigated because of the small sample and general equality of the age distribution by sex. It could be, though, that Tlajinga is not necessarily different from other skeletal samples that have more young female than young male adults among the dead. However, given current understandings, this pattern does not necessarily indicate higher young female mortality, but only a larger female cohort. The explanation for the common paleodemographic pattern may not be childbirth, anyway.

Chronological Differences

The complete Tlajinga 33 age distribution was constructed from early and late period samples (see Table 6–2). These were not equal, as the early sample is larger. A Kolmogorov-Smirnoff two-sample test was used to compare the age distributions, as suggested by Lovejoy (1971), and revealed a significant difference between the two chronological periods. The Late Period sample is younger, having 82% of the individuals under age 30, whereas only 59% of the Early Period were younger than 30. Thus, there are differences to be explored.

As a starting point, the stationary-population life tables, with a maximum lifespan of 85 years, are presented for both periods in Table 6–5 and 6–6. The difference in the age distributions is immediately evident in the tables in the life expectancy at birth or mean age of death, which is 24.04 years for the Early Period and 16.09 for the Late. The only correction to the untransformed age distributions that will be investigated is the migration one, as the old-age correction has no effect on the Late Period because of the few individuals over 40, and only minor impact on the Early in the older life expectancies. Migration, however, did have an effect in most analyses done above and changes both chronological age distributions. As the suggestion was made that perhaps migration was

TABLE 6-5
Tlajinga 33 Stationary-Population
Life Table, Early Period

Age	D_x	d_x	l_x	q_x	L_x	T_x	e_x
Perinatal	29	.27	1,000	.24	147	24,042	24.04
Infant	2	.04	760	.03	625	23,895	31.44
1	14	.12	740	.16	2,720	23,270	31.45
5	3	.02	620	.03	3,050	20,550	33.15
10	6	.05	600	.08	2,875	17,500	29.17
15	3	.02	550	.04	2,700	14,625	26.59
20	5	.04	530	.08	2,550	11,925	22.50
25	7	.06	490	.12	2,300	9,375	19.13
30	3	.02	430	.05	2,100	7,075	16.45
35	8	.07	410	.17	1,875	4,975	12.13
40	18	.15	340	.44	1,325	3,100	9.18
45	8	.07	190	.37	775	1,775	9.34
50	10	.08	120	.40	400	1,000	8.33
55+	5	.04	40	1.00	600	600	15.00
Totals	121	1.00					

more important during the Late Period, and this was the age distribution with a preponderance of the young ages when migrants would enter the compound, it was decided to model a worst-case migration scenario weighted toward the Late Period.

The 20% impact on peak migration ages, modeled for the complete untransformed age distribution, entailed the removal of a total of 41 individuals. These were apportioned between the two chronological periods. A 5% migration effect was modeled on the Early Period age distribution, with 10 individuals removed proportionately from ages 0–4 and 15–34, and a 15% effect on the Late Period, with 30 individuals removed proportionately from the same age ranges (one individual of the original 41 was not removed here, because that would have left a zero in one age cohort) (see Table 6–7). The effect is to raise the mean age at death of both periods. It is only about one year for the Early but a more dramatic three years for the Late Period.

A comparison of the D_{30+}/D_{5+} ratios (Buikstra et al. 1986) for the two untransformed chronological distributions yields 52/76 or 0.6842 for the Early Period, and 19/49 or 0.390 for the Late Period, much lower than any other calculated for Tlajinga 33. When one calculates the 95% com-

TABLE 6-6
Tlajinga 33 Stationary-Population
Life Table, Late Period

Age	D_x	d_x	l_x	q_x	L_x	T_x	e_x
Perinatal	26	.31	1,000	.31	142	16,091	16.09
Infant	6	.07	695	.10	549	15,949	22.95
1	4	.05	625	.08	2,400	15,400	24.64
5	8	.09	575	.16	2,650	13,000	22.61
10	4	.05	485	.10	2,300	10,350	21.34
15	6	.07	435	.16	2,000	8,050	18.51
20	11	.13	365	.34	1,513	6,050	16.58
25	1	.01	240	.04	1,175	4,537	18.91
30	4	.05	230	.22	1,025	3,362	14.62
35	4	.05	180	.28	775	2,337	12.99
40	4	.05	130	.39	525	1,562	12.02
45	3	.03	80	.44	312	1,027	12.97
50	1	.01	45	.22	200	725	16.11
55+	3	.03	35	1.00	525	525	15.00
Totals	85	1.00					

parison intervals as before and uses the same Illinois skeletal samples, except to use a five-sample comparison to calculate the intervals, one arrives at the results graphically displayed in Figure 6–8. There is no overlap between the Early and Late Periods, which indicates statistically significant differences in the ratio at the 0.05 level. This result is not surprising, considering the difference in the two age distributions. There is also no overlap of either Schild site population from Illinois and the Tlajinga Early Period distribution, which seems to indicate a possible increase in fertility from the Early to the Late Period. As the Schild Mississippian is thought to indicate high fertility, the change through time at Tlajinga is from moderate to high fertility.

If the migration-corrected ratios are calculated, the Early Period is 51.5/73 or 0.7055, and the Late 17/38 or 0.4474. The comparison intervals for these, also based on a five-sample comparison, are shown in Figure 6–8. With the migration correction, the two periods now overlap and are not statistically different, although a trend of increasing fertility through time is still suggested. The Early Period also still does not overlap with the two Schild samples, which thus still suggests significant fertility differences between Tlajinga and a high-fertility skeletal population. The

TABLE 6-7
Migration-Corrected Age
Distributions of Deaths by Periods

Age	Early Period		Late Period	
	Number	d_x	Number	d_x
Perinatal	24	.22	12	.22
Infant	2	.02	3	.055
1	12	.11	2	.035
5	3	.03	8	.15
10	6	.05	4	.07
15	2.5	.02	3	.055
20	4	.04	5	.09
25	6	.05	1	.02
30	2.5	.02	2	.035
35	8	.07	4	.07
40	18	.16	4	.07
45	8	.07	3	.055
50	10	.09	1	.02
55+	5	.05	3	.055
Totals	111		55	

Mean age at death = 24.5   Mean age at death = 19.9

effect of the migration correction is fairly dramatic upon the Late Period, to moderate the ratio and suggest that a more moderate fertility may be characteristic of this period than the transformed age distribution would lead one to believe.

In comparison to the child mortality ratio of D_{1-5}/D_{1-10} of Buikstra et al. (1986), the Early Period has a ratio of 14/17 or .8235, and the Late Period 4/12 or .3333. These are graphically presented with 95% comparison intervals and some Illinois skeletal samples in Figure 6-9. The small samples in Tlajinga yield such large intervals that they overlap with each other and all the Illinois samples. Thus, although a chronological trend may be present for a decrease in weaning mortality, this could just be a result of chance differences in the samples. When the migration-corrected ratios are calculated (and also graphed in Figure 6-9), the Tlajinga Late Period does not overlap with the Schild Late Woodland. Thus, there may be a difference in weaning mortality between these two samples, with Tlajinga having less. However, small

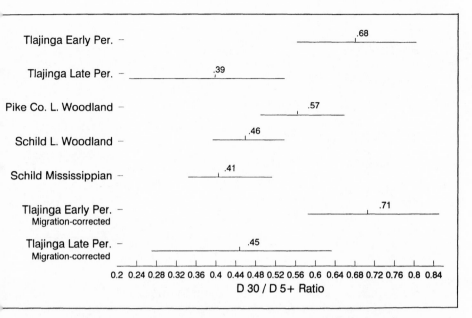

Figure 6-8. Fertility Ratios in Two Tlajinga 33 Chronological Periods and Three Illinois Skeletal Populations (95% comparison intervals; Illinois populations from Buikstra et al. 1986)

sample size hinders the usefulness of this ratio, and not much can be concluded about the nature of child mortality on this basis. However, as before, the large numbers of infants and perinatals are excluded, and their information is not utilized in this ratio.

When the chronological periods are compared with Milner et al. (1989) reference populations (Figure 6-10), both show a generally high fertility profile, with high ratios of deaths 0–5 to 45+. Again, the Tlajinga age distributions do not quite resemble any of the others in all categories. Clearly visible are the distinct patterns of the Late Period in the 15–25 age category and the Early Period in 35–45. Also evident is the youthful nature of the Late Period versus the more common later ages in the Early Period. The latter is generally more similar to the Yanomamö and Oneota distributions, except for the one category. The Late Period is similar to the Yanomamö and Oneota in three age categories and similar to Libben in the other three. As it behaves erratically, it is quite possible that the Late Period age distribution is being distorted by migration.

The migration-corrected age distributions (Figure 6-11) show the effect of reducing the proportion of very young individuals and increasing that of older individuals in both cases, though as might be expected,

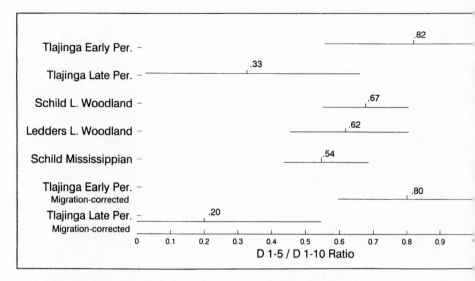

Figure 6-9. Juvenile Mortality Ratios in Tlajinga 33 Chronological Periods and Three Illinois Skeletal Populations (95% comparison intervals; Illinois populations from Buikstra et al. 1986)

the effect is more pronounced in the Late Period. These corrected distributions still do not resemble the low-fertility population but suggest perhaps more moderate fertility than the untransformed distributions, as the ratio of 0–5 to 45+ is still higher than one. The ratio is 1.95 in the Early Period and a large 5.1 in the Late untransformed distributions. With the correction, the ratio drops to 1.65 in the Early and 2.6 in the Late. These Tlajinga distributions are still not like the other reference populations and have their own pattern.

The Henneberg (1976) measures reveal that the Early Period maintains a lot more of its reproductive potential and has a better capacity for increase than the Late Period. The reproductive potential rate for the Early Period is 0.79, for an R_0 equal to 1.5 if completed fertility is seven, and 1.3 if the fertility is six. The Late Period has a lower reproductive potential rate of 0.64, and because of the large proportion of juveniles in this age distribution, the R_0 is 0.99 if completed fertility is seven, and 0.84 if it is six. Thus, Henneberg's measures seem to indicate a deterioration through time in the ability to replace the population and grow at Tlajinga 33. This is the opposite conclusion to the other models discussed above, where the Late Period appears as a high-fertility population.

If these measures are calculated for the migration-corrected age distributions, the Early Period has a reproductive potential of 0.82 and

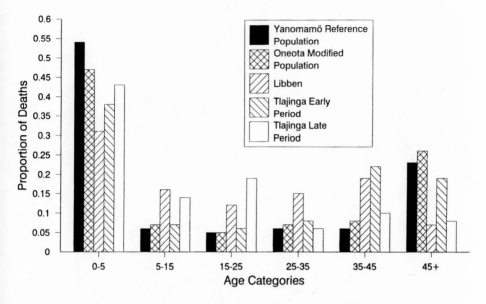

Figure 6-10. Proportions of Deaths in Six Age Categories in Tlajinga 33 Chronological Periods and Three Reference Anthropological Populations (reference populations from Milner et al. 1989; Lovejoy et al. 1977)

an R_0 of 1.6 with seven as the completed fertility, and 1.4 with six. This one improves slightly over the untransformed. The Late Period also moderates slightly, with a reproductive potential of 0.65 and an R_0 of 1.07 with seven children as the completed fertility, and 0.92 with six. Thus, it looks more as if the Late Period was able to barely maintain itself, even when corrected for migration. Again, the Henneberg measures reveal that with a reasonable fertility, the Tlajinga 33 age distributions show the potential for stability or moderate growth, although in one case decline is also indicated. The difference is that the Henneberg pattern reverses the other comparisons made, where the Late Period was shown to perhaps have the higher fertility, whereas with the Henneberg pattern it has the most potential for decline. This difference, of course, is due to the fact that Henneberg tries to take mortality into account, judging it by the reasonableness of a stability measure. His method can be criticized, because the internal consistency tests of his rates reveal that the assumption of stability is often not justified, and if so, then the juvenile mortality cannot be measured at just face value from the stationary-population life table. However, his method generally shows

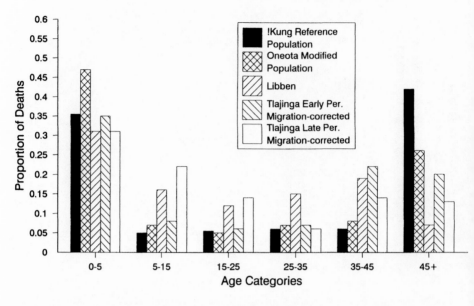

Figure 6-11. Proportions of Deaths in Six Age Categories in Tlajinga 33 and the !Kung, Oneota, and Libben Populations (reference populations from Milner et al. 1989; Lovejoy et al. 1977)

similarities to the other ones used to reveal that fertility is important in the age distribution of deaths at Tlajinga 33.

Summary

The untransformed age distributions of deaths over all of the occupational history of the Tlajinga 33 compound were analyzed by methods suggested by paleodemographic researchers, as modified by the insight that age distributions of deaths are highly influenced by fertility. The untransformed age distribution was subjected to two corrections for possible biases in the original: an old-age one for slight underaging of older adults and a worst-case migration scenario, where up to 20% of the young adults plus young children and infants would be recent migrants who died soon after arrival in the compound. These are the ages at which the migration rates are highest and could have the most distorting effect upon the demography. Though migrants would be represented throughout the lifespan, it is hypothesized that their effect upon the other age categories would be negligible. In fact, the worst-case scenario would be true only if there were significant influxes of young families into the compound. The migration of single young adults would not have much effect upon the age distribution of deaths.

All methods used, including the two corrected age distributions, revealed that Tlajinga 33 had a high to moderate fertility profile. Investigation of this pattern by examination of the chronological differences in age distribution currently available for the compound revealed that there were some statistically significant differences between the Early and Late periods in the untransformed age distributions. These differences became nonsignificant or less divergent when a migration correction was applied, a correction that hypothesized that the greatest impact of the migration would have been during the Late Period. Nevertheless, the results were similar to the total analysis in that Tlajinga 33 was shown to be generally characterized by moderate to potentially high fertility.

That the residents of the pre-Columbian urban center of Teotihuacan might have had a high fertility resembling that of contemporary, sedentary, noncontracepting populations is no surprise. There is no *a priori* reason to assume that Teotihuacan would have a low fertility like the San. This conclusion really gives little insight into Teotihuacan as a demographic phenomenon. Especially puzzling are the indications of high fertility and perhaps a moderate population growth trend in a compound and a city that basically shows no growth during the period under investigation. Although it is possible that there was significant migration out of the city to its hinterland, this is generally not common of preindustrial cities (McNeill 1984). The settlement history of Teotihuacan seems to indicate a great nucleation of people very early in its history, which then saw a return of settlement to the surrounding rural areas early in the Middle Horizon (see Sanders et al. 1979: Chapters 5 and 6). That this rural growth at this time was due, at least partly, to reverse migration out of the city is likely, but it may be also due to migration from other parts of Teotihuacan's hinterland or from other parts of Mesoamerica. The growth rate of the Basin of Mexico rural population during the Middle Horizon is not so great that it could not be due to natural increase of that population—0.3–0.1% per year (Sanders et al. 1979: 183–184). Thus, the evidence for a vigorously growing and expanding Teotihuacan is not visible in the demographic pattern of Tlajinga 33 or of the city during the occupational period of that compound. To better understand Tlajinga 33 and its city, one needs to investigate the effects of more than fertility.

Paleodemography has come to realize that the age distribution of deaths of a skeletal population is a complex result of both the fertility and mortality rates of the living population that produced it (Johansson and Horowitz 1986). Except when the stationary condition is assumed, birth rates and mortality cannot be directly calculated from an age distribution of deaths (Johansson and Horowitz 1986; Horowitz and Armelagos 1988). However, the trend toward stressing just fertility analyses will be counterproductive in the long run in paleodemography, because of their ability to yield only *relative* measures of fertility and not get at the *dynamics* of vital rates that produced the age distribution. These dynamics, and how they differ for different skeletal populations that result from different cultural and environmental conditions, are what will allow paleodemography to contribute to our understanding of the past. Some method must be used that enables us to estimate mortality and thus investigate the dynamics of fertility and mortality. Johansson and Horowitz (1986) have suggested using independent estimates derived from archaeological evidence to model mortality and fertility.

However, the skeletons themselves also contain evidence of possible causes of morbidity and mortality, which can be studied by paleopathology. Paleopathological patterns need to be investigated to learn if they, too, can provide independent evidence of possible health problems that could indicate mortality problems that need to be modeled in any final determination of mortality patterns at Tlajinga 33. Thus, before trying to estimate mortality in Tlajinga 33, we must study the paleopathological indicators to look for patterns of cause and age occurrence that might be significant to our understanding of the way the living population produced the age distribution of deaths recovered from the compound.

Paleopathology, Health, and Mortality at Tlajinga 33

THE INVESTIGATION of mortality patterns at Tlajinga 33 should focus, at least partially, on possible causes of death in the population. Mortality is obviously related to the health and adequacy of diet of a population. Thus, evidence of potential problems in the lifestyle at Teotihuacan is important in any assessment of the demographic characteristics of the Tlajinga 33 population.

Recently there has been an increasing effort to study the health and nutritional status of past populations (e.g., Wing and Brown 1979) and to perform biocultural analyses of human skeletal remains (Cohen and Armelagos 1984). Archaeological examination of food remains is one way to study past nutrition, but more direct evidence of the adequacy of diet and health status can come from the human bones. Unfortunately, bones are not a very efficient source of information on health and diet. Although pathological states are fairly common on bones, identifying the exact disease or cause of death on the basis of such evidence is often impossible (Ortner and Putschar 1981) because the skeletal system is relatively well-buffered from disease and nutritional insults. As the supporting structure of an organism and protector of the brain and other critical organs, bone seems to be involved in disease and stress primarily when the resources of soft tissues can no longer handle the insult. Thus, many illnesses and nutritional deficiencies are not preserved in bone pathoses, and only those that are severe and chronic, that is, of long duration, tend to be preserved in the skeleton (see Goodman et al. 1988). Therefore, the skeleton reflects only certain types of health problems encountered by the individual during life and too often does not record the cause of death.

Also, the response of bones to disease and nutritional deficiencies is often generalized, because many disturbances act on the same processes of bone growth and mineralization to produce similar results (Huss-Ashmore et al. 1982; Goodman et al. 1984b). The response of bone is characterized by either proliferative or resorptive responses (see Powell 1988). A differential diagnosis of the cause of a skeletal lesion depends on age, sex, and the pattern of skeletal involvement (Ortner and Putschar 1981). Because of the multiple causes of proliferative or resorptive responses or the poor preservation of the skeleton or both, a diagnosis of the cause for a pathosis may not be possible.

However, recent models for approaching bone pathoses have begun to increase the knowledge that can be derived from skeletons of health and nutritional conditions in the past. The work of Armelagos, Goodman, and coworkers have presented a stress model that uses indicators in the skeletons to infer past stress and thus help us to understand how cultures both respond to and may cause stress (Goodman et al. 1984b and 1988; Martin et al. 1985). Stress may be thought of as physiological disruption resulting from the three potential sources (see Goodman et al. 1984b: Figure 2.1) of environmental constraints, cultural stressors, and host resistance failures. Environmental constraints generally consist of limiting resources, insults, and noxious stimuli; culture-buffering systems are able to control some and not others. Culture itself, besides being able to provide some buffers, also can be the source of stress (Goodman et al. 1988), as in the case of differential access to resources by sex or by social class. Host resistance factors can vary by age, sex, and genetic factors, and it is their ultimate failure to cope with stressors, both environmental and cultural, that leads to the physiological disruption. Skeletons record the indirect indicators of physiological disruption during the lifetime of the individual in both bones and teeth.

Goodman et al. (1984b) divide the skeletal indicators of physiological stress into three types: general, cumulative stress indicators; general, episodic stress indicators; and indicators of specific insults. The general or nonspecific stress indicators are so designated because many diseases and deficiencies in diet can cause the same pathoses in bone. In fact, when a stress is strong enough to affect bone, it is very often the result of multiple causes, the synergistic effect of nutritional inadequacy complicated by disease, for example. Thus, there is usually not a sole cause underlying a pathosis. The importance of these indicators is that they are clues to stress, and the impact of that stress on a skeletal system can be studied. The general, cumulative indicators are informative of long-standing problems and body responses. The general, episodic indicators are very important because often the age pattern of these can be determined for a population, and thus understanding of potential causes of stress and the effects of lifeways can be inferred. The specific indicators then reveal both environmental conditions and cultural factors that impinge on individuals. All types are indicative of failures of both cultural-buffer and host-resistance factors, and observation of the patterns and relations among the types of indicators allows more sophisticated inference about the long-term adaptive potential of a population and its culture. In a recent article detailing the integration of the concept and use of stress in biological anthropology (Goodman et al. 1988), the linking of physiological response to both environmental and greater sociocultural factors is urged. All three types of skeletal indicators of stress are discussed for the Tlajinga 33 population. These are also linked to an understanding of both environmental and cultural sources of stress, including the socioeconomic conditions likely to have been experienced by the residents of Tlajinga 33, to provide insight into the life of the people and an understanding of the adaptive potential of the urban center of Teotihuacan.

Mortality is the ultimate measure of stress, being the complete failure of physiological response, and one of the reasons for studying paleopathological indicators of stress in the skeletons of Tlajinga 33 is to try to better understand mortality at the compound. The translation of paleopathological indicators into mortality equivalents is not clear-cut (see Johansson and Horowitz 1986 for this criticism). That is because the skeletal indicators are actually of morbidity, not direct mortality, and the translation of morbidity into mortality is not simple, even in modern demography. It is felt that morbidity affects mortality, but it is a variable and often time-lagged effect. As shall be seen when the individual skeletal stress indicators are discussed, many are actually visible because of the ability of the host to survive an insult and continue living. Those that die directly of an insult often carry no evidence of that insult skeletally.

When stationary-population life-table analysis was the dominant mode of analysis in paleodemography, it was thought that linking age patterns of stress to jumps in the proportions dying at the ages involved was sufficient to make paleopathology directly informative about mortality in the population. With the new understanding about what the age distribution of deaths in a skeletal series potentially does and does not represent, such a simplistic one-to-one correlation of stress and mortality is no longer warranted. More careful inference is needed, and the linking of stress to its possible mortality consequences must be more clearly justified. That paleopathological indicators may have consequences for mortality is shown by the studies that reveal lower mean ages at death for individuals with skeletal stress indicators than for those without (Cook 1981; Goodman and Armelagos 1989). The challenge for skeletal studies is "to show the linkage between markers of stress and adaptive consequence" (Goodman et al. 1988: 195). That is, paleopathological indicators should be used to indicate possible mortality consequences in a population. Although an age distribution of deaths can be greatly affected by fertility, a true picture of the demographic conditions that caused the deaths is forwarded only when we also understand the mortality rates that affected the different cohorts.

Paleopathological indicators are one source of that kind of information, but the challenge is to be able to use their morbidity information to estimate mortality effects. That challenge is attempted here on the Tlajinga 33 population. Paleopathological indicators are used to derive both age-specific and general conditions that might affect mortality rates of certain cohorts. The estimation of the impact of the paleopathological indicators is derived from comparison with present-day populations and from impacts directly measured in the skeletons. For these to have mortality impacts, the morbidity factors need to be understandable in terms of the lives and cultural adaptations of the living populations that produced the age distribution of deaths. In a new synthesis for paleodemography, the insights of the recent researchers regarding fertility and mortality effects upon an age distribution of death are combined with the insights of stress analysis of the skeletons to form a reasonable hypothesis of the demographic and cultural conditions that produced the skeletal series under study. An attempt at this kind of synthesis is being made here with the Tlajinga 33 study. It is expected, and hoped, that future researchers will be able to improve on the results presented here.

Porotic Hyperostosis and Periosteal Reactions

These are skeletal markers that directly indicate specific stress insults in an individual. The differential diagnosis of various diseases and nutrient deficiencies, such as rickets, tuberculosis, and treponematosis, is possible on skeletons (Ortner and Putschar 1981; Powell 1988). These are important pathoses within a population, but in this study of Tlajinga 33 only more general diagnoses of disease and nutrient deficiency from skeletal indicators are used. Porotic hyperostosis and periosteal lesions fall into this category, and these are used to look for the incidence of problems in the Tlajinga 33 population as a general measure of health and resiliency, and also of potential morbidity.

Porotic hyperostosis is a common and well-studied lesion of the cranium. It is easily identified by a thickened bone and a porous, sieve-like appearance of the outer tabular surface. It is most commonly found on the superior part of the orbits (where it is often referred to as *cribia orbitalia*), and on the outer table of the frontal and parietals. Recent studies have linked the condition to a variety of anemias (Mensforth et al. 1978). There are both hereditary anemias, like sickle-cell or thalassemia, and nutritional, from a lack of sufficient dietary iron. The difference between the two is distinguished by the skeletal elements involved and ages affected. In North America no hereditary anemias have been identified for pre-Columbian populations, and thus the porotic hyperostosis seems to be nutritional. It can then serve as a useful indicator of nutritional stress in a population when studied in conjunction with subsistence practices. In North American pre-Columbian populations several studies have linked the iron-deficiency anemia to an excessive reliance on maize in the diet and a lack of meat, especially during weaning (El-Najjar et al. 1976). Like most cereals, maize is low in iron and, in addition, contains phytates that inhibit the absorption of iron (Wing and Brown 1979), compounding the problem.

Lallo et al. (1977) and Mensforth et al. (1978) were able to establish associations between the occurrence of porotic hyperostosis and evidence of infection on the skeletons of infants and young children in the Dickson Mounds and Libben skeletal samples. The synergism of nutrition and infection has been implicated in weanling diarrhea and childhood mortality in many contemporary populations of the developing world (Scrimshaw et al. 1968). What seems to happen is that nutritional deficiency, the anemia, lowers the body's ability to counteract infection, and then the infection often inhibits the ability of the digestive system to absorb the nutrients necessary to survive through diarrhea, making a vicious circle that is the leading cause of mortality of infants and young children in present-day developing nations (Gordon et al. 1963 and 1967). In the skeletal studies the co-occurrence of porotic hyperostosis and periosteal lesions (which indicate infection) was common in children, and infections seemed to be more serious when occurring with the hyperostosis (Lallo et al. 1977; Mensforth et al. 1978). Thus, the mortality of young children in prehistoric populations seem to have been significantly affected by the effects of weanling diarrhea.

The techniques for thorough analysis of porotic hyperostosis on a skeletal sample have been provided by Mensforth et al. (1978). They suggested scoring skeletal lesions according to whether there is any evidence of healing (remodeling of the lesion) and giving careful attention to the pattern of co-occurrence and ages affected. At Libben these researchers found that infections, judged by the unremodeled lesions, peak during the first year, whereas porotic hyperostosis peaks around the third year. Infections, then, happen early and seem to precipitate the nutritional deficiency of anemia. The presence of individuals under three years of age in the skeletal sample is probably largely due to the interaction of infection and nutritional deficiency.

The ability to reconstruct the diet archaeologically also allows the determination of the causes of the condition. For example, the occurrence of porotic hyperostosis at Libben, in spite of adequate meat sources, reveals the importance of infectious disease in causing the problem there, whereas in prehistoric Nubia, the dependence on a cereal diet low in iron indicates that nutrition was the precipitating cause of the skeletal lesion in that population (Martin et al. 1985). Thus, it is possible to find differences in cultural adaptation underlying the same skeletal pathosis. Recent work has also refined the aging indications of porotic hyperostosis, with the finding that the porosity and sieve-like appearance occur only during childhood, reflecting the greater effects of iron deficiency on rapidly growing individuals (Stuart-Macadam 1985). Adults often bear the remodeling porosity indicative of their survivial of a childhood bout of anemia.

Since it seems likely that the synergistic combination of anemia and infectious disease around the time of weaning contributes greatly to the mortality of prehistoric and contemporary populations, it would be logical to find a similar pattern at Tlajinga 33. However, one of the surprises of the paleopathological study was that there was very little evidence of porotic hyperostosis. One child, Burial 60b, had a very serious, unremodeled lesion on both parietals, indicating a problem that probably contributed to death around the age of nine, older than would have been expected (Figure 7–1). Although iron-deficiency anemia probably contributed directly to the death of this individual, it was probably not because of weanling diarrhea. This individual had several small, healing (remodeling underway), infectious lesions on the long bones, but no other pathological indicators. No other infants or juveniles had active lesions, even of the orbital type. Only four individuals, two adults and two subadults, had remodeled porotic hyperostosis lesions. Though it is likely that these represent survivors of weaning stress, this does not constitute evidence that it was a significant problem at Tlajinga 33.

With one of the more usual skeletal markers of nutritional stress missing, the interesting question is how the population avoided the problem. In Tlajinga 33 either the diet must have been such that iron intake was adequate, even for children under five, or infection was not seriously impacting the young children, as it was at Libben. Both of these possibilities must be explored to explain the lack of iron-deficiency anemia in this population.

Figure 7-1. Unremodeled Porotic Hyperostosis on the Parietals of a Nine-Year-Old Child from Tlajinga 33

Maize is the main staple of the Mesoamerican diet, so the question is why the reliance on maize does not have the same effect as in North American populations, like Dickson Mounds (Lallo et al. 1977). With the use of figures from the study of the Institute of Nutrition of Central America and Panama (INCAP) of food composition for Latin America (INCAP 1961), the possible iron content of the pre-Columbian diet that would have been consumed at Teotihuacan was investigated. The most promising sources from known pre-Columbian food items are listed in Table 7–1, along with other common items in the diet for comparison. As can be seen from the table, the diet seems to have contained adequate iron, but many of the foods, though generally probably common in the diet, do not seem appropriate for a weaning diet. For example, dried peppers, the basis of many pre-Columbian sauces in this area, probably were too hot in taste to feed to small children in any quantity. The best candidate is probably beans, as the broth from their cooking and the mashed beans could have been fed to young children and would have provided good nutrition. As can be seen from the table, beans have higher iron content than meat and actually are close to that of raw beef liver, which has 8.8 mg per 100-g edible portion (Watts and Merrill 1962). Of course, the Dickson Mounds population also had beans in the diet but still had problems. It could be that beans were used at every meal in the diet in Teotihuacan, much as they are today in Mexico, and thus were much more important here than in the diet of other populations, a situation that is certainly found today. For example, the traditional Mexican diet of corn, beans, and chiles has more iron than a typical United States meal (DeVore and White 1978). Therefore, at this point, one can only postulate that there was a difference in the diet given to weanlings between the two populations, and perhaps the Central Mexicans had enough iron in theirs to prevent that nutritional deficiency.

Of course, in the Libben study discussed above, diet was probably not the cause of the anemia either. It was the weakening effects of infection that seem to have precipitated the deficiency (Mensforth et al. 1978). Even though the Tlajinga 33 population did not have much porotic hyperostosis, there were periosteal lesions on bones that indicated infectious disease episodes for individuals. A periosteal reaction is an area of poorly woven, or porous, new bone laid down on the periosteal surface in response to inflammation from infection of the overlying periosteum. If very serious, the reaction can cover a large part of the bone and distort its normal contours. It can also be quite small and localized. If the infection disappears, the bone will continue normal growth, and the reaction will be remodeled and the porosity filled in. Because periosteal reactions occur commonly with many diseases, it is usually not possible to diagnose a specific disease, although certain infectious diseases do have specific enough patterns of age and bone involvement to be recognizable in paleopathology (Powell 1988). Periosteal reactions are the result of an insult of considerable duration and serious enough to affect the bone.

In Tlajinga 33 both unremodeled and remodeled periosteal lesions were scored, by the use the methodological recommendations of Mensforth et al. (1978) for identifying and recording both conditions. Only 41 individuals had enough long bones and cranial fragments to be accurately scored for the presence or absence of lesions. If a lesion was present, it was usually found on several bones, which indicates a possible systemic infection. Here, the lesion is treated nonspecifically; no specific diagnosis is sought. The decision to take this approach was made because of the generally small numbers involved, although future work will discuss some of the diagnoses possible with the Tlajinga 33 material. Of the scored individuals, 13 or 32% had no evidence of any lesions. Of the majority with lesions, 9 or 22% had unremodeled, active lesions at death, and 19 or 46% had remodeled lesions. Of those with unre-

TABLE 7-1
Iron Content of the
Pre-Columbian Diet

Dietary Item	Mg. Iron per 100g Edible Portion
Cereals: maize treated with lime	1.6
Vegetables	
Pulque	0.9
Epasote	5.2
Dried red peppers, bush	12.0
Dried red peppers, cherry	6.4
Dried red peppers, long	7.5
Squash blossoms	1.0
Dried beans	7.6
Squash seeds	9.2
Meat	
Venison, roasted	3.5
Venison, semi-dried, salted	1.9
Turkey	3.8
Rabbit liver	14.0

Source: INCAP 1961
Note: Green and red tomatoes and all fruits are low in iron content.

modeled lesions, 6 were adults, 1 was an adolescent, and 2 were children (see Figure 7–2). The remodeled lesions were on 14 adults, 1 infant, 1 child, and 2 adolescents.

The numbers of infants and young children were too small to justify identifying a good pattern of age of onset and highest frequency of occurrence, as suggested by several researchers (Mensforth et al. 1978; Palkovich 1987). The two young children with unremodeled lesions were both three years old, and the other individual this age that could be scored had a remodeled lesion. However, the one infant that could be scored had a remodeled lesion, and the one-to-two-year-old had no lesions. The one child with remodeled porotic hyperostosis had remodeled periosteal lesions. The unremodeled porotic-hyperostosis subadult case also had remodeled lesions. Thus, no pattern of high co-occurrence of both indicators is present. It is probably important that of the individuals that could be scored under ten years of age at death, only one of six appeared to have no evidence of lesions. There does seem to be evidence that infections, al-

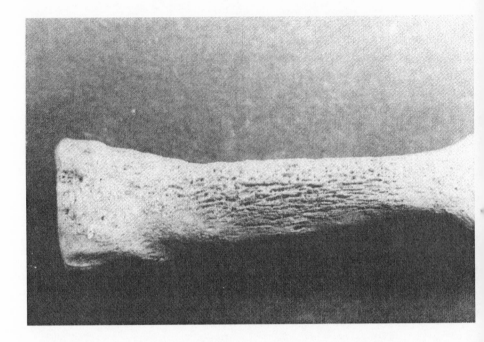

Figure 7-2. Unremodeled Periosteal Lesion on the Metatarsal of Burial 57. This individual was found with the most elaborate grave offering in the compound.

though not fatal, were common during the childhood years. The pattern identified by other researchers of a potential infection-diarrhea interaction is not found in Tlajinga 33, mostly because of the small sample size.

In the further investigation of periosteal reactions, it is interesting to note that many adults showed evidence of healed lesions and also had the majority of the active ones at death. It is not possible to determine the age of occurrence of a remodeled periosteal reaction, so lesions that may have occurred in childhood cannot be distinguished from those that occurred during adulthood. Therefore, it is not possible to tell if there may have been a pattern of significant adult infectious episodes that an individual would tend to recover from in the population. However, the prevalence of adults and adolescents with unremodeled lesions probably indicates that adult infections were present and could be serious.

Although the numbers of individuals that could be studied were too small for age-related analysis, it does seem as if the Tlajinga 33 population was subject to bouts of infection that were serious enough to leave skeletal lesions on the majority of individuals, 68% of those that could be scored. Although most lesions are remodeled and indicate that the diseases were not fatal, infection was probably an important contributor to the overall morbidity, a general weakening of physical constitutions of the population. The kinds of diseases that might have affected a New World pre-Columbian population like Tlajinga 33 are staphylococcal and streptococcal infections, viruses, gastroenteritis, tuberculosis, treponematoses, and fungi (Mensforth et al. 1978; Ubelaker 1989; Powell 1988), plus the effects of parasites, which are likely to be common in tropical environments (Reinhard 1987). Some of these diseases were likely to be more prevalent among infants and young children than adults. For example, gastroenteritis is one of the most common infections of these young ages in preindustrial societies (Gordon et al. 1967). What evidence is available does seem to indicate that infectious diseases were common in Teotihuacan, and individuals were susceptible all through the lifespan. The fact that 5 of 6 individuals who died as children had lesions, 3 of 3 who died as adolescents, but only 20 of 32 adults, indicates that young individuals were more susceptible and perhaps the effect on their health was ultimately more drastic.

Since infection and a probable significant parasite load did not lead to the nutritional deficiency of anemia in Tlajinga 33, other skeletal markers are needed to determine if these disease episodes had other effects on individuals. Just because iron-deficiency anemia is not serious enough to have caused skeletal problems during childhood at Tlajinga 33 does not mean that Tlajinga 33 did not suffer from nutritional problems. The porotic hyperostosis indicator points only to problems in the young child (Stuart-Macadam 1985) and not to possible complications of anemia in older subadult and adult years. Also, the main problem in young children at Tlajinga 33 is not among two- to three-year-olds, as is often common in paleodemographic samples such as Dickson Mounds (Goodman et al. 1984a) and Libben (Mensforth et al. 1978), but in the large numbers of perinatals and newborns, who would not live long enough to show iron deficiency anyway (Palkovich 1987). Thus, infection is clearly present, but the evidence for iron-deficiency nutritional problems is mainly negative.

Harris Lines and Dental Enamel Hypoplasias

Harris lines and dental enamel hypoplasias are two indicators of general, episodic stress. Again, they are nonspecific because the possible causes are legion (Huss-Ashmore et al. 1982) and can be either disease or nutritional problems, or the interaction of both. These markers are important, however, because the age pattern of their occurrence can be determined. These are episodic indicators because they result from physiological disturbances of normal growth processes during childhood from which the individual recovered.

Harris Lines

Transverse or Harris lines (named after an early researcher) are lines that can be seen radiographically in the growing ends of long bone shafts or diaphyses. The lines may vary in thickness and density and may also be oblique or fail to traverse completely the diameter of the bone. Although the oblique or incomplete transverse lines probably do not differ in their cause from full transverse lines, the reasons for differences in density and thickness are not clear, although all variations in the lines are affected by bone susceptibility and remodeling processes (Martin et al. 1985). At any rate, none of the variations appear to be clearly related to the severity of the stress causing the line. The mechanisms of the line formation are attributed to resumed growth after a time when growth had been slowed down or stopped at the junction of the growth cartilage and metaphysis. During the time the growth is disrupted, mineralization is continuing so that when growth resumes, a radiopaque ring of increased mineralization is left behind (Park 1964).

Transverse lines are thus lines indicating recovery from growth arrest (Park 1964). However, not all long bones are equally sensitive to the formation of transverse lines. Studies indicate that the tibia, femur, and radius are the long bones with the highest frequency of lines, and that the distal end of the tibia is the single best area of the three for investigating transverse lines (Garn et al. 1968; Mansilla 1980). The tibia and femur are the best to study, because these bones grow quickly and thus space their transverse lines well. These bones also have good aging sequences, up to the age of eighteen, for timing the occurrence of lines (Hunt and Hatch 1981; Maat 1984).

Harris lines appear to be caused by a wide variety of stresses. Vitamin deficiencies, pneumonia, measles, scarlet fever, protein-calorie malnutrition, and mechanical restriction all have been associated with the formation of transverse lines (Park 1964). It seems that an organisim responds to a temporary stress by slowing down bone growth, especially when nutritional shortfalls and illness are making great demands on the individual's constitution. Thus, the lines are nonspecific indicators of stress but can also be the result of the synergism of illness and nutritional deficiency.

Harris lines, representing temporary growth disruptions, can also be resorbed as the individuals age because of the continuous remodeling processes of bones (Garn et al. 1968). Thus, it is probable that not all Harris lines ever formed during the growing years will be found in the adult bones. The thicker lines and probably those formed later in life are the ones most likely to persist. A study of the adult tibias and femurs may then be missing some portion of Harris lines that indicate growth disturbances due to stress during the growing years.

For the Tlajinga 33 population, all available tibias and femurs, including any reasonably sized fragment of bone, if that was all that was recovered, were X-rayed. Harris lines were then identified and counted, including any oblique or transverse line that was at least one-third of the diameter of the bone. The lines were studied to determine, on average, how many lines or episodes of growth disruption individuals had, and to determine at what ages the episodes occurred. The method for determining the age of the occurrence of a Harris line was taken from Hunt and Hatch (1981), although other similar methods are also possible (e.g., Maat 1984).

Hunt and Hatch's method takes the diaphyseal length of the adult bone and then locates the origin, the first point of ossification. Then, with the use of information compiled on the pattern of growth of modern American children, it was determined what proportion of the growth of the long bone is represented by each end. In the femur, 71% of the growth is in the distal end of the shaft and only 29% is represented by the proximal end. For the tibia, the distal represents 43% and the proximal 57%. In an adult bone the origin of the bone can then be found by measuring the appropriate proportion from an end. Once the origin is found, one measures from it to the line. Then, using a program developed by Hunt and based on the growth proportion per year (see Hunt and Hatch 1981), one calculates the age at which a line occurred on the basis of the number of centimeters from the origin. When available, the actual diaphyseal length of an adult can be used to calculate the age measures. For immatures and incomplete adult tibias and femurs, the calculations based on the average diaphyseal length of the adults is used. For example, the average adult male tibia had a diaphyseal length of 33 cm, and the growth between age eight and nine on the distal end was from 9 to 9.5 cm. Thus, a Harris line falling between those measures was considered to occur between the age of eight and nine. Of course, as the average adult length is often used, this can be considered only an estimate, but a reasonable one, as it is determined on the basis of the population.

For Tlajinga 33, only 34 individuals from infant through adult could be included in the Harris-line study. From examination of the X-rays, it was evident that few lines were visible on the bones, and those present were not very dense or clear, regardless of whether the bone was complete or fragmentary. Part of the problem is that fragmentary bones were probably not preserving enough cross-sectional integrity for some of the shaft to enable one to see any Harris lines. But, as the complete bones also had few lines, this population does not appear to have been very sensitive to Harris-line formation or preservation or both. With so few lines visible, the average number of Harris lines for adult individuals was 1.5, and for the five children, 2.4. This is lower than the average of 2.7 per individual from the Dallas population of North America (calculated from Hatch et al. 1983). Also, a post-Classic highland Mesoamerican population (A.D. 1325–1500) from Cholula, Puebla, had an average of 6.1 Harris lines per tibia and 3.7 per femur (Mansilla 1980). The lines from Tlajinga 33 are therefore distinctly fewer than expected and certainly much fewer than another Mesoamerican population in a similar environment.

The total sample number is too small for chronological distinctions, so only the overall sample can be studied. All lines occurring at an age were counted, whether on the tibia or femur. Lines on different bones at the same age for an individual were counted only once. However, this was a fairly rare occurrence, as most lines occurred only once, on the distal tibia. The incidence of lines per age, not per individual, is presented in Table 7–2. There is no doubt that the highest occurrence of lines is in ages 0 through 2 years old. This is slightly earlier than the peak around 2–3 years found in the Dickson Mounds population (Goodman and Clark 1981), whereas in the Dallas population, the peak also occurs around 1–2 years (Hatch et al. 1983). Both Dickson and Dallas also reveal a peak in the early adolescent years that is not present at Tlajinga. Unfortunately, aging of the Harris lines at Cholula was not attempted, so that pattern cannot be compared with Teotihuacan's.

The Tlajinga Harris-line pattern reveals that most lines form up through age 2, after which low levels of growth disruptions are present from age 3 to 17. This pattern is consonant with the earlier evidence of common infectious episodes, because in contemporary developing populations infections tend to be most prevalent during the first two years (Gordon et al. 1967). Since infectious diseases are linked with the formation of Harris lines, it could very well be that the Tlajinga residents, like contemporary populations, suffered from high rates of infection early in life, which disrupted their growth.

The individuals studied for Harris lines were those who lived at least a couple of months past birth. Although some fetal-age lines were identified, the main interest was in the evidence of growth disruptions arising directly from interaction of the individual with the postnatal environ-

TABLE 7-2
The Incidence of Transverse
Lines by Age

Age at Occurrence	Age at Death					
	Infant	1–9	10–19	20–30	30+	Total
Fetal		3			1	4
<1	2	3			4	9
1		3			5	8
2		3			3	6
3					2	2
4					2	2
5				1	2	3
6					3	3
7				1	1	2
8				1		1
9					1	1
10					3	3
11				2		2
12			1	1	1	3
13					2	2
14			1			1
15				1	1	2
16						0
17					1	1

Perinatal Lines

	Age at Death		
	7th mo.	8th mo.	9th/term
6th mo. *in utero*	2		
7th mo. *in utero*		2	2
8th mo. *in utero*			10
Neonate	2		4

ment. For perinatals, Harris lines could occur through disruptions mediated through the mother. Prenatally, individuals are usually well buffered from insults by the mother's system, even in many cases by taking from the mother's stores of nutrients, if necessary (Guthrie 1975). Therefore, any stress that could cause a fetal Harris line would probably be the result of a serious stress, and most perinatals should not show any lines. However, an X-ray study of the Mesoamerican population from Cholula included 16 perinatals, and of these, 56% had evidence of Harris lines (Mansilla 1980). Therefore, it was expected that there would be Harris lines on Tlajinga perinatals, especially since that was such a large age group in the skeletons of the compound.

Nineteen Tlajinga 33 perinatals were X-rayed. Of these, 16 (84%) had evidence of fetal lines. Table 7–2 lists their occurrence by month. The timing of a line was calculated by applying the Hunt and Hatch (1981) method. The length of the bone was measured, and the origin identified at 71% of the distance from the distal end of a femur and 43% from the distal end of a tibia. The lines were measured from the origin. Fetal growth is not one of even increments from month to month, because the eighth month has the most growth (Guthrie 1975). Thus, allowance was made for more growth in the eighth month than the last month, by the use of proportions derived from crown-rump length standards in the last two months (standards from Krogman 1962).

The bulk of the lines are aged during the eighth month *in utero* and around birth. Since the eighth month is the one with the most growth demands, the fetus appears to be susceptible to a slowdown if the mother's system cannot fulfill the demand (Stini 1985). Also, no matter what the age of the individuals at death, most lines occur the previous month, implicating the stress in their deaths but with a delay in effect. It seems that growth disruptions during gestation are not propitious for survival, as 12 of 14 newborns, 2 of 2 eighth-month individuals, and 2 of 3 seventh-month individuals that could be studied had fetal disruptions before death. However, individuals that survived past birth do not seem to have many fetal growth distruptions; only 4 out of 34 show them, although resorption of these lines is likely and perhaps occurs early in life.

In addition to the fetal disruptions, 6 of the perinatals had opaque bands at the metaphyses, or ends, of the long bone shafts. These bands may indicate a possible growth disruption occurring right before and up to death. The bands could indicate that the individual was born and lived for a few days or a couple of weeks before dying, hence the term "neonate" in Table 7–2. Of course, an individual who was born but did not long survive would have no dense area develop and would have no neonatal line. Those with bands are clearly the minority of the perinatals tested. One interpretation is that most neonates who die probably perish almost immediately after birth, and only about a third live for some time. Unfortunately, the bones alone apparently do not clearly indicate how many perinatals might be stillbirths, and so the presence of some stillbirths cannot be totally ruled out, although it is felt to be unlikely in the case of most of the Tlajinga 33 perinatals.

Dental Hypoplasias

Another skeletal marker with characteristics very similar to Harris lines is the dental defect referred to as enamel hypoplasia. It has been proposed as a marker for paleopathological investigation because it is a sensitive indicator of physiological stress during growth (Huss-Ashmore et al. 1982; Rose et al. 1985). An enamel hypoplasia is defined as a deficiency in enamel thickness that occurs because of a premature degeneration of ameloblast (enamel-forming) activity due to a metabolic disturbance (Rose et al. 1985). The result is a transverse dent or line of pits that can be seen macroscopically on the buccal (outside) surface of a tooth (Goodman et al. 1980).

The transverse pattern of hypoplasias, like that of Harris lines, is due to the ring-like growth of enamel when it is calcifying. The timing of the enamel formation is rhythmic and orderly (Sarnat and Schour 1941) and means that the age of the formation of the defect can be determined. This chronological feature of hypoplasias makes them very useful for studying the incidence of stress in the growing years, although only for the limited time that enamel is forming. The other advantages of hypoplasias are that teeth are hard, and thus often recoverable archaeologically, and that hypoplasias are not affected by later metabolic events and are not resorbed after formation. Thus, unlike Harris lines, hypoplasias record accurately all incidents of stress severe enough to produce them.

Like transverse lines, hypoplasias also seem to be caused by a wide variety of insults and thus are nonspecific indicators of stress. Both diseases and nutritional inadequacies can cause them, but a hypoplasia requires an insult of from several weeks to two months to cause it (Rose et al. 1985: 289). These are then evidence, like Harris lines, of growth disruptions, even though teeth in general are less severely affected by environmental influences than long bones (Ubelaker 1989). And indeed, hypoplastic teeth appear to reach their genetically determined enamel height and to finish development in keeping with the proper timetable.

Although a hypoplasia is evidence of a systemic stress that affects the development of teeth, growth is only temporarily disrupted and not totally stopped, as the enamel is only thinner.

The method for studying enamel hypoplasias follows that of Alan Goodman (Goodman et al. 1980 and 1984b). He stresses the importance of using a chronological technique to determine populational patterns and the use of a "best teeth" technique. That technique uses multiple teeth to record hypoplasias, instead of depending on one tooth, like a canine, for study. This technique allows one to measure the overall span of development of the crowns of the anterior permanent dentition, from 0.5 to 6.5 years, and it increases the sample size of defects. In addition, hypoplasias from the same stress episode can now be identified on several teeth from an individual, and thus one can distinguish obvious systemic stress (instead of stress that might affect only one tooth) and the age at which it occurs. The mandibular canines and maxillary central incisors are recommended, as they are more sensitive to hypoplastic formation than the premolars and molars (Goodman et al. 1980). As the Tlajinga 33 sample is generally fragmentary, all available incisors and canines were employed.

For Tlajinga 33, the permanent dentition of 32 individuals could be studied. There was an average of 2.7 hypoplasias or growth-disruption episodes per individual. These are systemic stresses that cause hypoplasias on more than one tooth at the same age. An average of close to three is fairly high, especially compared with the Middle Mississippian Dickson Mounds average of 1.61 on 46 individuals (Goodman et al. 1980). This average also contrasts with the estimation of 1.2 hypoplasias per individual in Imperial Rome (data in Angel 1984 on the basis of 39 individuals). The Oaxaca study, on the other hand, lists only the frequency of individuals with hypoplasias, 65% of the males and 83% of the females, in the skeletal group of the Classic Period that would be comparable in time and social complexity with Teotihuacan (Hodges 1987). In the Tlajinga sample all permanent dentitions that could be studied had at least one hypoplasia. Of course, most individuals in the population could not be included in this study, so the actual occurrence in the population cannot be assumed to be 100%, but it was likely to have been at least as prevalent as in Oaxaca.

The chronological pattern of hypoplastic formation among Tlajinga 33 individuals was determined by use of the chart from Goodman et al. (1980), which is modified from the graph of enamel crown development of Massler et al. (1941). The age-occurrence chart for hypoplasias in Tlajinga 33 is given in Figure 7–3, and the values of the crown heights from cemento-enamel junction to tip have been modified to reflect the larger

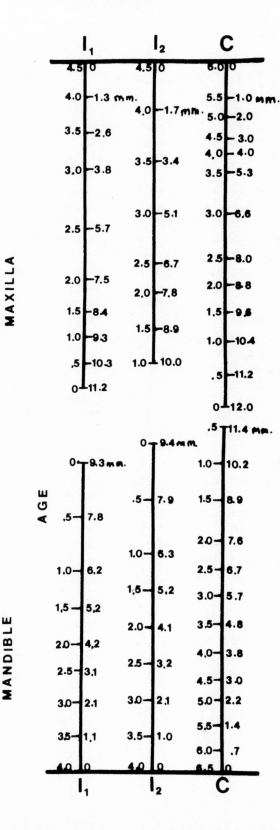

Figure 7-3. Chronological Values for Hypoplastic Formation of Tlajinga 33 Permanent Dentitions

average size of the Tlajinga 33 teeth. These average sizes were determined by measurement of the unworn permanent dentition of two juveniles, but all teeth but one were within 0.5 mm difference. The one different tooth was the maxillary central incisor, which had a 1.2 mm difference. The average of these two measures was used, but a few incisors that were not very worn supported the average as a reasonable one for this population.

Hypoplasias were measured from the cemento-enamel junction to the center of the dent or pits, using a thin-tipped Boley gauge that measured to tenths of millimeters. The present crown height of a tooth was measured to estimate how many years had been lost to attrition. Attrition was fairly high in the population, and most adults had lost the evidence of the first two years. Measured hypoplasias could then be estimated within a half-year of their occurrence. Table 7–3 shows the pattern of occurrence by age, dividing those that occur on more than one tooth of an individual from those that occurred on only one tooth of an individual. The hypoplasias on more than one tooth indicate a probable systemic stress and actual growth disruption (see Figure 7–4).

The systemic disturbances have a definite high point from 2.0 to 3.5 years, and overall high frequencies until age 5.0. The solitary hypoplasias have a similar pattern, although the peak is slightly later at age 4.0–4.5. Of course, since most adults have lost through attrition the first two years of enamel, it could be that the pattern of stress in those years was as high as the 2.0–3.5 years. However, Goodman and Armelagos (1985) have found that not only do teeth vary by susceptibility to hypoplasias, even among the anterior teeth used here, but also the medial third of a buccal surface is more susceptible. This means that the teeth are not equally prone to hypoplasia formation throughout the time of enamel formation, and even if the first two years were generally present, they would probably not have as high an incidence as the later years anyway. Thus, the age pattern noted here is not surprising, as it would cover the most susceptible ages in incisors, and the slightly later peak of canines (Goodman and Armelagos 1985). Thus, 63% of the systemic hypoplasias occur between ages 2.0 and 4.0, which would be the peak susceptible ages for the anterior teeth used here. And according to Goodman and Armelagos (1985), hypoplasias would be rare before one year and after age 5.0 on these teeth. Only three systemic and three solitary episodes are aged to these periods in Tlajinga (see Table 7–3), which would fit that pattern.

In comparison with other studied populations, the peak at 2.0–3.5 years is consistent with the 2.5–3.5 peak found with Dickson Mounds (Goodman et al. 1984a) and a Swedish medieval population (Swardstedt

TABLE 7-3
The Age of Occurrence of Hypoplasias
in the Permanent Dentition in Tlajinga 33

Age of Occurrence	Systemic Disruption (> One Tooth)	Solitary Hypoplasia (Only One Tooth)
0.5–1.0	2	3
1.0–1.5	2	0
1.5–2.0	3	4
2.0–2.5	9	3
2.5–3.0	12	6
3.0–3.5	10	7
3.5–4.0	8	6
4.0–4.5	6	11
4.5–5.0	5	8
5.0–5.5	4	4
5.5–6.0	0	0
6.0–6.5	1	0

1966). These are all indications of stress during and following weaning. Although the fact that teeth are more susceptible to hypoplastic formation during these ages means that growth arrest at this time is more likely to be preserved in the skeleton, this fact does not mitigate the significance of the existence of systemic problems during these ages that are present in the majority of the individuals tested. The hypoplasias record significant systemic stress during the ages at which the teeth are vulnerable, but this does not mean that no systemic stress is present at other ages. Thus, the low occurrence of hypoplasias before the age of 2.0, largely due to attrition anyway, and after the age of 5.0 may cause one to underestimate the problems during these ages, not to assume their absence. This question is discussed in more detail below.

Another pattern that can be investigated with hypoplasias is whether there is any seasonality to the occurrence of stress. A yearly pattern would imply that the population suffered from yearly nutritional shortages. Such a pattern can be determined by comparing the spacing of hypoplasias in individuals who have more than one. In Tlajinga 33, 40 hypoplasias were separated by half-year intervals and only 21 by whole years. There were also 11 hypoplasias separated by more than one year. This pattern was the opposite from that found in Dickson Mounds (Goodman et al. 1984a), where yearly spacing cases outnumbered the half-yearly. Tlajinga does not seem to have undergone a regular seasonal

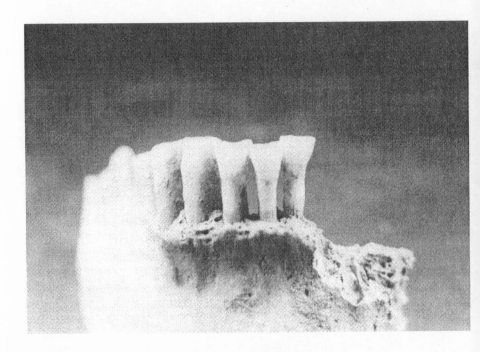

Figure 7-4. Systemic Growth Disruption Visible as Hypoplasia. From the anterior dentition of a female from Tlajinga 33.

time of food shortage, even during its dry season. It is probably logical that an urban market would have had at least some type of food available all year round, and that the craft specialists would always be producing objects to exchange for food throughout the year as well. Troubles would occur during times of general agricultural failure, and these would probably be episodic in the history of the city and in the lives of its people. There is no reason to expect a seasonal problem. The pattern seen at Tlajinga is actually more indicative of the slowness of individual constitutions to recover from stress, since they seem to be quite susceptible to a recurrence or relapse within a year. However, these individuals survived these episode(s) or the hypoplasias would not have been recorded, so in this case the stress was not the direct cause of mortality. But, the evidence indicates chronic conditions within the compound that subject children to more than one episode of growth disruption and, usually, a slow recovery.

So far, the focus on hypoplasias has been on the permanent dentition, where a pattern of weaning and postweaning stress is indicated.

However, it is of interest to investigate *any* evidence for stress that might explain why there are so many perinatal and infant skeletons. For these ages, the deciduous dentition can be used for hypoplastic defects, since the formation of enamel begins about the fourth month *in utero* and is completed several months after birth (Lunt and Law 1974). Another enamel defect that can be studied is hypocalcification, and it is fairly common on deciduous teeth. Hypoplasias affect the formation of an enamel matrix, where the result is reduced thickness of the enamel because of stress. But during the tooth maturation stage when the enamel calcification is completed, if the process is disrupted by stress, the enamel will be opaque in appearance because of a lack of calcified salts. Hypocalcification is usually easily observed, but the defect is rare in permanent teeth and so is not usually studied (Huss-Ashmore et al. 1982). For deciduous dentitions, however, it is a useful marker of stress. It has been noted that the teeth of poorly nourished children are more poorly calcified than those of well-nourished ones (Rose et al. 1985). Like hypoplasias, hypocalcifications are nonspecific indicators of stress, but they tend to implicate poor nutrition at the base of the problem.

Defects of the deciduous dentition are studied with a similar methodology as for the permanent. The age at which a defect occurred was determined by dividing the crown height by the number of months the enamel calcified to determine the monthly increment (method from Blakey and Armelagos 1985). The standards for the time of initial formation and end were taken from Lunt and Law (1974). The thickness of a hypocalcification was measured to each edge of the opacity from the cemento-enamel junction, as these seem to persist for up to several months (Blakey 1981). Hypoplasias were measured from the cemento-enamel junction to the center of the dent or pit. The age was determined by finding how many monthly increments the defect was from the bottom of the crown and subtracting from the end of enamel formation. As with the permanent dentition, only canines and incisors were used, but only the incisor crowns are largely formed prenatally. To illustrate the aging technique: a defect four monthly increments from the cemento-enamel junction of a mandibular central incisor would have occurred at about eight months *in utero*, since the crown finishes calcification at two months past birth.

The advantage of the method is that if the tooth was incomplete (as it would be in perinatals), the monthly increment in size and the month of the defect could still be calculated if the age of the individual was known. For example, a defect could be aged by where it fell in relation to one of the five monthly increments on the mandibular central incisor that would have taken place if an individual was a term-age perinatal, since calcification began at the end of the fourth month *in utero*. For the incomplete teeth, those still being formed, of perinatals and infants, the buccal surfaces were examined under a microscope to verify a defect, which are present as dents and as linear gaps of enamel. Defects were counted if present on more than one tooth.

The hypoplastic defects that were present in 16 deciduous dentitions in Tlajinga 33 are aged in Table 7–4. Not surprisingly, they are most common in the last months of fetal development, when growth is most rapid, especially in body weight. Table 7–4 also presents the hypocalcifications, most of which fall in the same period as the hypoplasias. It is logical that if growth were to be disrupted prenatally, it would occur when the demand on the mother was greatest. The enamel defect pattern thus supports the evidence from Harris lines for the fairly common occurrence of a developmental disruption at the end of the prenatal period.

Of course, this method assumes that these teeth are not more susceptible at certain months to hypoplastic formation, as permanent teeth obviously are (Goodman and Armelagos 1985), but there has been no equivalent test of this assumption. If such an assumption were true, then the end of the prenatal period might very well be the most recordable in the deciduous dentition. However, this does not seem to be true, as other studies that have used dental defects on deciduous dentition have found different age peaks. For example, considerable proportions of prenatal defects among children were also found in the deciduous dentition of skeletal series from the Lower Illinois Valley (Cook and Buikstra 1979) and Dickson Mounds (Blakey and Armelagos 1985). In the Illinois population the most severe defects occurred before the seventh fetal month, earlier than at Tlajinga. In Dickson hypocalcification is highest in the eighth fetal month, but hypoplasias peaked at the first month after birth, a slightly later peak than at Tlajinga. Thus, almost the entire range of ages available in the deciduous dentition have had peaks, which discounts the notion that these teeth might be more susceptible at a given phase.

Unfortunately, the Tlajinga 33 sample is rather small, and there are not enough infant and children's teeth to judge whether prenatal stress may have been a morbidity factor that could explain the death of these children in the first few years, as Cook and Buikstra (1979) demonstrate in the relation of prenatal enamel defects and death during weaning age for their Illinois skeletal series. In Tlajinga the only individuals with no defects had died as perinatals; all infants and children that could be studied had evidence of prenatal stress. Thus, it does seem that there is a

TABLE 7-4
The Age of Occurrence of Hypoplasias
in Deciduous Dentition in Tlajinga 33

Age of Occurrence	7th Mo.	8th Mo.	Term	Infant	2–3 Yrs.	3–5 Yrs.	5–9 Yrs.	Total
Age at Death								
Before Birth								
6th mo.			1	1	1		1	4
7th mo.	1				1	2		4
8th mo.	1	3				2		6
9th mo.				1				1
After Birth								
1 mo.				1	1	1		3
2 mos.						1		1
3–6 mos.						1		1
6–9 mos.								0
9–11 mos.								0

Hypocalcifications
(by age of occurrence)

1 from 7.5 fetal months to birth
1 from 8 fetal months to birth
1 from 2.5 to 4 months after birth
2 from 7th to 8th fetal months

relation between young children's dying and prenatal stress at Tlajinga 33, but the pattern cannot be quantified as the Illinois case could.

Although again the sample number is rather small, all 5 term-age newborns that could be studied had evidence of prenatal stress, too. Interestingly, the 2 seventh-month individuals with teeth had none, and neither did 2 of the eighth-month perinatals available. Therefore, it seems that dying around birth was related to stress in the last trimester of pregnancy. Extrapolation from the data suggests that a pattern of late prenatal stress may have existed for perinatals and infants. It is a pattern that could explain why there are so many perinatals in the skeletal sample.

Stress Patterns Revealed by Harris Lines and Dental Hypoplasias

The prenatal stress pattern in the deciduous dentitions that shows a peak in the eighth month *in utero* is consonant with the prenatal stress pattern found in Harris lines, and the two skeletal indicators support a pattern of late prenatal problems in the population. However, for the permanent dentition hypoplasias, the peak frequency was from 2 to 3.5 years, which is slightly later than the peak of 0–2 years found in Harris lines. This lack of correspondence between the two markers has been found before. For example, McHenry and Schultz (1976) did not find any significant association between the two markers in a study of California Indians. Goodman and associates (Goodman and Clark 1981; Goodman et al. 1984a) found that there is a year or more difference in the peak of Harris lines and that of enamel hypoplasias in the Dickson Mounds population. The Tlajinga pattern is one of peaks about two years apart (Figure 7–5), but as in the Dickson case, the Harris line peak is earlier. The Tlajinga peaks are around a year earlier in Harris lines but slightly later in hypoplasias than Dickson. It is possible that the times of generalized stress started earlier in the life cycle in Tlajinga and lasted a little longer. Perhaps weaning began earlier, and it took children who would survive a little longer to get past significant growth disruptions under the age of five. The 2.7 hypoplasias per individual may be the indicator of a longer potential stress period at Tlajinga 33.

The differences between Harris lines and enamel hypoplasias are not surprising. Harris lines are generally more common and may be formed by stresses that are not as severe or as long-lasting as those that cause enamel hypoplasias, as quickly as a result of a few days' illness (Martin et al. 1985; Rose et al. 1985). They can also be caused by psychosocial stress (Mays 1985). They also may be more prone to formation during peak growth-velocity periods (Goodman et al. 1984a), such as under three years, and certainly are more likely to be resorbed by catch-up growth after the stress is over (Mays 1985). The hypoplasia peak, as discussed above, is largely due to the differential susceptibility in age of a tooth crown and is not likely to record stresses in people under two years old, unless severe (Goodman and Armelagos 1985). Why Harris lines would not still maintain a peak during the time of high frequency of hypoplasias is not clear from the literature. Perhaps long bones, too, are more susceptible at certain ages or lines formed at the younger ages are denser and less likely to be resorbed than those formed from ages 3 to 5.

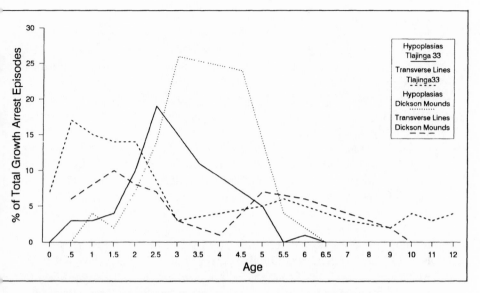

Figure 7-5. Transverse Lines and Permanent-Dentition Hypoplasias in the Tlajinga 33 and Dickson Mounds Populations

Nevertheless, Harris lines are expected to be more common than hypoplasias (McHenry and Schulz 1976), although in Tlajinga 33 hypoplasias were more common and revealed a higher average number of growth disruptions during childhood per individual than did transverse lines. Of course, Harris lines are subject to resorption and can be detected only on well-preserved bones. Tlajinga did have too many fragmentary bones, but even on complete, well-preserved bones there were few Harris lines, and many were not very radiographically dense. One reason might be that this population was undergoing very rapid bone remodeling, which would have prevented the preservation of many lines. The best way to test this is through microscopic analysis of long-bone cross-sections to look at the evidence of remodeling (e.g., Martin and Armelagos 1979; Huss-Ashmore et al. 1982). This test has not yet been done for Tlajinga 33, so a more macroscopic method was used to look for evidence of possibly strong remodeling effects in the Tlajinga 33 population.

Cortical Thickness

The compact cortical bone of long bones in humans does not remain unchanged throughout the lifespan, but increases and decreases during growth and aging. Bone is a dynamic system and is constantly affected by remodeling processes, the formation of new bone matrix by osteoblastic cells and the absorption or removal of bone by osteoclastic cells. The interaction of osteoblasts and osteoclasts actions continues throughout life, affects growth and, of course, cortical thickness. Cortical thickness fluctuates as bone is added to its outer or periosteal surface and either stays stable or is lost on its inner or endosteal surface, which adjoins the marrow cavity.

The general patterns of cortical thickness throughout the lifespan have been identified by the use of various modern populations. Cortical thickness increases through childhood, although some endosteal bone is lost, so that the marrow cavity increases (Massé and Hunt 1963). The cortical thickness then remains relatively stable until the beginning of the fourth decade of life, when it starts to decline (Garn 1970). After middle age, endosteal bone is apparently lost more rapidly than periosteal bone is added, meaning that cortical thickness decreases, the marrow cavity widens, and the general bone mass is less. This condition is called osteoporosis, and it is a common process of aging, especially among postmenopausal women.

There are, however, indications that nutrition can affect cortical thickness. Protein-calorie malnutrition in children has resulted in thinner cortices, less bone mineralization, and osteoporosis (Garn et al. 1966; Himes et al. 1975; Martin and Armelagos 1979). The effect on the cortical bones in the malnourished appears greater than on other indices, such as weight (Garn et al. 1964). The osteoporosis of aging, however, does not appear to have a nutritional basis (Garn et al. 1967). A prehistoric Nubian skeletal population had early and dramatic decline in cortical thickness in young females (Dewey et al. 1969). A multiple-method study of this loss revealed that it was both endosteal resorption and decreased mineralization, as bone and mineral were being sacrificed to support the increased demands of childbearing and lactation on the young female population (Martin and Armelagos 1979; Martin et al. 1985). Thus, it seems that nutritional problems can cause problems with cortical thickness and can increase the turnover rates of bone (see Martin et al. 1985).

For the Tlajinga 33 study, cortical bone thickness was measured at the midshaft of each femur and at a point two-thirds of the bone length from the proximal end of the tibia, the same measures as used by Hatch et al. (1983) on the Dallas population. The measurements were taken from an X-ray and measured to the nearest 0.5 mm. Although it is recognized that such measurements are less accurate than actual measurement of the cortex (Martin et al. 1985), it is a reasonable measure when the actual bone measure is not possible. The lengths of the bones were already known from measurements taken from an osteometric board, although in a few cases the lengths were estimated because the bones were incomplete. These lengths were estimated by measuring sections of the long bone present and using regression formulae to calculate the length of the bone, a method pioneered by Steele (Steele and Bramblett 1988). Cortical thickness was determined by subtracting the width of the medullary cavity from the total shaft width. From this, the cortical index, which indicates the proportion of cortex to the total bone, is calculated as cortical thickness/total width x 100 (Hatch et al. 1983). Both measures are an indication of how much bone mass is present and can be used to compare populations, if the methodology is comparable.

Table 7–5 provides the measures for Tlajinga 33 by age and sex. Only adults were measured, since these are the individuals who are lacking many transverse lines. Reduced cortical thickness in the Tlajinga population might be evidence of active remodeling and resorption. This then might be a clue to the relative lack of Harris lines. The sample is unfortunately quite small, especially for females and young adults. Thus, the averages cannot be used with any statistical validity to show a dramatic pattern of bone loss with age, although a trend toward less bone mass and cortical thickness with age is present in both sexes.

The Tlajinga cortical thickness measures can now be compared with those from the Dallas study (Hatch et al. 1983), which had about double the Harris lines of the Tlajinga sample. The averages of the two measures by bone and sex were calculated from the Dallas measurements by age in decades (see Table 7–5). The Dallas cortical thickness averages are definitely higher than those for Tlajinga 33. It seems as though the Tlajinga population has somewhat thinner cortices throughout the adult years than at least one other population that has large numbers of infants and young children in the skeletal series and a higher incidence of Harris lines. The thinner cortices in the case of Tlajinga, therefore, appear to be evidence for more active destruction of endosteal bone and more resorption among both sexes. That may be why Harris lines are not preserved.

However, the thinner cortices are actually better evidence for general nutritional stress in the population, because chronic protein-calorie malnutrition may affect the thickness of the bone cortices all through the lifespan. More investigation of the cortical thickness and bone mass will be undertaken in the future, but the preliminary evidence of probable thinner cortices may indicate a chronic, cumulative stress that in turn is

TABLE 7-5
Cortical Thickness in Tlajinga 33 and
Dallas Population Adults

	Tlajinga 33			
	Femur		**Tibia**	
Age	**Thickness**	**Index**	**Thickness**	**Index**
15	12.0	53.3		
20				
25				
30	11.0	46.8	5.0	29.4
35	10.5	38.9	9.5	38.7
	15.0	57.7	7.5	31.9
	8.0*	40.0	5.5*	26.2
	(12.75)	(48.3)	(8.5)	(35.3)
40	12.5*	48.1	7.5*	31.9
	15.5	48.4	6.5	27.7
			8.0	36.4
			9.5	35.8
			(8.0)	(33.3)
45	12.5	48.1	7.0	28.0
	8.0	33.3	7.0	25.9
	11.0	44.0	4.0	11.1
	(10.5)	(41.8)	4.0	19.0
			6.5	31.0
			(5.7)	(23.0)
50+	10.5*	40.4	5.0*	25.6
	14.0	58.3	7.5	32.6
	12.0	46.2	7.0	33.3
	(13.0)	(52.5)	3.5	14.9
			(6.0)	(26.9)

*Female measure

TABLE 7-5 Continued

			Dallas Population				
	Female				Male		
	Femur		Tibia		Femur		Tibia	
Age	Thick.	Index	Thick.	Index	Thick.	Index	Thick.	Index
20	13.6	57.2	7.9	37.37	16.6	62.8	10.3	46.2
30	13.0	53.2	6.7	31.48	16.3	55.1	9.5	40.1
40	13.1	50.4	5.0	23.71	16.8	60.6	10.6	44.3

Note: Numbers in parentheses are averages for males for each age class.

evidence of nutritional insufficiency throughout the lifespan, and not of stress just during the growing years, as hypoplasias were able to indicate.

Growth and Stature in Tlajinga 33

Other cumulative measures of stress involve the growth patterns and ultimate stature of the population (Goodman et al. 1984b). The indicators of growth disruption discussed above, if serious enough, should have an effect on the growth of children and the adult stature attained, and thus these could indicate the general severity of stress in the population.

The lengths of long bones were used to age the Tlajinga 33 perinatals and children, usually where the most accurate indicator of age, teeth, was not available. Long-bone lengths can also be used to study the growth pattern of a population. It has long been thought by researchers that growth and adult stature are affected by nutritional stress, although it is recognized that it is difficult to control totally the influence of other environmental and genetic factors on growth and stature in isolation from nutritional contributions (Huss-Ashmore et al. 1982). In modern populations growth delays have been attributed to protein-calorie deficiencies (Frisancho and Garn 1970), and among the high-altitude Quechua of Peru it has been postulated that delayed growth and small adult size are part of the biological adaptation to an energy-poor environment (Thomas 1973). There is a suggestion from growth-and-development studies that growth delay may be an adaptive response to a situation of protein-calorie malnutrition (see Nickens 1976). In fact, the shorter stature of many prehistoric Mesoamerican populations, especially from the complex societies like Teotihuacan, may be the result of adaptation to chronic malnutrition (Nickens 1976).

In prehistoric populations growth delays have been found in Nubian populations (Armelagos et al. 1972) and the North American population of Dickson Mounds (Lallo 1973). In both cases there is evidence of growth continuing into the twenties, which is later than in most modern populations. In addition, prehistoric populations also may present evidence of serious short-term disturbances in growth during childhood. Possible weaning stress may be indicated by a slowdown in growth between 2 and 6 years of age in the Dickson Mounds, Indian Knoll, and Nubian populations (Huss-Ashmore et al. 1982; Johnston 1962; Armelagos et al. 1972). Comparisons with growth curves from relatively well-nourished modern children (Maresh 1955) point up the developmental differences among the prehistoric populations and point to possible nutritional involvement, plus some disease effects.

To construct reliable growth curves for a prehistoric population, it is best to have a large, fairly well-preserved subadult population that has been aged by tooth eruption. Unfortunately, Tlajinga 33 has few well-preserved subadults that can also be aged by their teeth. Thus, although growth curves can be constructed for Tlajinga 33, the small numbers mean that the curves are not very detailed, and the average values per age may not be truly representative of the actual populational values. Interestingly, only the perinatal age class had enough individuals to yield meaningful averages. Table 7–6 presents the average values of long-bone lengths that could be measured at Tlajinga 33. The numbers were too small for chronological distinctions, so all have been lumped together. Also, it can be seen that some bones are not represented in every age class.

The pattern of the growth curve for femurs is presented in Figure 7–6. Here, the curve for white children (Maresh 1955) and the North American Arikara (from Ubelaker 1989) are also given for comparison. It was apparent from the available adult data that there was no difference in average size between individuals in their twenties and thirties, so that it appears that maturation in Tlajinga 33 was not unusually delayed. Although data are limited, it appears from the curve that the Tlajinga 33 population experienced a typical adolescent growth spurt.

There are, however, two rather interesting and important patterns that can be seen in the curve. One is, of course, that the population is much smaller in stature at various childhood ages than the modern

TABLE 7-6
Average Long-Bone Lengths
(in mm) by Age at Tlajinga 33

Age	Femur	Tibia	Humerus	Radius	Ulna	Ilium
7th mo.	43.6(4)	43.0(2)	40.1(4)	37.0(2)	40.0(1)	24.8(3)
8th mo.	69.2(5)	61.3(5)	61.0(5)	52.0(6)		32.2(5)
Neonate	71.9(9)	61.6(5)	61.6(5)	51.0(3)		32.8(5)
Infant	90.0(2)	74.5(2)	72.0(2)	58.0(2)	60.0(2)	46.0(2)
1–3	150.0(2)	121.0(2)	118.0(2)	86.0(2)		63.0(2)
3–5	162.0(2)	134.0(2)		95.0(1)		
5–10						96.0(1)
10–15			214.0(1)	170.0(1)		105.0(2)
15–20	445.0(1)					
Adult male	460.0(9)	370.0(8)		236.0(2)		

Note: Figures in parentheses are numbers of individuals used in the calculations.

white population. In comparison with another Native American population from North America, the Tlajinga 33 individuals were shorter at most ages than the Arikara standards compiled by Ubelaker (1989). There is evidence then that Tlajinga 33 is short all through the growing years, even by prehistoric North American standards.

The more important pattern visible in Figure 7-6, however, is the evidence of two significant growth slowdowns. The femurs show a flattening of the growth curve at 3 to 5 years. This pattern is reminiscent of the possible weaning stress problem noted earlier and seems to be directly due to the systemic stress that is so prevalent in the population between ages 2 and 4, according to the hypoplasia data. Thus, there is another indicator of weaning stress, a flattening of the growth curve between ages 3 and 5, in the Tlajinga 33 population.

The most severe slowdown, however, is during the last month *in utero*. In all five long bones measured, average lengths for this late prenatal month showed no appreciable difference of size (see Table 7-6). Thus, it appears that contrary to the normal pattern, the fetus is not growing in the last month of pregnancy.

This possible perinatal-growth slowdown has to be evaluated, because although 9 of the perinatals were aged to the month by dental standards (Kraus and Jordan 1965), all others in the skeletal population had been aged by their relation in the perinatal size seriation (see Chapter 5) to those aged by teeth. So that it could be determined whether the

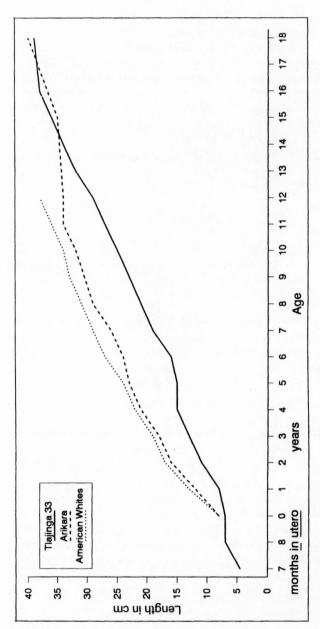

Figure 7-6. Growth Curves for Femurs of Three Populations

slowdown was real or an artifact of mixing long-bone lengths with dental ages in the seriation of the perinatals, the long bones available were aged separately and only then compared with any dental ages for an individual. By the use of maximum diaphyseal length of any complete long bones present, gestational age in weeks (from mother's last menstrual period) was estimated by the use of the regression formulae of Scheuer et al. (1980). The ages determined from the regressions were compared with those determined for Arikara perinatal femurs (Table 7–7). Where multiple bones were available for an individual, all estimated ages for Tlajinga were in close agreement, with not more than one week's difference in estimates. The pattern of the Tlajinga ages, however, is quite different from those estimated for the Arikara (Owsley and Bradtmiller 1983). The majority of the Arikara femurs fall in the 39-week and above range, whereas Tlajinga femurs and other bones are mostly in the range of 36–38 weeks. The percentages given in the table clearly reveal the differences. The Kolmogorov-Smirnoff statistical test on the cumulative proportions reveals that the two distributions of femur ages are statistically significant at the 0.001 level. Even with the disparity in sample sizes, this difference is not surprising, because 95% of the Tlajinga femurs were 37 weeks and younger, but only 25.6% of the Arikara were within this age range.

The reality of the slowdown is revealed by a comparison of the dental ages with the long-bone ages available for the 9 perinatals with teeth (Table 7–8). There was a significant discrepancy here, especially if it is remembered that the long bones have approximately two weeks added to the estimate compared with that of teeth, because of the use of the mother's last menstrual period as the beginning of the age standard. As can be seen in the table, the 4 individuals who were clearly at 32 weeks *in utero* are the same size as those aged as being over 36 weeks. Thus, although there is at least four weeks' difference in age, there is not much difference in sizes of any long bones. If teeth are the more accurate indicator, as most researchers feel, then it appears from this sample, although small, that perinatals from Tlajinga 33 were virtually not growing during the last month *in utero*, at least not those who were dying as perinatals.

This pattern actually complicated the size-rank seriation of the perinatals in general. It revealed how prevalent the pattern was among all perinatals. As the seriation was performed, the small individuals less than 32 weeks were apparent, but the other perinatals, who were to be aged as eighth-month and term-age, were very similar in size. Drawing the line above the largest 32-week perinatal aged by molars (Burial 21C) resulted in an estimate of 19 eighth-month individuals and 20 term or ninth-month ones. This is a very high prematurity rate, as adding those individuals aged seventh month and younger means that the majority of the Tlajinga 33 perinatals were premature. The average length of gestation for humans is 38–41 weeks from the mother's last menstrual period (Tanner 1978). The Arikara only have 21% of the sample under 38 weeks. According to a study of gestation period in American white and black infants (Anderson et al. 1943: Table 9), only 14% of white infants and 20% of black infants were born before 38 weeks.

Since it seems highly unlikely that such a large proportion of infants would be premature, it is perhaps possible that the average gestation length of Tlajinga females is one or two weeks shorter than normal. However, a more reasonable explanation is that Tlajinga infants are *shorter* at birth than modern and Arikara infants, and that the size of 37 weeks was that actually attained in 39 weeks of gestation. The evidence is that this is not the result of a normal pattern, but of pathology.

There is a *growth slowdown in the last month of pregnancy* as evidenced in the discrepancy of dental ages with size. The slowdown seen in the growth curves is real. Moreover, this evidence is consistent with the paleopathological indicators of Harris lines and enamel hypoplasias discussed above. Perinatals that could be studied commonly had evidence of Harris lines and hypoplasias that occurred during the eighth month. Thus, episodes of prenatal growth arrest were present in most of the perinatals and seem to correlate with a growth slowdown. A pattern of uterine growth retardation would have resulted in *small-for-gestational-age infants*. That is, Tlajinga perinatals would have attained a "proper" 39-week size at birth, except for some factor causing intrauterine growth retardation. In this population it is probably impossible to calculate the proportion of definitely preterm births, and it is more logical to consider most of the "preterm" perinatals as being term but simply small. The growth curve and long-bone ages reveal a pattern that indicates that many of the Tlajinga 33 perinatals were highly likely to be small for gestational age. The importance of this pattern is that in present-day developing nations, small-for-gestational-age infants also form a large proportion of low-birthweight infants, who have higher risks of mortality and complications in development (Faulkner 1981; Martorell and Gonzalez-Cossío 1987). This provides an important clue to account for the extremely high frequencies of perinatals in the skeletal sample of Tlajinga 33, an issue discussed below.

Another test using the data graphed in the growth curves is provided by calculation of the average diaphyseal lengths of femurs and tibias that would be expected from a mathematical model of growth (Hunt and Hatch 1981). This model was used to age Harris lines. Given

TABLE 7-7
Long-Bone Ages for Perinatals
in Tlajinga 33 and the Arikara

Gestational Age in Weeks	Tlajinga				Arikara	
	Femurs (%)		Other Bones (%)		Femurs (%) *	
28	1	(5.3)			4	(1.1)
29	2	(10.5)	2	(8.7)	1	(0.2)
30						
31					3	(0.8)
32					7	(1.9)
34	1	(5.3)	3	(13.0)	6	(1.6)
35			2	(8.7)		
36	5	(26.3)	5	(21.7)	13	(3.5)
37	9	(47.4)	6	(26.1)	62	(16.5)
38			4	(17.4)		
39	1	(5.3)	1	(4.3)	175	(46.7)
41					85	(22.7)
42					19	(5.1)
Totals	19		23		468	

*Adapted from Owsley and Bradtmiller 1983: Table 2.

the mean diaphyseal lengths for adult males, the theoretical length of the diaphysis at each age can be calculated. Figures 7–7 and 7–8 compare the theoretical lengths from Hunt and Hatch's model with the actual lengths obtained from femurs and tibias. In both cases the theoretical and actual are fairly similar, especially for the tibia. The femurs do tend to lag slightly behind what they should, so there is probably some catch-up growth represented in the actual data. The tibias are larger than predicted up to age 5, but the actual data are based on few examples, and not too much statistical importance should be placed on the deviations. What is interesting, though, is that the actual birth sizes determined for both long-bone measures are larger, even using Hunt and Hatch's correction for the neonatal size. The indication is that Tlajinga 33 infants may indeed be larger than what would be expected. This result occurs even in the presence of a slowdown of late-fetal growth. One hypothesis is that perhaps there was enough nutritional stress in the population to slow down the overall growth from what it might have been, once an individ-

TABLE 7-8
Tlajinga 33 Perinatal Burials:
Aging by Dentition and Long Bones

Tooth Age by Weeks *in utero*			
<32	32	32–36	36+
Burial 36	Burial 5	Burial 9	Burial 3
(35)	(37)	(37)	(37)
	Burial 8	Burial 21d	Burial 29a
	(36)	(37)	(37)
	Burial 21c		
	(36)		
	Burial 41e		
	(37)		

Note: Long-bone ages in weeks are in parenthesis. There is approximately a two-week difference in estimation between the two methods, because long-bone age is from mother's last menstrual period.

ual was born. This would be difficult to prove, but it may be that if malnutrition is chronic, small body size may result and the population never fulfills the potential that was present at birth, even with fetal retardation. This interpretation could reinforce the previous indicator of cortical thinning that Tlajinga 33 was characterized by a chronic nutritional inadequacy.

Measurement of the long bones of adults were also used to calculate stature. Calculating stature of the living adults from long bones depends on the known proportions of the latter to the former, which does vary among different populations (Ubelaker 1989). For Tlajinga 33, the formulas developed by Genovés (1967) for prehistoric Mesoamericans and based on living statures of indigenous Mexicans were used. Also, the formulas are different for the sexes. For stature, the long bones of the leg, the femur and tibia, are the most accurate and the only ones used by Genovés. However, other stature formulas for Mexicans, developed by Trotter and Gleser (1958), also use the humerus, radius, and ulna. The arm bones are less accurate, and Genovés believed that Trotter and Gleser's Mexican samples were too tall to be accurate for prehistoric Mesoamericans. However, these arm formulas were used wherever only complete arm bones were available.

By the use of the tibia and femur lengths only, the average stature was calculated for the Tlajinga 33 population. On the basis of 7 males, the average stature was 165 cm, and for 2 females, it was 159 cm. The statures of the sexes were fairly close. The male average stature is definitely shorter than that found for the Arikara, on the basis of the shorter long-bone lengths of Tlajinga as compared with the Arikara during growth (Ubelaker 1989), but is similar to the 160-cm estimate for La Ventilla B males, which was obtained by use of the same formula (Serrano and Lagunas 1974). The Tlajinga females are also apparently taller than the 146-cm average of La Ventilla B. Thus, the Tlajinga population is shorter than many North American populations but comparable to another Teotihuacan population. Mesoamericans, especially from the complex societies, were fairly short, which may have been an adaptation to chronic protein-calorie malnutrition (Nickens 1976). Thus, the cumulative stress indicators available for Tlajinga 33 seem to indicate thinner cortices in long bones and shorter stature than might be predicted. Both of these indices are linked to chronic undernutrition. The growth-arrest episodes seen in Harris lines and enamel hypoplasias are implicated in these effects on growth and stature, as well.

Morbidity and Mortality in Tlajinga 33

The paleopathological study has examined a variety of skeletal markers that indicate probable nutritional and disease problems for an individual, especially during the growing years. Many of these markers are evidence of growth disruptions during childhood that resulted when sufficient stress on the organism caused a temporary diversion of skeletal resources from growth to deal with the stress. In most cases the stress is similar to the effects of the interaction of infection and nutritional inadequacy seen in growing children in contemporary populations. Some markers also seemed to indicate chronic, lifelong undernutrition.

However, most of these indicators are of *morbidity* and do not translate directly into mortality. In fact, the markers, like enamel hypoplasias, are present because the individual actually survived the stress episode, delaying mortality for some time. One of the current challenges of paleopathology is to develop methods to estimate the effects of stress on mortality for individuals and the population.

Under the assumption of stationarity, it was thought possible to link the ages of peak occurrence of stress with peaks of mortality in the life table. Weaning stress as indicated in the hypoplasias of adults was reflected in the jump in the mortality of two and three-year olds in a skeletal population, for example (Huss-Ashmore et al. 1982). But with the

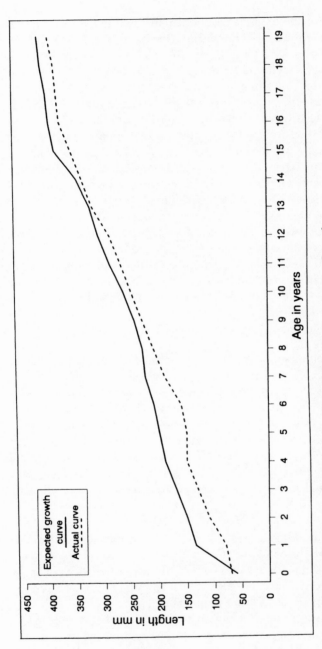

Figure 7-7. Actual and Theoretical Predicted Lengths of Femurs during Growth

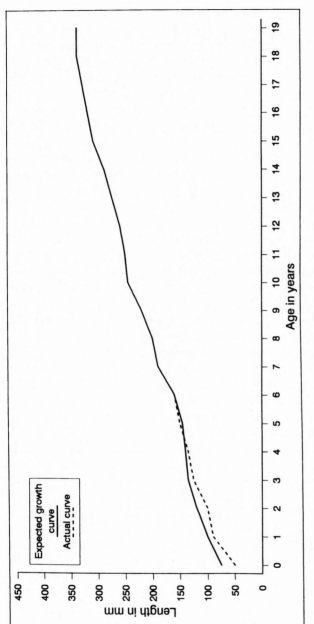

Figure 7-8. Actual and Theoretical Predicted Lengths of Tibias during Growth

new paleodemographic reconstruction of skeletal series as primarily affected by differences in fertility, this straightforward assumption has been challenged. Thus, several of the studies of North American skeletal populations with some time depth have shown that differences in the mean ages at death indicate not *rising mortality* but *rising fertility* associated with the intensive agriculture underlying the Mississippian culture, as in Dickson Mounds (Johansson and Horowitz 1986) and in Schild (Buikstra et al. 1986). These are then reconstructed as growing societies, and the increase seen in the paleopathological indicators of stress that characterize the Mississippian populations, when they are compared with the earlier, less complex cultures that preceded them, is then seen as baffling. Thus, in west-central Illinois an increase in dental defects that had been linked with differential survival (Cook and Buikstra 1979) and an increase in childhood mortality is no longer supported by an analysis of the pattern of subadult ages-at-death, which is now seen as supporting a *decreasing* subadult mortality from the Middle Woodland to the Mississippian (Buikstra et al. 1986). In this case, and in the Dickson Mounds case as well, then, what does the rise in stress indicators indicate?

As Johansson and Horowitz (1986) and Horowitz and Armelagos (1988) point out, the assumption of rising fertility for skeletal series assumes no mortality change between periods, and in the absence of other information, this is the best course, because fertility has a more direct effect upon mean age at death (Johansson and Horowitz 1986). However, it is imperative for accurate paleodemography that not only the effect of fertility but also how mortality might be changing be modeled. Paleopathological indicators can provide important clues to that mortality.

In a recent article Goodman and Armelagos (1988) showed that the mean age at death in Dickson Mounds was 4.4 years greater for individuals with no hypoplasias than for those with one hypoplastic episode, and a startling 10.2 years greater than for individuals with two or more hypoplastic episodes occurring between the ages of 3 and 7. Somehow, it does not seem logical that the lower mean age of death of individuals with two or more cases of systemic stress is due to their higher fertility within the population than those without lesions. Mean age at death, in this case, is reflecting the causal influence of greater morbidity upon mortality—in this case, costing some individuals perhaps up to 28% of the potential average lifespan.

But then how does this difference between those individuals who were stressed as children and those who were not translate into mortality rates? Since the Dickson Mounds population probably had higher fertility during the intensive agricultural phase, was there also a mortality rise that accompanied the increase in stress markers on individuals? The importance of the funding of Goodman and Armelagos (1988) is that the effect has impact not solely upon young children but also into the young adult years. The effects, then, of morbidity are likely to have been complex. Using a calculated growth rate for this population during agriculture, Johansson and Horowitz (1986) estimated that the decline in life expectancy in this case, as opposed to the earlier hunter-gatherer population from Dickson Mounds, would have been probably no worse than two or three years, and not the six implied by comparing population life tables based on stationarity. They then indicate that the problem paleodemogrpahy faces is that even if a reasonable life expectancy at birth is determined, the Coale and Demeny tables (1983) contain four sets of radically different age-specific death rates that are compatible with that life expectancy (Johansson and Horowitz 1986: 248).

However, that is exactly where it is believed the paleopathological indicators are important. The potential age-specific death rates can be compared with indications in the age distribution of deaths of susceptible individuals so that a reasonable mortality profile for the skeletons can be estimated. In Dickson Mounds weaning-age individuals are at risk, and the effect is to lower the mean age of death, in the worst-case scenario, to 25 years (Goodman and Armelagos 1988). *Thus, the problem becomes one of fitting the age distribution of deaths to the most reasonable fertility rates, population growth rate estimates, and the most reasonable mortality rates* (see Paine 1989).

Before exploring the potential mortality profile of Tlajinga 33, then, we should summarize the paleopathological information for Tlajinga 33 to identify the possible crucial factors in mortality. In Tlajinga 33 all individuals who could be tested had enamel hypoplasias on their permanent teeth, and all children and most perinatals who could be tested had evidence of prenatal stress. Thus, there is no control available to estimate the likely reduction in mean age of death between those who were impacted by stress and those who were not. The common presence of stress markers also probably means that virtually no one escaped physiological stress in the Tlajinga 33 population during the prenatal months or young childhood or both. Thus, the lifestyle of the residents of the compound probably had the effect of an *overall lowering of life expectancy,* which probably would not have occurred if the stress had not been present.

In the Tlajinga 33 age distribution of deaths, the greatest bulk of the individuals are ages 0–5 years. The proportions of individuals 5–35 are lower (see Figures 6–6 and 6–10). Thus, interest in possible impacts of mortality at Tlajinga 33 seem to focus on these early years. There are 55 perinatals (27%), 8 individuals from around two months to one year (4%), 3 individuals age one, 3 individuals age two, and 9 individuals age three and four. Thus, the last age and the first (perinatals) have the highest numbers. The three- and four-year-old deaths occur during and just after the peak in the hypoplasia frequency for the entire population. The fact that many Tlajinga hypoplasias were spaced within a year of each other suggests that these dead children, given evidence for prenatal stress and probably having been subject to physiological stress for about a year before death, may not have survived one more bout of illness or nutritional inadequacy. Those who died at older ages in Tlajinga but who reveal that early childhood stress period in their teeth, then, may have been "damaged" immunologically, too, which might have resulted in their dying at an earlier age as adults (Goodman and Armelagos 1989). The evidence that stress may have been lifelong is evident in the cortical thinning that characterized this population, and in the generally small stature of adults. This chronic stress plus the early childhood effects would be responsible for a shorter lifespan. Thus, a possible rise in mortality at ages three and four *is* indicated, with a related inference of generally shorter adult lifespans than would have been possible if physiological stress had not been present in virtually every resident of the compound (as inferred from the 100% incidence of stress indicators in tested individuals).

Of course, the most dramatic numbers of deaths occurred in the perinatals, in individuals who had just been born and survived little time after birth. The paleopathological indicators had shown that prenatal stress was common in those individuals and young children, and, more importantly, that there was a growth retardation in the last month of pregnancy that resulted in infants that were small for gestational age. Such infants still today have distinctly higher risks for mortality, even in developed countries, as demonstrated by an Australian study that found the perinatal mortality of growth-retarded infants was ten times that of infants of normal size, even with uncomplicated pregnancies (Dobson et al. 1982)! The importance of the growth retardation is that such infants are also low-birthweight babies (Faulkner 1981). Low-birthweight babies in a modern hospital setting in the early 1980s still had only a 60% chance of surviving the neonatal period (Brans et al. 1984). The problem is that in developing nations the overwhelming number of low birthweight babies are small for gestational age, whereas in developed nations prematurity accounts for the majority of low-birthweight infants (Faulkner 1981; Villar and Belizán 1982). The potential medical problems with the two groups are not the same, and unfortunately, much knowledge about neonatal death is from the populations where smallness for gestational age is the lesser problem. Nevertheless, the infants diagnosed as growth-retarded in a modern hospital setting in the United States during the early 1980s had 1.5 times the mortality that would have been predicted on the basis of the obstetrical characteristics of their mothers (Brans et al. 1984). The prognosis in prehistoric times, before modern medicine, for such infants was not good. Thus, the common presence of small-for-gestational-age infants among those dying as neonates in the Tlajinga sample is a clue that infant mortality in this population was high, and estimates of losses of around 30%–40% are probably not excessive. Thus, the paleopathological studies have identified three potential effects on mortality in the Tlajinga 33 population: higher deaths among three- and four-year-olds and perinatals, and shorter adult lifespans. For the latter, the general evidence of early childhood stress in *all* adults, combined with the evidence of potential cortical thinning and small stature from chronic stress, indicates that excessive morbidity could have (and probably did) affect the longevity of the residents of Tlajinga 33.

The next analytic procedure is to model mortality and fertility in Tlajinga 33 so that valid demographic parameters that might have characterized the population can be determined. The implications of these demographic parameters will then be investigated for the ways they aid in understanding, not only the Tlajinga 33 compound as a living entity, but also the workings and internal dynamics of the pre-Columbian city of Teotihuacan.

Mortality Models and the Demographic Significance of Tlajinga 33

H AVING OBSERVED the paleopathological indicators present in the skeletons from Tlajinga 33, we now need to integrate them into mortality profiles for the skeletal sample. As discussed in Chapter 6, the mean age at death has an understandable relation with life expectancy at birth, and also with mortality, if the growth rate can be estimated (Johannson and Horowitz 1986). The best that paleodemography can do is to make reasonable estimates and provide a range of likely demographic parameters for the past population. Although the specificity of mortality in this case is not likely to be as detailed as that possible if true q_xs, or the probabilities of dying in an age class, could be estimated, it is the contention here that some indication of the mortality experience not only is available from the age distribution of deaths, but that paleopathological indicators also indicate age patterns of mortality that will help in the selection of the best mortality model for a skeletal population.

Mortality Models for Tlajinga 33

To summarize relevant patterns so far discussed, Tlajinga 33 has a moderately high to high fertility profile, but it could not be determined by the use of those models if it also had a high mortality profile. The existing methodologies, most of which exclude the use of perinatals and infants because these are often underrepresented in archaeological populations, also did not indicate particularly elevated subadult mortality that would have prevented the population from replacing itself or offsetting the high fertility.

The paleopathological information indicated that two age groups might be at risk of elevated mortality: the perinatals, probably as a result of intrauterine growth retardation, which was common among those who died; and three- to four-year-olds, probably because prenatal stress and the stress of weaning and young childhood in the compound were common (see Chapter 7). Some young individuals would then finally have perhaps depleted their ability to rebound from stress and died at these ages. The paleopathological information also indicated that life expectancy in the compound would have been lowered because of universal stress during childhood and chronic undernutrition during the whole lifespan. At Dickson Mounds, Goodman and Armelagos (1988 and 1989) found a reduction of four years in mean age at death with one hypoplasia and ten years with two or more episodes. There are several plausible biological explanations for the earlier adult deaths as a consequence of childhood stress resulting from possible "immunological damage" (see Goodman and Armelagos 1988). If a similar process was present at Tlajinga 33, and it is reasonable to assume it was, Tlajinga 33 adults also could have lost anywhere from five to ten years of average adult life expectancy as a result of the health conditions present in the compound. Added to the other clues regarding the demographic conditions of the compound is that neither the city nor the compound was growing, but seemed nearly stable, during the time the Tlajinga 33 skeletal sample was deposited. All these clues must be taken together in any attempt to model the mortality of the living population that produced the skeletal sample.

Several methods have been suggested for determining the best mortality model for a paleodemographic sample. Johansson and Horowitz (1986) suggest using mean age at death together with growth rate estimates to locate the best model in the Coale and Demeny (1983) series of model life tables. Paine (1989) suggests using maximum likelihood curves and tests to determine the best fit between a given skeletal age distribution of death and that of a model from Coale and Demeny (1966). Once the best-fitting model is determined by the use of either of these methods, other demographic characteristics of the population can be determined.

A very useful feature of the second edition of the Coale and Demeny model life tables (1983) is that they determine the age distribution of deaths for all their models, including several with declining and increasing growth rates. Thus, it is fairly easy to compare a skeletal series to the models and determine the best fit by some appropriate statistical test. The only drawback to the procedure is that these model tables have several underlying assumptions that may or may not be reasonable when they are applied to anthropological populations. One problem is that there are four families of tables, three that are based on historical records and a fourth, West, determined by other available records that do not have one of the other recognizable patterns. Thus, although many anthropologists use the West tables as being the more appropriate for their populations, *these are nevertheless based on mostly European life tables, and the patterns in them may not be similar to those of non-Western prehistoric populations.* However, suitable life tables available to Coale and Demeny (1983) were not used as the basis for the families of life tables when they deviated from the general pattern they had identified. The uniformitarian assumption would stress that those populations should be similar to known populations, but the Coale and Demeny life tables *do not encompass all possible human demographic patterns;* they simply present four modal patterns derived exclusively from the industrial period. They do not contain ones that are still very plausible in terms of human population dynamics. Their use has tended in many ways to reify their patterns, by default, as those necessary for all human populations to mimic to be valid for study, and the danger is that we will shoehorn anthropological populations into patterns ultimately derived from mostly nineteenth-century European populations.

This issue is relevant to the other possible drawback of using the model tables for skeletal series. All draw out the lifespan to age 90. This problem of whether skeletons are systematically underaged, or that in the past very few individuals lived to ages over 70, has been discussed before. The effects of longer lifespans upon life tables based on stationarity was discussed in Chapter 6, as was the argument that these lifespans may have appeared fairly recently. In many anthropological and skeletal populations individuals undoubtedly lived to advanced ages, but the numbers would have been so few and sporadic that they would have relatively little influence over most life table measures. In the Tlajinga case a modeled lifespan of 85, as opposed to 65, added at least two years to all life expectancies. This model did not reapportion the older individuals but only treated as reasonable that in the last age cohort some small percentage of the survivors would have lived into their eighties. Whether it is more accurate to extend the lifespan will not be decided to everyone's satisfaction solely on the basis of Tlajinga. The only point here is that model life tables use the longer lifespans and that was why the life tables based on stationarity in Chapter 6 also did. However, it is probable, given the general lack of indices of very advanced age in Tlajinga 33 (see Mensforth and Lovejoy 1985), that a lifespan of 65 to 70 is reasonable for that population. This possibility is tested below.

The Tlajinga 33 study has seven possible age distributions, developed in Chapter 6: the complete, untransformed age distribution for all residents; the old-age-corrected age distribution; the migration-corrected age distribution; the two chronologically distinct, untransformed age distributions; and these latter two with a migration correction. These age distributions are all fitted to the best Coale and Demeny (1983) model tables, and then these age distributions and, more importantly, the cumulative age distributions of deaths are then fitted by the use of the Kolmogorov-Smirnov (K-S) test. Although Paine's (1989) likelihood method is good, the K-S test is easy to apply and more appropriate, especially since the cumulative distributions are given by Coale and Demeny. Also, the K-S test is preferred in this case because it is sensitive to both the shape of the distribution and the information contained in the ordinal data of the age classes. As an age distribution of death has both a shape and is ordinal, this test is preferable here over any chi-square test, which loses the ordinal information. Here, it will be used as a goodness-of-fit test. There are two ways to judge the best fit with this test. The usual measure is to determine the single largest divergence or difference in one age class between the cumulative proportions of the age classes of a model distribution and the skeletal distribution being fitted. The best-fitting model is the one whose largest difference is quantitatively the smallest of all the models fitted. Another measure is to total all differences between cumulative proportions in the age classes of a model and a skeletal population to indicate how well the actual skeletal age distribution approximates the models. The smallest quantity of total differences should also be the best-fitting model. The mean age at death of the model and of the Tlajinga data should also be similar.

The best fits were in the West tables, as has been found with other anthropological populations, although some North tables were fairly close. The East and South families were too divergent in age distributions of death. All distributions tested were in the first five levels of mortality of each family of tables, the "high mortality" tables, as other levels were distinctly more divergent from the Tlajinga 33 age distribution of deaths.

The model age distributions closest to the untransformed, complete age distribution for the apartment compound are given in Table 8–1. Both the total differences between the cumulative age distributions and the largest differences between model and Tlajinga in an age class are listed. As is evident from the table, a range of levels of mortality *and growth rates* are present. Although most are declining or stationary, two are growing. The best fit of all these model distributions is the one that is the lowest in both largest difference and total differences between cumulative proportions and is the closest to the mean age at death. That is model Male West Level 1, declining at 0.5% per year (see also Figure

8–1). This model is also reasonable in terms of archaeological evidence, which indicates general stability of population size, and certainly not explosive growth, in the city of Teotihuacan during the occupation of Tlajinga 33. The model also seems to suggest that the Tlajinga 33 residential population might have been declining slightly, as had also been found with other preindustrial urban populations in Europe.

However, it is also evident that there were gross differences between the cumulative age distributions, and Tlajinga 33 is not particularly close to the Coale and Demeny models. The quantities of the total differences between cumulative proportions nearly equal 1.0. Also, the Tlajinga 33 age distribution of deaths is statistically significantly different from each of the models in this table. A value less than or equal to 0.095 in the largest difference, the D statistic, was necessary for Tlajinga to be considered as having the same distribution as a model. In all cases this value was exceeded. The reasons are not hard to fathom, as evidenced in Figure 8–1, where the Tlajinga and the two closest models are graphed. Tlajinga has fewer cumulative deaths under age 5 than all models and catches up by age 25, with more deaths in ages 5 to 25. Also, the differences in proportions of older adults from the models are visible, because in Tlajinga few live past age 55. These are the kind of differences that are often seen when skeletal age distributions are compared with Coale and Demeny (see Howell 1982), even though Tlajinga has more infants than many skeletal populations and also a proportion of total deaths over 40, which resembles the models. That is, there is more moderate infant and young child mortality, higher mortality of older children through young adults, and fewer old adults over 50 in many skeletal populations. These were the differences that are apparent when Tlajinga and some other skeletal populations are compared with reference populations (see Chapter 6).

Again, we must return to the vexing question of whether the fault lies with skeletal age estimations and recovery technique, or with assuming that the Coale and Demeny models represent all of the possible human mortality profiles. It is still possible under uniformitarian assumptions for human demography that patterns of mortality for children and young adults were slightly different, or that adult lifespans were on the average shorter in the past. For example, only 4% of the deaths in Tlajinga occur after age 55, whereas Male West Level 1 has 15%. In Tlajinga most older adult deaths are clustered in the forties and early fifties, rather than being spread over all ages from 40 to 85, as in the models. This pattern has critically important implications for fitting the models of Coale and Demeny to the Tlajinga population. This difference is visible in Figure 8–1. It is entirely possible that mortality could have

TABLE 8-1
Best-Fitting Model Tables with the
Tlajinga 33 Untransformed Age Distribution

Model Life Table	Total Differences between Cumulative Distributions	Mean Difference between Distributions	The Value of the D Statistic, Largest Difference	Age Class with D	Mean Age at Death
Female West Level 2					
$r = 0$	.794	.061	.136	at 55	22.50
Female West Level 1					
$r = -0.5\%$	.824	.063	.143	at 55	23.25
Female West Level 5					
$r = +1\%$	.827	.063	.138	at 55	22.33
Male West Level 1					
$r = -0.5\%$	.795	.061	.120	at 5	20.96
Male West Level 4					
$r = +0.5\%$	.811	.062	.120	at 55	21.82
Male North Level 3					
$r = 0$	.820	.063	.135	at 55	22.34

Note: Tlajinga mean age at death = 20.49 years.

followed the Tlajinga pattern rather than the model one. The paleo-pathological evidence discussed in Chapter 7 indicates that the Tlajinga residents had a shortened lifespan because of physiological stress during childhood and perhaps all through the lifespan. This does not mean that no one lived into the eighties at Tlajinga 33 or in the city of Teotihuacan, although no one clearly that old was identified skeletally at Tlajinga, but it does mean that such individuals would have been rare. Unfortunately, these differences between historical models and prehistoric skeletons cannot be resolved here, as doing so depends on which assumptions regarding mortality one finds more convincing—those of historical, relatively recent, national European populations, or those of paleo-demographic samples from non-European, preindustrial, prehistoric

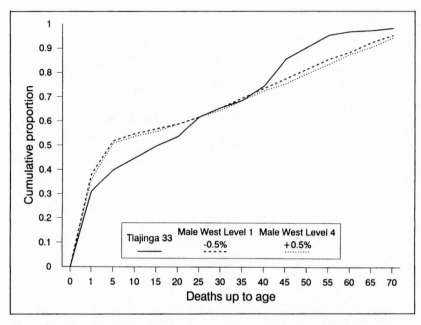

Figure 8-1. The Cumulative Proportions of Ages at Death in the Tlajinga 33 Untransformed Age Distribution and Two Coale and Demeny (1983) Model Tables

contexts. The former models potentially may represent only a limited range of the mortality of populations, and therefore would not be suitable for representing the entire range of "uniformitarian" mortality patterns. This researcher believes that although model tables are important and useful, they are not necessarily preferable to actual data. In this case the mortality patterns, though deviant from models, are not so different as to preclude their characterizing a human population, particularly since the cultural context of the data is so dramatically different.

The underlying structure of the Coale and Demeny model tables is revealed when the Tlajinga old-age-corrected age distribution of deaths is fitted to them. In this corrected distribution, deaths are more evenly spread from ages 40 to 80, such that 13% of the deaths are over age 55. Table 8–2 presents the best-fitting models. Now, all the largest differences are at age 5, and both measures of best fit, largest difference and total differences, are less than with the untransformed. However, there is more of a divergence in the measures of best fit, as those models with the smallest quantity of total differences have the greatest *D* statistic and differ in mean age at death. There is no one table lowest or next to lowest

TABLE 8-2
Best-Fitting Model Tables with the
Tlajinga Old-Age-Corrected Age Distribution

Model Life Table	Total Differences between Cumulative Distributions	The Value of the *D* Statistic, Largest Difference	Age Class with *D*	Mean Age at Death
Female West Level 1				
r = -0.5%	.564	.08˙	at 5	23.25
Female West Level 2				
r = 0	.546	.09˙	at 5	22.50
Female West Level 3				
r = +0.5%	.477	.108	at 5	21.50
Male West Level 1				
r = -0.5%	.489	.120	at 5	20.96
Male West Level 3				
r = 0	.570	.09˙	at 5	22.85
Male North Level 4				
r = +0.5%	.534	.109	at 5	21.82

Note: Tlajinga mean age at death = 22.52 years.
˙No statistically significant difference between Tlajinga and the model.

in all three measures of fit, so choosing among the models is not as easy. Perhaps the best fit here is Female West Level 2 Stationary, which has the same mean age of death as the Tlajinga distribution, one of the lowest *D* statistics and a moderate quantity on the total differences. Figure 8–2 compares this model with Male West 1 *r* = −0.5% per year, which remains one of the best fits along the total distribution. The effect of the old-age correction for the Tlajinga distribution is to make it definitely more compatible with the Coale and Demeny models, *although certainly not necessarily more correct for the data*. The differences with Coale and Demeny are now concentrated in ages under 25, in the same pattern as discussed above.

Thus, there is still the problem of whether lifespans such as those indicated in Tlajinga are realistic. The problems have been dramatically discussed by Howell (1982) in relation to the Libben age distribution, which has fewer older individuals and also less infant mortality than Tlajinga. In the Libben case she reveals the high dependency ratio (numbers 0–14 and 60+ to the productive adults 15–59), the probable high work load of adults, the lack of "elders" for cultural continuity, and the instability of marriages and kinship relations implied by the Libben distribution, where there are generally so few adults. The Tlajinga dependency ratio is 1.08, resembling Libben's (1.0), but the bulk of the Tlajinga subadults are perinatals, who die soon after or before birth. The Tlajinga age distribution and paleopathological indicators clearly imply high infant mortality, so that these individuals would not really be dependents. If perinatals are removed, then there are only 52 dependent individuals to 99 productive adults in the distribution, for a low dependency ratio of 0.53, in the stationary-population case. Although Tlajinga is not likely to be a stationary population, the dependency ratio should not be excessive, and in the model Male West Level 1 $r = -0.5\%$ per year, it is 0.63 (Coale and Demeny 1983: 105). Thus, Tlajinga does not appear to have had a deficiency of productive adults in proportion to total population. However, the adult mortality in Tlajinga would also mean that marriages often would not last the whole female reproductive span and children would lose one or both parents with some frequency, although the pattern would not be as dramatic as in Howell's Libben reconstruction. Half the adults would be dead by age 40 in the Tlajinga stationary-population case, so that most surviving individuals would probably have lost at least one spouse, and teenagers one parent. The bulk of the surviving adults die between age 40 and 54, although by this time, most would probably be grandparents of one child by one older surviving offspring. Thus, as in the Libben case, most young adults would have lost their parents soon after beginning their own families. The few individuals that were "elders" were likely to be important within the daily life of the Tlajinga compound and crucial in guiding the young adults and as resources of experience. The favorable burial treatments accorded such individuals (see Chapter 4) thus makes perfect sense in such a demographic condition. Also, a relation between a kin-based organization of the Teotihuacan apartment compound and the craft specialization would also make sense: young adults work under the guidance of a few elders, who would be relatives, and start to pass on the craft to teenagers. In such a case, the shorter lifespans and the mortality of adults are not likely to completely disrupt the economic workings of the compound. The picture of life within the Tlajinga compound is thus one of high

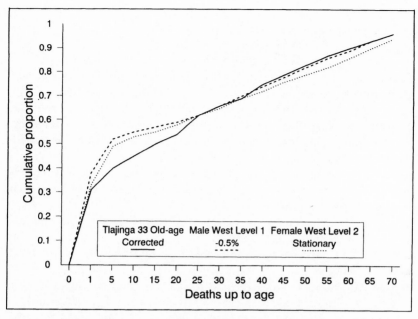

Figure 8-2. The Cumulative Proportions of Ages at Death in the Tlajinga Old-Age-Corrected Distribution and Two Coale and Demeny (1983) Model Tables

infant mortality; probable great care and worry over surviving children; women with common, closely spaced pregnancies (because of the quick loss of infants and the need for high fertility to try to compensate); teenagers with one parent and perhaps a step-parent (if remarriage was common) learning to be productive adults; and young adults with young families and probably some younger siblings in their apartment suites. A large proportion of younger siblings in a family would become dependent on their extended relations for guidance and continuity, as many would be orphaned before reaching maturity. Although the implication is that a faster achievement of mature behavior was expected than is characteristic of contemporary populations, such an expectation was not unreasonable in comparison with expectations regarding maturity in many cultures. Thus, Tlajinga 33 could have continued with some economic and cultural stability, in spite of the infant losses and shorter adult lifespans implied by the age distribution of deaths and the paleopathological indicators. A population like that envisioned here at Tlajinga is not unrealistic from a cultural perspective. Thus, the Coale and Demeny older-age pattern may not be appropriate for fitting to a skeletal population like Tlajinga and could actually obscure the actual demographic pattern by forcing it into a pattern derived from national populations from another time, place, and culture.

However, the use of model tables is useful for smoothing out the fluctuations of small populations like Tlajinga 33 and allowing its comparison with an existing standard, which has other known demographic properties, that otherwise would not be obtainable from just the skeletons themselves. At this point, the best-fitting model distributions have been those of stationary or slightly declining populations, especially those closest in mean age at death. The implication is that probably some migration could have been important to Tlajinga, as to most urban populations, either to keep the resident numbers stationary or to keep them from declining even more.

Table 8–3, which uses the migration-corrected age distribution for all Tlajinga 33 residents, lists the best-fitting models to that distribution. Although in Chapter 6 it was indicated that the smoothest age distribution obtainable at Tlajinga was that which combined the migration correction with the old-age correction, this was not fit here because of the objections to the old-age correction discussed above. The differences are of a greater magnitude than those in Table 8–1. Here, average age at death is the most divergent from all models, but the lowest in both total differences and D statistic is Male West Level 3 $r = -0.5\%$ per year, a declining population. Removal of some of the possible distorting effects of recent migrants on the Tlajinga age distribution seems to magnify the general differences between the Tlajinga pattern and the Coale and Demeny West one, although again the majority of reasonable models are declining or stationary populations. In this case the effect of migration was actually to increase the mortality levels from West Level 3 to Level 1.

Because the migration-corrected age distribution may be the best approximation of what was occurring to the truly resident and native population of Teotihuacan among the lower-class artisans, it is important to try to improve the fit between Tlajinga and the Coale and Demeny models. This can be accomplished if one ignores the cumulative age distributions over age 40, where the great differences between skeletons and models occur. When one compares the fits up to age 40 and selects the eight best-fitting models (Table 8–3), the largest difference and total deviations fall dramatically. Here, it can be seen that the best fit is probably Male West Level 5 stationary, although in total differences, Female West Level 3 $r = -0.5\%$ is about the same.

These both imply fairly similar underlying life tables. In the Male West Level 5, the life expectancy at birth is 27.6 years, 30% of the infants born are dead within one year, and survivorship at age 15 is 53% (Coale and Demeny 1983: 44). For the Female West Level 3, life expectancy at birth is 25 years, 30% of the infants born are dead within the first year, and survivorship to age 15 is about 49% (Coale and Demeny 1983: 43). These figures are reminiscent of those calculated for residents of European preindustrial cities like London and Amsterdam (see Chapter 2). They imply significant infant and child mortality for Tlajinga 33, implications certainly supported by paleopathological indicators for this population. Although it is possible that a population with such a mortality level can maintain numbers with high enough fertility, many indications present in the age distribution point to the distinct possibility of a slight shortfall. Over the 500 years of the Tlajinga 33 occupation, it is very likely that, with such mortality, migration may have been needed to maintain a steady number of residents within the compound and within the overall city itself.

Thus, like the European preindustrial cities discussed earlier, Teotihuacan was probably not able to maintain its numbers and was dependent on at least some migration. Again, as in the other preindustrial cities, infant and child mortality was a large reason for the demographic difficulties. In Tlajinga, with generally shorter adult lifespans, the loss of so many infants would have led to small average family sizes, as many adults would not live out their total reproductive span. It is easy for resident fertility to fall short of what would be needed to replace the population. The migration-corrected Tlajinga age distribution of deaths is compatible with moderately declining population of 0.5% per year, which probably was offset over time by enough migration for the compound and city to maintain stable numbers. The effect of the presence of possible migrants in the skeletal population, interestingly, as seen in the untransformed age distribution, was only at best to help the population maintain stationarity, and most likely it also contributed to the decline. The Male West Level 1 underlying life table, the best fit for the untransformed, has a life expectancy at birth of 18 years, 41% of the individuals born die as infants, and only 38% of the population survives to age 15. Thus, migrants might add to the mortality without affecting fertility, a pattern that has also been postulated for European preindustrial urban populations (Sharlin 1978). With the same adjustment made to the model fitting as for the migration correction, the untransformed age distribution was compared only through age 40. The best fit in total differences is Female West Level 6 with $r = +1\%$ per year growth rate, but the age distribution was also closely matched by Female West Level 1 with $r = -0.5\%$ per year and Female West Level 2 Stationary. The model table with the smallest D statistic was Male West Level 1 $r = -1\%$ per year. Thus, although one growing population was a good fit to the age distribution, all others were declining or stationary populations, the

TABLE 8-3
Best-Fitting Model Tables with the
Tlajinga Migration-Corrected Age Distribution

Model Life Table	Total Differences between Cumulative Distributions	The Value of the *D* Statistic, Largest Difference	Age Class with *D*	Mean Age at Death
Female West Level 1 $r = -1\%$	.915	.176	at 55	26.82
Female West Level 2 $r = -0.5\%$	.977	.168	at 55	26.05
Female West Level 6 $r = +0.5\%$	.976	.202	at 55	28.30
Male West Level 2 $r = -1\%$	.925	.166	at 55	27.17
Male West Level 3 $r = -0.5\%$	.907	.159	at 55	26.34
Male North Level 5 $r = 0$	.913	.180	at 55	27.67
Male West Level 5 $r = +0.5\%$	1.072	.137	at 55	23.99

same pattern seen before. The Female West 6 life table has a life expectancy at birth of 32.5 years and infant mortality of just 23% of those born. This table is the most favorable mortality model yet found for Tlajinga 33, but it does not seem plausible, given the paleopathological evidence and the compound size. This evidence indicates that Tlajinga is more likely to resemble the high-mortality declining populations that generally have provided the best models.

There is substantiated evidence, both from the age distribution itself and the implications of the paleopathological indicators, that Teotihuacan's lower-status artisans, like those of Tlajinga 33, resembled the poor of other preindustrial cities in mortality and were not able to re-

Model Life Table	Total Differences between Cumulative Distributions	The Value of the D Statistic, Largest Difference	Age Class with D	Mean Age at Death
	Comparisons Up to Age Forty			
Female West Level 1 $r = -1\%$	.311	.106		
Female West Level 2 $r = -1\%$	.337	.074		
Female West Level 3 $r = -0.5\%$	.278	.081		
Female West Level 5 $r = 0$	.300	.069		
Male West Level 2 $r = -1\%$	.337	.102		
Male West Level 5 $r = 0$	.277	.063		

Note: Tlajinga mean age at death = 23.90 years.
'No statistically significant difference between Tlajinga and the model.

place themselves demographically. Migration was ultimately necessary to keep economic units like Tlajinga 33 going, probably by bringing in marriage partners in most cases, but sometimes by adding young families as well.

The chronological information presently available for Tlajinga 33, showing a population whose mean age at death dropped somewhat dramatically through time, perhaps is a clue to the dynamics of demographic loss in the poorer sectors of Teotihuacan. The lowering of the average age of death (see Tables 6–6 and 6–7) across time, which in many cases would indicate an explosive growth rate in the population, cannot be indicating the same in Teotihuacan, as the city barely maintained stability even during the Late Xolalpan. It is possible, of course, that the growth was being sent out to the countryside, but that is contrary to what is usually seen in the preindustrial city. In fact, in a society like Teotihuacan where human labor was the main source of energy within a culture that lacked draft animals, direct control of a population increasing in size would have been the way to increase political power and outcompete nearby societies and dominate the countryside. The rulers of Teotihuacan should have preferred a growing city population, especially during the Late Xolalpan when other urban centers like Xochicalco and Cholula were starting to compete with Teotihuacan for political, economic, and demographic hegemony in central Mexico. The paleopathological patterns of prenatal stress that led to high infant mortality and even affected young children is evidence that the increase in numbers of infants by the Late Xolalpan was not the result of an increasing birth rate, but more probably the worsening of the health conditions underlying prenatal stress. The younger mean age of death is evidence of real trouble in the Teotihuacan system. A population dying so young is probably evidence of the destabilization of Teotihuacan demography, as that kind of mortality would make the population crash within a short time. By Late Xolalpan times, it may not have been possible for the city to overcome the shortfall. Thus, the Late Xolalpan age distribution is probably not one that can be considered a stable population, but one that is declining beyond the rates compatible with stable-population theory. Even with a correction for migration, which also assumes that migration increased through time, the same pattern of increasing youth in the age distribution is still evident (Table 6–8), with the same implications. It is probable that the Early Period age distribution represents a population more able to maintain stability, whereas the Late Period is no longer stable, but losing population dramatically. In fact, the end of Teotihuacan as a major polity and preindustrial city "suddenly" in the archaeological record may represent the evidence of such dramatic population loss as to destroy societal cohesion. In the future the more recent methods for demographic study of nonstable populations will be employed to investigate the potential problem visible through time in the Tlajinga 33 chronological age distributions.

One could attribute the raw age distribution of deaths of the Tlajinga population to either moderate growth or decline as well as to a stationary condition, by fitting the Coale and Demeny West model tables; however, one must use other information to determine what demographic conditions might be present (Johansson and Horowitz 1986). Some of the indicators, in particular the large numbers of infants and young children and the generally young mean age at death, are believed to indicate a high-fertility, and probably growing, population (see Chapter 6). However, this assumption is contradicted by archaeological evidence for size trends in the Tlajinga 33 compound and the city of Teotihuacan and by paleopathological indicators, especially those of prenatal stress and large numbers of perinatals. The evidence for late fetal growth retardation and potential small-for-gestational-age infants would mean an elevated infant mortality. Such mortality, coupled with a shorter average adult lifespan caused by ubiquitous childhood stress, would easily create a situation where fertility, though high at six or seven children in completed fertility, would not be able to offset mortality and population decline. The age distribution often fit well with moderately declining populations. Therefore, a reconstruction of the demographic conditions of Tlajinga 33 as moderately declining is preferable, given all the evidence.

An age distribution of death must be judged not only as the result of fertility, which does have a dramatic effect on its shape, but also in the light of the possible age pattern of mortality that produced it. In Tlajinga 33 mortality is likely to be dominant in infancy and under the age of 5 in producing the proportions seen in the age distribution of death. It is also likely to affect the ability of adults to survive to the end of the reproductive span. The loss of reproductive capacity (see Henneberg 1976) probably affected the ability of families to offset all the mortality losses. Thus, from the evidence of Tlajinga 33, which is only one compound but likely to be representative of the poorer artisanal sector of the city population, it is likely that Teotihuacan had a declining resident population and was thus subject to the "Law of Natural Urban Decrease" (de Vries 1984), as were other urban populations, in spite of the environmental, cultural, and epidemiological differences from the Old World. Preindustrial cities create population densities and living conditions that are not conducive to survivorship and prosperity for many of their inhabitants. The reasons for this, as well as the implications of Teotihuacan as a typical preindustrial city in its particular environmental and cultural milieu, must be discussed if one is to understand the implications of the Tlajinga 33 paleodemographic study.

The Demographic Implications of the Tlajinga 33 Study

The demographic profile of the Tlajinga 33 apartment compound is one of high infant and child mortality; the study found substantial evidence of stress episodes during growth and perhaps a shortened average lifespan because of the stress during childhood and probable chronic undernutrition throughout the lifespan. It was a population that may have just barely been maintaining itself, but more likely was slightly declining, even with some effects of migration accounted for and modeled. It is also probable that mortality may have increased through time, such that the population was not a stable one by the Late Xolalpan and cannot be accurately characterized by such models. In this case the population would have probably been declining rapidly and the city losing population quickly, as the end of the polity approached. The Tlajinga 33 population does not appear to have lived in a very healthy environment.

It is not surprising that the dense population of Teotihuacan may not have been conducive to a healthful environment. Preindustrial cities in Europe are believed to have had problems with public sanitation and contaminated water supply, which help explain their high disease load and high mortality (Wrigley 1969; McNeill 1976). Teotihuacan is in an arid highland environment, which would be beneficial in cutting down on some diseases present in the New World (the insect-borne diseases, for example), and perhaps by hampering individual-to-individual infection through the air. Although the arid environment might be beneficial for a dense population in some ways, it certainly would not have prevented contamination of the water supply.

Teotihuacan has a monsoonal rain pattern; 80% of all precipitation falls between June 1 and October 1 (Sanders et al. 1979). For a substantial portion of the year there is not much rainfall to refresh reservoirs. Teotihuacan did benefit from the year-around output of springs just below the city, but they probably were not the main or only source of water for much of the population. An important source of water for city residents would have been the reservoirs dug around the city (Millon 1973), which were filled by rain. During the long dry season water was probably carefully rationed from these reservoirs. But more importantly, the rain pattern means that trash and human waste would not have been flushed out of the city for several months, and cleaning would generally have been more difficult. This situation probably created quite a health hazard, a potent breeding ground and source of contamination for parasitic and endemic intestinal infections among the population. Thus, Teotihuacan probably did have problems with its public sanitation and water supply that consequently fostered ill health in the population.

A modern example of the morbidity due to a lack of a clean water supply is provided by the besieged city of West Beirut, Lebanon, during the summer of 1982. When water had been cut off for two weeks, John Desalis, the Red Cross regional director, reported that infectious diseases such as scabies, conjunctivitis (a viral inflammation of the eye membranes), gastroenteritis, and diarrhea were prevalent among the population (Associated Press interview with Desalis, August 9, 1982). It is not hard to imagine that Teotihuacan would have had similar problems during its dry season. Thus, in spite of its having an environment unlike that of the Old World and the lack of many Old World pathogens, Teotihuacan still would have had problems with disease, infection, and the continual circulation of endemic infections to infect and reinfect the population, especially every dry season. It would not have been a healthy place to live.

Tlajinga 33 yields clear evidence of health and mortality problems, but how representative of the city of Teotihuacan is it? This has been, of course, a demographic study of just one of an estimated 2,000 compounds (Millon 1973), and one that is on an edge of the city and somewhat distinctive in its characteristics from other excavated compounds (see Chapter 3). However, it is a craft specialists' compound and of low status. Thus, it is likely to be more representative of a significant proportion of the population than a more wealthy compound would be. The lower strata of the city, which included the large proportion of resident food producers as well, should have far outnumbered the upper classes in the city. Tlajinga 33 is probably different from a food producers' compound in some ways, especially as it might be more food-poor and nutritionally stressed because of its nearly complete dependence on the market for subsistence items. However, it can characterize the demographic situation of the lower strata of the city until more evidence is available.

The demographic problems of Tlajinga 33, if representative of the poorer compounds, as seems likely, had significant implications for the Teotihuacan social system. Mortality was high, especially around birth, although there is also evidence of weaning and postweaning stress, which affects the morbidity of children and apparently also of adults. However, the loss of approximately 30% of the infants born, as the best models for the population indicate, could have created a problem in replacing the population. It is more likely that most neonates were lost from natural causes. There are two general classes of pathoses that may have caused neonatal death: prenatal problems and the variety of infections that can strike mortally in the first few days.

It was suggested in Chapter 7 that growth disruptions during late fetal development may have resulted in small-for-gestational-age and low-birthweight babies. The etiology of such growth disruptions is not simple. Mean birthweights for ethnic groups do vary. For example, a survey of North American Indian groups found a difference of 400 g between the high and low means of birthweights (Adams and

Niswander 1968). Interestingly, in that study birthweight coincided closely with the pre-Columbian subsistence patterns, and the maize agriculturalists of the Hopis and Pueblos have the smallest, while the bison-hunting Sioux, Cheyennes, and Crows the largest. If this is true of Mesoamerica, one would expect the Tlajinga 33 infants to have small mean birthweights as well. But the pattern in Tlajinga implies a near absence of growth during the last month *in utero* in many perinatals, which is evidence that individuals were being born smaller than they should have been.

Retardation of the growth of some individuals in the uterus so that they are born smaller than the mean has been attributed to a variety of factors and is considered to have a number of sequelae. A review of evidence for the relationship of maternal nutrition and low birthweight found that the latter is related to neonatal and infant mortality, problems in growth and development, and to future reproductive problems in girls (Martorell and Gonzalez-Cossío 1987). Ultrasound technology has made it possible to distinguish between two patterns of growth disruption (Cronk 1983). One pattern, "low profile," appears to be present throughout the pregnancy. The other, "late-flattening," appears to characterize the Tlajinga pattern, where growth is normal until 32 weeks, then decreases abruptly, so that infants are born somatically small with large heads. The known causes of this are varied but may not totally be applicable to the Tlajinga case, because the information comes from modern developed nations where sanitation, nutrition, and socioeconomic factors may be underrepresented in the given etiologies (see Martorell and Gonzalez-Cossío 1978). Although normal growth rates for fetuses by month are not yet clearly known (Cronk 1983), we do know that most growth and nutrient demands are greater toward the end of gestation (Tanner 1978). The problem at Tlajinga is very likely to have involved, in some way, maternal failure to support these increased nutrient demands.

The relation between maternal nutrition and low birthweight or intrauterine growth retardation has been the focus of recent research, although not all the potential relationships are well understood. Some researchers feel that the most important component of adequate maternal nutrition is the mother's lifetime nutrition and potential reserves, rather than the diet she takes during pregnancy (Guthrie 1975). In this case, by the time of pregnancy it is too late to undo many of the nutritional problems that could have an adverse effect upon the fetus. However, other recent studies have clearly shown that maternal nutrition during pregnancy has a direct effect upon birthweight (the Bogota, Birmingham, and Guatemala studies quoted in Martorell and Gonzalez-

Cossío 1987; Gebre-Medhin and Gobezie 1975). In these cases nutritional supplementation increased mean birthweights, especially in the more poorly nourished women. Maternal nutrition is directly implicated in low birthweight.

The health of the mother can also affect prenatal and infant growth. Infections, heart problems, and toxemia have been implicated in producing low-birthweight babies (Ounsted and Ounsted 1973; Coid et al. 1977). Other factors that might affect maternal diets and the body's ability to utilize what nutrients are available include seasonal difference in food availability and work, general strenuous physical work during pregnancy, cooking smoke, and culturally prescribed food taboos on pregnant women (Martorell and Gonzalez-Cossío 1987). All of these might have been present in Tlajinga 33 and could have caused low birthweights.

The problems faced by a low-birthweight infant seem to be more clearly known than exactly how maternal factors cause intrauterine growth retardation. There are possible organ problems, as some are too small, and heart problems (Naeye 1970), but these seem more common in premature, very low-birthweight babies. Low-birthweight babies in general seem to be at greater risk from neonatal asphyxia, poor thermoregulatory mechanisms, hypoglycaemia, and dehydration (Ounsted and Ounsted 1973). Small-for-gestational-age infants also generally lag behind in physical growth and, although normal in maturational development, have much smaller stature than adequate-weight infants (quoted in Martorell and Gonzalez-Cossío 1987). There is also the potential for cognitive problems, but these seem to be less severe in "late-flattening" than in "low profile" retardation (Martorell and Gonzalez-Cossío 1987). There is also evidence that intrauterine growth-retarded infants probably have an increased susceptibility to infections that can last years (Ferguson 1978).

The susceptibility to infection is crucial, because an important cause of neonatal mortality is infection. Infants can be infected while still *in utero* and when coming down the birth canal by such diseases as conjunctivitis, pneumonia, septicaemia, meningitis, osteomyelitis, and urinary tract infection (Gamsu 1977), to name those that were probably present in the pre-Columbian New World. Bacteria that cause diarrhea are easily given to infants at birth from an infected birth canal or the hands of both attendants or parents (Marcy 1976). These diarrheal infections are the kind of disease that could have been a real problem at Teotihuacan, where inadequate disposal of human wastes and a lack of water for cleaning, especially during the dry season, would have created a very good environment for the bacteria. Neonatal tetanus, a similar infection from unsanitary conditions, could also have been important, and probably was present in pre-Columbian times.

The age distribution of deaths at Tlajinga 33 included many perinatals, and the demographic modeling and paleopathological analysis both revealed that this is likely because of the high neonatal mortality. At Tlajinga 33 there certainly were reasons for such mortality in a combination of prenatal growth retardation and infection. Infection was likely to be rife in that water-poor, densely populated environment with poor sanitary practices. Also, mothers probably entered pregnancy with insufficient reserves because of chronic undernutrition throughout the lifespan, and they probably could not have been provided a special nutritional supplement during pregnancy in a lower-class compound. The probable result was undersized infants, many of whom would die soon after birth.

The high mortality of infants would have presented the Tlajinga 33 residents with the problem of raising children to adulthood, a problem that was probably faced by most of the lower-class strata of Teotihuacan. Every Tlajinga 33 individual, without exception, that could be studied presented evidence of stress after infancy, which undoubtedly accounts for the demographic model showing Tlajinga to have lost around half of the individuals ever born before the age of 15. Thus, the problem was for the population to have enough fertility to overcome the mortality present. The evidence from the age distribution of deaths is that Tlajinga was a moderately high-fertility population, so that the potential for maintaining population was there. It is hard to estimate what this high fertility would mean in terms of an age distribution of death. The best-fitting models (Coale and Demeny 1983) indicate gross reproductive rates of nearly three, for an average completed total fertility of around six children for women who have survived their whole reproductive span. Is this high enough for the indices and to overcome mortality at Tlajinga 33? It is slightly less than the seven or eight children thought to be the normal completed fertility of noncontracepting sedentary populations (see Hassan 1981 for discussion of this evidence), but higher than that estimated for the !Kung San (Howell 1979), who might be thought of as having moderate fertility, with just under five children in completed fertility. There are reasons, however, to suspect that Tlajinga 33 might not have been able to attain higher fertilities than six.

Frisch (1978) believes that the evidence for many historically known populations is for subfecundity to the eight to ten total children born commonly found in modern noncontracepting populations, especially among those in lower socioeconomic statuses. This is because females, if chronically undernourished and subject to hard physical labor to survive, are likely to have shorter and less efficient reproductive spans. Frisch amplifies the application of her "critical fat" hypothesis by postulating that if undernourished, a female is likely to have later menarche, earlier menopause, and a higher frequency of irregular menstrual cycles, because her fat reserves are not great enough to support a regular cycle. Also, lactational amenorrhea after a birth would probably last longer, and birth intervals would be longer. The result would be for a lower completed fertility of between six and seven.

Of course, the "critical fat" hypothesis has been criticized, and Frisch's points have not always been borne out in modern field studies (Scott and Johnston 1985). It does not seem to be something as simple as fat that has an effect upon menstrual cycles. However, there are various behaviors and health measures that can have an effect on the length of the birth interval (see Bongaarts and Potter 1983), but Frisch marshals good evidence that low socioeconomic status and lower fertility are related in historical demography. Similarly, longer birth intervals were also found among the poorer parishes in seventeenth-century London (Finlay 1981). Also, modern studies have shown that low-birthweight girls grow up to give birth to low-birthweight babies, which indicates a transgeneration effect (Martorell and González-Cossío 1987). Thus, problems in mortality, growth, and health could be present each generation.

It is, therefore, not inconceivable that Tlajinga 33 residents would have had less total fertility than may have been possible under better lifestyle conditions. This, together with the high mortality, increases the likelihood that over time Teotihuacan's poorer sectors would decline, even if there were periods of stability, and they would have been dependent on migration to keep up. The size of Tlajinga 33 seems about the same from the Late Tlamimilolpa to the Early Metepec, and the city population is considered stable during this period as well (Cowgill 1979). Thus, like European preindustrial cities, Teotihuacan was probably not able to reproduce itself internally and was dependent on some migration to maintain its numbers.

Teotihuacan and Its Hinterland

Preindustrial cities in the Old World had a complex relationship with their rural hinterlands on which they were dependent for food and new urban recruits. As a preindustrial city, Teotihuacan undoubtedly also had a complex relation with its rural areas. However, it also differed from Old World ones because of certain constraints present in the pre-Columbian New World. Sanders and Webster (1988: 529) have summarized these as the result of a society powered largely by human muscle, such that Meso-american agriculture was comparatively inefficient, per capita production of food surpluses was limited, ratios of food producers to nonagricultural specialists had to be high, and food extracted from hinterlands would have had to be fairly close so that the cost of human transport was supportable. Because of the dependence on human muscle, human labor was the main resource that could be controlled by an urban center.

Teotihuacan seems to have directly controlled its agricultural resources by concentrating a large proportion of the food producers within its borders, probably partially by some coercion. This may have buffered the Teotihuacan population from vagaries of food delivery, since the farmers lived in the city and could have been more easily monitored. However, such a concentration might have also left the city fairly vulnerable to serious local crop failures, because both the concentration of food producers and the limits of human transport meant that Teotihuacan usually met most of its food needs from a restricted area of nearby hinterland. If so, then certain characteristics of the history of the city became clearer.

The increase of Teotihuacan's size and population was very quick, after which it stabilized until the end (Cowgill 1979). Teotihuacan was obviously not growing, as many other Old World preindustrial cities were, even though the control of human labor and sheer size of its population were the keys to its polity's power and influence in Mesoamerica during its florescence. It might be thought that a growing Teotihuacan would have been in the rulers' best interest, but growth did not happen. It is possible that Teotihuacan could not get bigger and assure even poor compounds like Tlajinga 33 a bare living, given the agricultural-transport constraints. Thus, it is possible that stability of population was or became the main goal of the Teotihuacan polity. Getting smaller certainly would not have been in the best long-term interest of the city, but maintaining 2,000 functioning apartment compounds was. Thus, the internal decline of population would have meant that the city needed enough migration to at least overcome the shortfall.

Cities cannot be understood apart from their sociocultural settings (Fox 1977). In terms of Fox's analysis of urbanism, Teotihuacan was definitely an administrative city (see also Sanders and Webster 1988), combining both ceremonial or ideological functions with political ones as the capital, the home of the rulers and elites of the polity. The truth of this statement is clear archaeologically (see Chapter 2). Fox (1977: 33–34) divides urban variability along two dimensions: the extent of state power and its economic autonomy, that is, to what extent a city depends on rural areas for wealth or is itself the generator of economic productivity. The importance of these dimensions, although Fox did not discuss them in this light, is that both have an effect on that underlying aspect of urban society, migration from the rural area to the city. Cities need migrants, but how do they attract and get them? Powerful states obviously can have great coercive power to get migrants, but conversely, the more powerful the state and rigid the social structure, the less opportunities a city might present for advancement or betterment to a migrant and the less attractive it would be. For economics, obviously, the more autonomy a city provides, the more economic opportunities it has for attracting migrants. Teotihuacan was a powerful state, with imposing public buildings and a definite social structure, whose rigidity cannot be well defined at present. That is, membership in the elite and ruling class was probably by birth, but whether there were avenues for social mobility, as there were in the later Aztec polity, is unclear. However, in the economic sphere Teotihuacan's craft specialists, like those in Tlajinga 33, and the presence of significant market exchanges dominating daily life for even subsistence purposes allow for a fair amount of economic opportunity to residents and migrants. Thus, Teotihuacan could very well have had the power to coerce and the economy to attract migration.

Studies of migration, both in historical situations and in the modern world, work by analyzing the potential migrants and the factors that "push" them out of their homes or that "pull" them into a place or both (de Vries 1984). The push factors are often at work in the case of subsistence migrants, those who move because they must to survive. Pull migrants are often looking for better chances, not that they necessarily or usually find them. Subsistence migrants were often not very welcome in European cities, as they often appeared in large numbers and could produce vagrancy, but pull migrants would be beneficial (Clark and Souden 1987). Nevertheless, preindustrial European cities were dependent on lower-class migrants to provide labor, and most migrants were unskilled young people (de Vries 1984; Clark and Souden 1987). Both push and pull were present in European migration, and the potential migrants were those individuals resulting from the rural natural increase for whom there was no available land and who required alternative means of subsistence (de Vries 1984). The migration in Europe is thus a combination of the push and pull of lower-class individuals needed in the cities to provide cheap and ready labor and to replace directly those sectors of the urban population that could not reproduce themselves. That is, urban mortality was highest among the lower strata, and that was where migration was greatest. Although there was a potential to make a better life, and certainly some did so, the truth was that unskilled labor was doomed to remain poor and probably to die young and have more children die in those preindustrial European cities.

The Teotihuacan situation is certainly not the same as that for Europe. For one thing, it is now apparent from historical sources that the European population was always quite mobile (Clark and Souden 1987), basically because of the general nuclear family organization of European society. There is no evidence of such mobility in pre-Columbian Mesoamerica, but many population movements into and out of the Basin of Mexico that occurred during pre-Columbian times (see Sanders et al. 1979: Chapter 5) were undoubtedly due to migration. The propensity of people to move has probably been generally underestimated by many New World archaeologists. Nevertheless, Teotihuacan probably had both push and pull migration as well. It may well have coerced people into migrating into the city in order to keep numbers stable. It is not clear that in Teotihuacan times rural growth would have resulted in people who were surplus in relation to the available agricultural land. The rural population in the Basin of Mexico was growing during that time but would in later times grow even larger (see Sanders et al. 1979), so that any potential migrants could probably very well have remained in the rural areas. Thus, Teotihuacan may not have had the pool of potential migrants that characterized the European situation, and it therefore seems likely that most Teotihuacan migration was accomplished by pull, by attraction. The compound organization and economic needs for labor would provide opportunities for migrants and also allow them to be incorporated into city social organization very efficiently and in a way that provided some sense of security and belonging. What would have been the attraction of the city that would offset its poor health conditions, especially in the kinds of situations into which the migrants were most likely to end up? An administrative city like Teotihuacan was obviously the center of its polity, the ideological heart, and exceedingly dominant over its hinterland, such that for much of its history there were few other settlements with much population. There were probably ideological and political advantages, besides potential economic ones, to being a resident of the city, even in the poorer sectors, than in rural hamlets. These advantages probably were attractive to potential migrants, much as cities today still attract for the same reasons, such that the drawbacks of the urban lifestyle do not discourage people from trying it. One of the true paradoxes of human history is that preindustrial cities were "demographic sinks" and known to be unhealthy, but people have always flocked to them if it was feasible, as if they were not going to be victims. Life in Teotihuacan may have been unhealthy, not to mention quite odiferous during the dry season, but it offered more variety and stimulation than rural hamlets because of the people and the market, the potential marriage partners, the rituals, and the civic functions. Teotihuacan probably attracted the migrants it needed fairly easily but may have controlled them to keep numbers stable and to avoid growing too much, although this is pure conjecture. Teotihuacan probably had its share of vagrants and perhaps slums in perishable structures. Maybe it wanted to grow but just could not because of a combination of mortality conditions and limitations on food availability. Teotihuacan must be thought of as similar to many preindustrial cities in its dependence on a hinterland for both food and migrants, although it probably was not the dynamic source of economic productivity that European preindustrial cities were.

If Teotihuacan was at least maintaining its population of 125,000 to 200,000, how many migrants were needed? Using Tlajinga 33 as a guide to the possible magnitude of the internal decline, the shortfall was probably around 0.5% per year, or 5 persons per 1,000 population. Thus, on a yearly basis, Teotihuacan was losing from 625 to 1,000 people, who would need to be replaced by migration. That is not an excessive number, but the additional people would have had to come from a larger area than just the rural population of the Basin of Mexico, which was about 70,000 people during the Middle Horizon of Teotihuacan florescence (Sanders et al. 1979: 218). The number of needed migrants represents the total natural increase of a rural population of around 200,000 growing at 0.5% per year. Realistically, the total natural increase was probably not moving to Teotihuacan, so at least double or triple the rural population, to around 600,000, would be needed to provide the migrants. If the rural growth rate was that which was characteristic for most of the Basin of Mexico, 0.3% per year (Sanders et al. 1979), then the total natural increase of 350,000 rural inhabitants would be needed. Again, more realistic would be double or triple these numbers, and it can be seen that Teotihuacan may have needed nearly a million people under its control or influence in the hinterland to assure its demographic stability. That is quite a large polity, and it is not clear that Teotihuacan controlled such numbers.

The history of the Teotihuacan rural populations studied archaeologically is informative, as reconstructed by Sanders et al. (1979: 105–129). Early in its history 80% of the population of the whole Basin of Mexico was at Teotihuacan itself in a massive relocation, which was probably partly coerced. But by the first century A.D., there was a resettlement in the basin but probably under the strong control of the city. During the Middle Horizon, or Classic period itself, the Basin of Mexico rural population doubled. Although dramatic, this growth was slower than earlier growth rates in the basin. The area around Teotihuacan and the central portion of the basin were where most of the population resided and probably formed the core of the Teotihuacan resource zone. The rest of the basin was sparsely settled.

Outside the Basin of Mexico, but near Teotihuacan, the effects of the city were also visible. Although these areas were probably under Teotihuacan influence, they were more likely part of a secondary resource zone, not depended on for daily subsistence (see Sanders et al. 1979). Settlement to the north in the Tula region and to the east in the Puebla-Tlaxcala area was oriented to Teotihuacan in terms of the spatial organization of larger settlements, the architecture, and the ceramics. Teotihuacan's influence was even felt to the southeast of the basin in eastern Morelos (Hirth 1978). The effect of the city on the hinterland could have been dramatic. For example, in the Puebla-Tlaxcala area the population was more rural, the total population was lower, and the area was rather more stagnant during Teotihuacan times (Tenanyecac Phase A.D. 100–650) than it had been earlier or later (García Cook 1981).

Thus, there is archaeological evidence of a large hinterland under Teotihuacan influence, if not direct control. Whether this hinterland countained enough people to provide the necessary migrants is not clear. It does seem that the city's effect upon the rural population was variable. There was growth in the Basin of Mexico and Tula but probable decrease in Puebla-Tlaxcala, for example. There are European examples where the migration to urban centers actually swamped the natural increase of the rural populations, and they declined (de Vries 1984). This may well have happened to some of Teotihuacan's hinterland. The doubling of the Basin of Mexico is slower than earlier growth rates, to 0.1% from 0.3% per year (Sanders et al. 1979: 183–184), so that even though the rural population grew, some of its surplus was probably being drawn to the city or perhaps to the other regions of Teotihuacan control. The shifts in rural population and the migration needs of the city would have put quite a premium on population during the Middle Horizon. To support both rural growth and urban replacement, the whole system would have required sustained growth from a fairly large rural population base. It is quite possible that even the rural growth, especially early in the Middle Horizon, had been fueled by migration from areas outside the hinterland. Nevertheless, the migrant needs of the city suggest a hypothesis for future testing. Was the size of the hinterland controlled by Teotihuacan influenced by its migration needs?

Again, with Tlajinga 33 as a model, there is evidence that perhaps mortality conditions worsened through time, such that the Late Xolalpan had a very high mortality rate and may have been more dependent on migration than the Tlamimilolpa period. It could be that it became more difficult to recruit new migrants as conditions worsened. The process would have been made even more difficult by some changes at Teotihuacan itself, as well as external events. Within the city, it was seen in Chapter 4, the social stratification system of the city may have become more simplified and perhaps more rigid. There was a clearer demarcation of wealthy and poor, and poorer compounds like Tlajinga 33 no longer had access to the exotic goods they had had earlier. Such social rigidity may have made the city less attractive to migrants just at the time that more might have been needed. Perhaps the need for, and influx of, more lower-class migrants made the elites uneasy and caused the system to more clearly separate the powerful and wealthy from others in the culture. Other urban centers were also growing during the Late Xolalpan, such as Atzcapotzalco, Cholula, and Xochicalco, and they may have started to siphon off increasing numbers of potential migrants.

If the population of Teotihuacan started to decline precipitously, especially among its poorer residents, and it could no longer attract the migrants, the process could have been an important factor in causing the downfall of the urban polity. Tlajinga 33 was probably abandoned at least 50 years before the end of the Teotihuacan polity it had existed under, an indication that the lifestyle of the city had failed its lower-class artisans. It may have become impossible to maintain the compound as a separate craft entity because of high mortality and the lack of new migrants. The remaining residents removed their sacred objects from the shaft tomb and perhaps joined another nearby compound. Tlajinga 33 probably no longer had enough productive adults available to do the craft specializations on its own.

A loss of population, perhaps every year more precipitously, for at least 50 years before the Teotihuacan central area was sacked meant the loss of power and dominance in that cultural system. People had been the source of Teotihuacan's dominance, and without them, the system could not go on. Teotihuacan remained a large settlement for the rest of the pre-Columbian period, but much of the city was abandoned, and it never again came to dominate more than its immediate surroundings. Population growth had been the cause of its rise, and population loss was probably instrumental in its fall.

Conclusion

A generalization that can be drawn from the Tlajinga 33 paleo-demographic study, pending further evidence, is that Teotihuacan was fairly similar in demographic characteristics to other preindustrial cities.

The importance of this reconstruction is that the effects of dense population upon mortality and health, where public sanitation systems are inadequate, are likely to be fairly uniform across environments and cultures. Although Teotihuacan may not have suffered greatly from waves of epidemic infectious diseases as had Old World cities (McNeill 1976), the evidence from Tlajinga 33 is that physiological stress in the form of infection and undernutrition was common, if not chronic, among the residents. It seems reasonable that the dense population together with a lack of water for part of the year would have supported a high load of endemic infections and parasitic diseases. These infections would have been continually circulating in the population. The evidence for probable lifelong undernutrition in Tlajinga 33 indicates that Teotihuacan was also not totally successful in supporting its populations, especially the full-time craft specialists in the lower social strata. As is common with known preindustrial cities, the Tlajinga 33 population is best modeled as barely stable, or slightly declining, with high infant mortality and a short average lifespan for adults. Over the long run, such a demographic profile would lead to a declining resident population, and as Teotihuacan would then not have been self-sustaining in reproduction, it was ultimately dependent on some migration.

Tlajinga 33 is the only skeletal population presently available and studied by the use of recent techniques for aging and paleopathological indications. Its evidence at the moment carries considerable importance and has to be treated as representative of the majority of the population of Teotihuacan until more information is available. It is not unreasonable that a dense population under the energy and sanitation systems present in the culture would have suffered deleterious effects on individual health and life expectancy. Thus, it is expected that future evidence will support the Tlajinga 33 reconstruction, especially for the poorer sectors. The wealthy sectors may very well reveal a much better health and mortality profile, although in Europe, wealthy sectors were generally just able to replace themselves. This study of the Tlajinga 33 skeletal population is only one window into the life of the city of Teotihuacan, but its demographic and health characteristics provide a wealth of information regarding what kind of place the city was to live in. Furthermore, the study successfully demonstrates that many of the methodological objections to the use of paleodemography disappear when the archaeological (cultural) context of the population is understood. Paleodemography provides valid and important insights into the lives and deaths of past populations.

Metric Measurements Used in the Discriminant-Function Sexing

Cranium

1. The maximum length of the skull, from the most anterior point of the frontal, in the midline, to the most distant point on the occipital, in the midline.

2. The greatest breadth of the cranium perpendicular to the median sagittal place and avoiding any supramastoid crest.

3. The maximum breadth of the palate taken on the outside of the alveolar borders, at the level of the second molars.

4. The length of the mastoid measured perpendicular to the plane determined by the Frankfort plane. The upper arm of the sliding calipers is aligned with the upper border of the auditory meatus, and the distance to the tip of the mastoid is measured.

Mandible

1. The mandibular body height as measured between the first and second molars on the buccal surface.

2. The maximum thickness of the mandibular body measured at the level of the second molar.

3. The smallest anteroposterior diameter of the ramus of the mandible.

4. The distance between the most anterior point of the mandibular body (gnathion) to the most posterior point on the ramus (not including the condyle).

5. The height measured from the uppermost point on the condyle to the middle of the inferior border of the body (height of ramus).
6. The maximum diameter, externally, between left and right gonion (bigonial breadth).
7. The gonial angle.

Dentition

1. The maximum mesiodistal diameter taken at the level of the cemento-enamel junction on all crowns of the mandibular and maxillary teeth. Note: This is not the standard measurement but was used as it was thought this might avoid problems of attrition and broken occlusal surfaces in taking the diameter. It was not particularly successful in the discrimination.
2. The maximum buccolingual diameter taken on all crowns of the mandibular and maxillary teeth.

Antimeres, where present, were not used in the analysis.

Postcranial Measurements

1. The greatest diameter of the femoral head.
2. The maximum femoral length.
3. The least transverse diameter of the femoral shaft.
4. The circumference at midpoint of the femoral shaft.
5. The width of the distal end of the femur (epicondylar breadth).
6. The height of the sciatic notch, measured as a perpendicular from where the superior border of the notch meets the auricular surface of the anterior border of the notch.
7. The acetabulosciatic breadth, measured from the median point on the anterior border of the sciatic notch (halfway between the ischial spine and the notch apex) to the acetabular border and perpendicular to both borders.
8. The maximum length of the humerus.
9. The minimum circumference of the humeral shaft.
10. The maximum diameter of the humeral head.
11. The maximum width of the distal end of the humerus (epicondylar breadth).

12. The maximum length of the clavicle.

13. The circumference of the clavicle at midshaft.

14. The maximum length of the radius.

15. The circumference of the radius at the midpoint of the shaft.

16. The circumference of the head of the radius.

17. The maximum mediolateral breadth of the distal epiphysis of the radius.

18. The maximum length of the ulna.

19. The maximum mediolateral breadth of the olecranon process of the ulna.

20. The transverse diameter of the shaft of the ulna taken just under the radial notch.

21. The maximum length of the tibia.

22. The maximum anteroposterior diameter of the tibial shaft at midpoint.

23. The maximum mediolateral breadth of the tibial shaft at midpoint.

24. The maximum anteroposterior diameter of the tibial shaft at the nutrient foramen.

25. The maximum mediolateral diameter of the tibial shaft at the nutrient foramen.

26. The least circumference of the tibial shaft.

27. The maximum breadth of the proximal epiphysis of the tibia.

28. The maximum length, from the most cephalic to the most caudal point, of the glenoid fossa of the scapula.

29. The maximum breadth of the glenoid fossa taken perpendicular to the maximum length.

30. The total breadth of the atlas vertebra measured between the apices of the transverse processes.

Note: These measurements are adapted from Giles (1970) and Bass (1987), but numbers 19 and 20 of the postcranial measurements were defined for this study.

References Cited

Acsádi, G., and J. Nemeskéri
1970   *History of Human Lifespan and Mortality.* Akadémiai Kiadó, Budapest.

Adams, M. S., and J. D. Niswander
1968   Birthweight of North American Indians. *Human Biology* 40: 226–234.

Altschul, J. H.
1987   The social districts of Teotihuacan. In *Teotihuacan: Nuevos Datos, Nuevas Síntesis, Nuevos Problemas,* ed. E. McClung de Tapia and E. Rattray, pp. 191–218. Universidad Nacional Autónoma de México, Mexico.

Ammerman, A. J., L. L. Cavalli-Sforza, and D. K. Wagener
1976   Toward the estimation of population growth in Old World prehistory. In *Demographic Anthropology,* ed. E. B. W. Zubrow, pp. 27–62. University of New Mexico Press, Albuquerque.

Anderson, N. A., E. W. Brown, and R. A. Lyon
1943   Causes of prematurity. *American Journal of Diseases of Children* 65: 523–534.

Angel, J. L.
1969   The basis of paleodemography. *American Journal of Physical Anthropology* 30: 427–428.
1984   Health as a crucial factor in the changes from hunting to developed farming in the eastern Mediterranean. In *Paleopathology at the Origins of Agriculture,* ed. M. N. Cohen and G. J. Armelagos, pp. 51–74. Academic Press, Orlando, Florida.

Angulo, J.
1987   Nuevas consideraciones sobre Tetitla y los llamados conjuntos departamentales. In *Teotihuacan: Nuevos Datos, Nuevas Síntesis, Nuevos Problemas,* ed. E. McClung de Tapia and E. Rattray, pp. 275–316. Universidad Nacional Autónoma de México, Mexico.

Armelagos, G. J., J. H. Mielke, K. H. Owen, D. P. Van Gerven, J. R. Dewey, and P. E. Mahler
1972   Bone growth and development in prehistoric populations from Sudanese Nubia. *Journal of Human Evolution* 1: 89–119.

Asch, D. L.
1976   The Middle Woodland population of the lower Illinois Valley: A study in paleodemographic methods. *Northwestern University Archeology Program, Scientific Papers* no. 1. Chicago.

Baker, B. J., and G. J. Armelagos
1988   The origin and antiquity of syphilis: Paleopathological diagnosis and interpretation. *Current Anthropology* 29: 703–737.

Baker, P. T., and W. T. Sanders
1972   Demographic studies in anthropology. *Annual Review of Anthropology* 1: 151–178.

Bass, W. M.
1987   *Human Osteology: A Laboratory and Field Manual.* Missouri Archaeological Society, University of Missouri, Columbia, Missouri.

Batres, L.
1906   Teotihuacan. *Memoria al XV Congreso Internacional de Americanistas, Quebec.* Mexico City.

Beloch, K. J.
1886   *Die Bevolkerung der grieschish-romishcen Welt.* Leipzig.

Benfer, R. A.
1968   An analysis of a prehistoric skeletal population, Casas Grandes, Chihuahua, Mexico. Ph.D. dissertation, Department of Anthropology, University of Texas, Austin.

Bennett, K. A.
1973   On the estimation of some demographic characteristics of a prehistoric population from the American Southwest. *American Journal of Physical Anthropology* 39: 223–232.

Binford, L. R.
1968   Post-Pleistocene adaptations. In *New Perspectives in Archeology*, ed. S. R. Binford and L. R. Binford, pp. 313–341. Aldine, Chicago.
1971   Mortuary practices: Their study and potential. In *Approaches to the Social Dimensions of Mortuary Practices*, ed. J. A. Brown, pp. 6–29. Memoirs of the Society for American Archaeology, no. 25. Washington, D.C.

Binford, L. R., and W. J. Chasko, Jr.
1976   Nunamiut demographic history: A provocative case. In *Demographic Anthropology*, ed. E. B. W. Zubrow, pp. 63–143. University of New Mexico Press, Albuquerque.

Black, T. K., III
1978   A new method for assessing the sex of fragmentary skeletal remains: Femoral shaft circumference. *American Journal of Physical Anthropology* 48: 227–232.

Blakely, R. L.
1977   Sociocultural implications of demographic data from Etowah, Georgia. In *Biocultural Adaptation in Prehistoric America*, ed. R. L. Blakely, pp. 45–66. Southern Anthropological Society Proceedings no. 11. University of Georgia Press, Athens.

Blakey, M. L.
1981   An analysis of hypoplasias and hypocalcification in deciduous dentition from Dickson Mounds. In *Biocultural Adaptation: Comprehensive Approaches to Skeletal Analysis*, ed. D. L. Martin and M. P. Bumstead, pp. 24–34. Department of Anthropology, University of Massachusetts at Amherst, Research Report no. 20. Amherst.

Blakey, M. L., and G. J. Armelagos
1985   Deciduous enamel defects in prehistoric Americans from Dickson Mounds: Prenatal and postnatal stress. *American Journal of Physical Anthropology* 66: 371–380.

Bocquet-Appel, J-P., and C. Masset
1982   Farewell to paleodemography. *Journal of Human Evolution* 11: 321–333.

Bongaarts, J.
1980   Does malnutrition affect fecundity? A summary of the evidence. *Science* 208: 564–569.

Bongaarts, J., and R. G. Potter
1983   *Fertility, Biology, and Behavior: An Analysis of the Proximate Determinants.* Academic Press, New York.

Boserup, E.
1965   *The Conditions of Agricultural Growth.* Aldine, Chicago.

Boucher, B. J.
1957   Sex differences in the foetal pelvis. *American Journal of Physical Anthropology* 15: 51–54.

Bourgeois-Pichat, J.
1966   *The Concept of a Stable Population: Application to the Study of Populations of Countries with Incomplete Population Statistics.* United Nations ST/SOA/ Series A139, New York.

Boyd, R., and P. J. Richerson
1985   *Culture and the Evolutionary Process.* University of Chicago Press, Chicago.

Brans, Y. W., M. B. Escobedo, R. H. Hayashi, R. W. Huff, K. S. Kayan-Hallet, and R. S. Ramamurthy
1984   Perinatal mortality in a large perinatal center: Five-year review of 31,000 births. *American Journal of Obstetrics and Gynecology* 148: 284–289.

Brass, W.
1968   A note on the Brass method of fertility estimation. In *The Demography of Tropical Africa*, ed. W. Brass et al., pp. 140–142. Princeton University Press, Princeton, New Jersey.

Brown, J. A.
1971   The dimensions of status in the burials at Spiro. In *Approaches to the Social Dimensions of Mortuary Practices*, ed. J. A. Brown, pp. 92–112. Memoirs of the Society for American Archaeology no. 25. Washington, D.C.

Buikstra, J. E., and L. W. Konigsberg
1985   Paleodemography: Critiques and controversies. *American Anthropologist* 87: 316–333.

Buikstra, J. E., L. W. Konigsberg, and J. Bullington
1986   Fertility and the development of agriculture in the prehistoric Midwest. *American Antiquity* 51: 528–546.

Burnet, M., and D. O. White
1972   *Natural History of Infectious Disease*. 4th ed. Cambridge University Press, Cambridge.

Cabrera, R., et al.
1982   *El Proyecto Arqueológico Teotihuacan, Teotihuacan 80–82, Primeros Resultados*. INAH, Mexico City.

Caldwell, J. C.
1981   The mechanisms of demographic change in historical perspective. *Population Studies* 35: 5–227.

Caldwell, J. C., and P. Caldwell
1977   The role of marital sexual abstinence in determining fertility: A study of the Yoruba in Nigeria. *Population Studies* 31: 193–217.

Caldwell, J., P. Caldwell, and B. Caldwell
1987   Anthropology and demography: The mutual reinforcement of speculation and research. *Current Anthropology* 28: 25–44.

Carneiro, R. L.
1970   Theory of the origin of the state. *Science* 169: 733–738.
1985   Comments on "Darwinian selection, symbolic variation, and the evolution of culture." *Current Anthropology* 26: 77–78.

Carneiro, R. L., and D. Hilse
1966   On determining the probable rate of population growth during the Neolithic. *American Anthropologist* 68: 179–181.

Carr-Saunders, A. M.
1922   *The Population Problem: A Study in Human Evolution.* Clarendon Press, Oxford.

Chagnon, N. A.
1975   Genealogy, solidarity and relatedness: Limits to local group size and patterns of fissioning in an expanding population. *Yearbook of Physical Anthropology* 19: 95–110.
1979   Mate competition favoring close kin, and village fissioning among the Yanomamö Indians. In *Evolutionary Biology and Human Social Behavior: The Anthropological Approach,* ed. N. A. Chagnon and W. Irons, pp. 86–131. Duxbury Press, North Scituate, Massachusetts.

Chandler, T., and G. Fox
1974   *3000 Years of Urban Growth.* Academic Press, New York.

Clark, J. E.
1986   From mountains to molehills: A critical review of Teotihuacan's obsidian industry. In *Research in Economic Anthropology,* supp. 2, ed. B. L. Isaac, pp. 23–74. JAI Press, Greenwich, Connecticut.

Clark, P.
1987   Migrants in the city: The process of social adaptation in English towns, 1500–1800. In *Migration and Society in Early Modern England,* ed. P. Clark and D. Souden, pp. 267–291. Barnes and Noble Books, Totowa, New Jersey.

Clark, P., and D. Souden
1987   Introduction. In *Migration and Society in Early Modern England,* ed. P. Clark and D. Souden, pp. 11–48. Barnes and Noble Books, Totowa, New Jersey.

Coale, A. J., and P. Demeny
1966   *Regional Model Life Tables and Stable Populations.* Princeton University Press, Princeton, New Jersey.

Coale, A. J., and P. Demeny with B. Vaughn
1983   *Regional Model Life Tables and Stable Populations.* 2nd ed. Academic Press, Orlando, Florida.

Cohen, M. N.
1977   *The Food Crisis in Prehistory: Over-Population and the Origins of Agriculture.* Yale University Press, New Haven, Connecticut.

Cohen, M. N., and G. J. Armelagos, eds.
1984   *Paleopathology at the Origins of Agriculture.* Academic Press, Orlando, Florida.

Coid, C. R., A. B. G. Landsdown, and I. R. McFadyen
1977   Fetal growth retardation and low birthweight following infection in pregnancy. In *Infections and Pregnancy,* ed. C. R. Coid. Academic Press, London.

Cook, D. C.
1981   Mortality, age structure and status in the interpretation of stress indicators in prehistoric skeletons: A dental example from the Lower Illinois Valley. In *The Archaeology of Death*, ed. R. Chapman, I. Kinnes, and K. Randsborg, pp. 133–144. Cambridge University Press, London and New York.

Cook, D. C., and J. E. Buikstra
1979   Health and differential survival in prehistoric populations: Prenatal dental defects. *American Journal of Physical Anthropology* 51: 549–554.

Cook, S. F.
1946   The incidence and significance of disease among the Aztecs and related tribes. *Hispanic American Historical Review* 26: 320–335.
1973   *Prehistoric Demography*. Addison-Wesley Modules in Anthropology no. 16. Reading, Massachusetts.

Corruccini, R. S., E. M. Brandon, and J. S. Handler
1989   Inferring fertility from relative mortality in historically controlled cemetery remains from Barbados. *American Antiquity* 54: 609–614.

Costa, R. L., Jr.
1986   Asymmetry of the mandibular condyle in Haida Indians. *American Journal of Physical Anthropology* 70: 119–124.

Cowgill, G. L.
1975   On causes and consequences of ancient and modern population changes. *American Anthropologist* 77: 505–525.
1979   Teotihuacan internal militaristic competition, and the fall of the Classic Maya. In *Maya Archaeology and Ethnohistory*, ed. N. Hammond and G. R. Willey, pp. 51–62. University of Texas Press, Austin.
1983   Rulership and the Ciudadela: Political inferences from Teotihuacan architecture. In *Civilization in the Ancient Americas: Essays in Honor of Gordon R. Willey*, ed. R. M. Leventhal and A.L. Kolata, pp. 313–343. University of New Mexico Press, Albuquerque, and Peabody Museum of Archaeology and Ethnology, Harvard University, Cambridge, Massachusetts.

Cowgill, G. L., J. H. Altschul, and R. S. Sload
1984   Spatial analysis of Teotihuacan: A Mesoamerican metropolis. In *Intrasite Spatial Analysis in Archaeology*, ed. H. J. Hietala, pp. 154–195. Cambridge University Press, London and New York.

Cronk, C. E.
1983   Fetal growth as measured by ultrasound. *Yearbook of Physical Anthropology* 26: 65–89.

Dávalos E.
1965   La osteopatología en los Teotihuacanos. *Anales* 18: 25–40. Instituto Nacional de Antropología e Historia, Mexico City.

Davis, K.
1973   *Cities and Mortality.* International Population and Urban Research, Institute of International Studies, University of California at Berkeley, reprint no. 433.

de Vries, J.
1984   *European Urbanization 1500–1800.* Harvard University Press, Cambridge, Massachusetts.

DeVore, S., and T. White
1978   *The Appetites of Man.* Anchor Press/Doubleday, Garden City, New York.

Dewey, J. R., G. J. Armelagos, and M. H. Bartley
1969   Femoral cortical involution in three archaeological populations. *Human Biology* 41: 13–28.

Ditch, L., and J. Rose
1972   A multivariate dental sexing technique. *American Journal of Physical Anthropology* 37: 61–64.

Dittrick, J., and J. M. Suchey
1986   Sex determination of prehistoric central California skeletal remains using discriminant analysis of the femur and humerus. *American Journal of Physical Anthropology* 70: 3–9.

Dobson, P. C., D. A. Abell, and N. A. Beischer
1982   Antenatal pregnancy complications and fetal growth retardation. *Australia and New Zealand Journal of Obstetrics and Gynaecology* 22: 203–205.

Dobyns, H. F.
1983   *Their Number Become Thinned.* University of Tennessee Press, Knoxville.

Dumond, D. E.
1975   The limitations of human population: A natural history. *Science* 187: 713–721.

Dunn, F.
1968   Epidemiological factors: Health and disease in hunter-gatherers. In *Man the Hunter,* ed. R. Lee and I. DeVore. Aldine, Chicago.

Durán, Fr. Diego
1964   *The Aztecs: The History of the Indies of New Spain.* Translated by Doris Heyden and Fernando Horcasites. Orion, New York.

Durand, J. D.
1960   Mortality estimates from Roman tombstone inscriptions. *American Journal of Sociology* 65: 365–373.

Dyke, B., and J. W. MacCluer, eds.
1974   *Computer Simulation in Human Population Studies.* Academic Press, New York.

Eaton, J. W., and A. J. Mayer
1953   The social biology of very high fertility among the Hutterites. *Human Biology* 25: 206–264.

El-Najjar, M. Y., D. J. Ryan, C. G. Turner III, and B. Lozoff
1976   The etiology of porotic hyperostosis among the prehistoric Anasazi Indians of the Southwestern United States. *American Journal of Physical Anthropology* 44: 477–488.

Faulhaber, J.
1965   La población de Tlatilco, México, caracterizada por sus entierros. *Homenaje Comas* 2: 83–121.

Faulkner, F.
1981   Maternal nutrition and fetal growth. *American Journal of Clinical Nutrition* 34: 769–774.

Ferguson, A. C.
1978   Prolonged impairment of cellular immunity in children with intrauterine growth retardation. *Journal of Pediatrics* 93: 52–56.

Finlay, R.
1981   *Population and Metropolis: The Demography of London 1580–1650*. Cambridge University Press, Cambridge.

Fix, A. G.
1977   *The Demography of the Semai Senoi*. Museum of Anthropology, University of Michigan, Anthropological Papers no. 62. Ann Arbor.

Fox, R. G.
1977   *Urban Anthropology: Cities in Their Cultural Settings*. Prentice-Hall, Englewood Cliffs, New Jersey.

France, D. L.
1988   Osteometry at muscle origin and insertion in sex determination. *American Journal of Physical Anthropology* 76: 515–526.

Frisancho, A. R., and S. M. Garn
1970   Childhood retardation resulting in reduction of adult body size due to lesser adolescent skeletal delay. *American Journal of Physical Anthropology* 33: 325–336.

Frisch, R. E.
1974   A method of prediction of age at menarche from height and weight at ages 9 through 13 years. *Pediatrics* 53: 384–390.
1978   Population, food intake and fertility. *Science* 199: 22–30.

Frisch, R. E., and J. W. McArthur
1974   Menstrual cycles: Fatness as a determinant of minimum weight for height necessary for their maintenance or onset. *Science* 185: 949–951.

Frisch, R. E., R. Revelle, and S. Cook
1971   Height, weight and age at menarche and the "critical fat" hypothesis. *Science* 194: 1148.

Frost, H. M.
1987   Secondary osteon populations: An algorithm for determining mean bone tissue age. *Yearbook of Physical Anthropology* 30: 221–238.

Gage, T. B.
1985   Demographic estimation from anthropological data: New methods. *Current Anthropology* 26: 644–647.

Gage, T. B., B. Dyke, and P. G. Riviere
1984   Estimating mortality from two censuses: An application to the Trio of Surinam. *Human Biology* 56: 489–502.

Gamsu, H.
1977   Health of mother, fetus and neonate following bacterial, fungal and protozoal infections during pregnancy. In *Infections and Pregnancy*, ed. C. R. Coid. Academic Press, London.

García Cook, A.
1981   The historical importance of Tlaxcala in the cultural development of the Central Highlands. In *Supplement to the Handbook of Middle American Indians*, vol. 1, *Archaeology*, ed. J. A. Sabloff, pp. 244–276. University of Texas Press, Austin.

Garn, S. M.
1970   *The Earlier Gain and Later Loss of Cortical Bone in Nutritional Perspective.* Charles C. Thomas, Springfield, Illinois.

Garn, S. M., C. G. Rohmann, and M. A. Guzman
1966   Malnutrition and skeletal development in the preschool child. In *Preschool Child Malnutrition*. National Academy of Science, National Research Council, Washington, D.C.

Garn, S. M., C. G. Rohmann, and B. Wagner
1967   Bone loss as a general phenomenon in man. *Federal Proceedings* 26: 1729–1731.

Garn, S. M., C. G. Rohmann, M. Behar, F. Niteri, and M. A. Guzman
1964   Compact bone deficiency in protein-calorie malnutrition. *Science* 145: 1444–1445.

Garn, S. M., F. N. Silverman, K. P. Hertzog, and C. G. Rohmann
1968   Lines and bands of increased density: Their implication to growth and development. *Medical Radiography and Photography* 44: 58–89.

Gebre-Medhin, M., and A. Gobezie
1975   Dietary intake in the third trimester of pregnancy and birthweight of offspring among nonprivileged and privileged women. *American Journal of Clinical Nutrition* 28: 1322–1329.

Genovés, S.
1967   Proportionality of the long bones and their relation to status among Mesoamericans. *American Journal of Physical Anthropology* 26: 67–77.

Gilbert, B. M., and T. W. McKern
1973   A method for aging the female os pubis. *American Journal of Physical Anthropology* 38: 31–38.

Giles, E.
1970   Discriminant function sexing of the human skeleton. In *Personal Identification in Mass Disasters*, ed. T. D. Stewart, pp. 99–109. Smithsonian Institution, Washington, D.C.

Goldstein, L. G.
1980   *Mississippian Mortuary Practices: A Case Study of Two Cemeteries in the Lower Illinois Valley.* Northwestern University Archeological Program, Scientific Papers, no. 4. Chicago.

Goldstein, M. C., P. Tsarong, C. M. Beall
1983   High altitude hypoxia, culture, and human fecundity/fertility: A comparative study. *American Anthropologist* 85: 28–49.

Goodman, A. H., and G. J. Armelagos
1985   Factors affecting the distribution of enamel hypoplasias within the human permanent dentition. *American Journal of Physical Anthropology* 68: 479–494.
1988   Childhood stress and decreased longevity in a prehistoric population. *American Anthropologist* 90: 936–944.
1989   Infant and childhood morbidity and mortality risks in archaeological populations. *World Archaeology* 21: 225–242.

Goodman, A. H., and G. R. Clark
1981   Harris lines as indicators of stress in prehistoric Illinois populations. In *Biocultural Adaptation: Comprehensive Approaches to Skeletal Analysis*, ed. D. L. Martin and M. P. Bumstead, pp. 35–46. Department of Anthropology, University of Massachusetts at Amherst Research Reports, no. 20. Amherst.

Goodman, A. H., G. J. Armelagos, and J. Rose
1980   Enamel hypoplasias as indicators of stress in three prehistoric populations from Illinois. *Human Biology* 52: 515–528.

Goodman, A. H., J. Lallo, G. J. Armelagos, and J. C. Rose
1984a   Health changes at Dickson Mounds, Illinois (A.D. 950–1300). In *Paleopathology at the Origins of Agriculture*, ed. M. N. Cohen and G. J. Armelagos, pp. 271–305. Academic Press, Orlando, Florida.

Goodman, A. H., D. L. Martin, G. J. Armelagos, and G. Clark
1984b   Indications of stress from bone and teeth. In *Paleopathology at the Origins of Agriculture*, ed. M. N. Cohen and G. J. Armelagos, pp. 13–50. Academic Press, Orlando, Florida.

Goodman, A. H., R. B. Thomas, A. C. Swedlund, and G. J. Armelagos
1988   Biocultural perspectives on stress in prehistoric, historical, and contemporary population research. *Yearbook of Physical Anthropology* 31: 169–202.

Gordon, J. E., I. D. Chitkara, and J. B. Wyon
1963   Weanling diarrhea. *American Journal of Medical Science* 245: 345–377.

Gordon, J. E., J. B. Wyon, and W. Ascoli
1967   The second year death rate in less developed countries. *American Journal of Medical Science* 254: 121–144.

Greenwood, D. J.
1984   *The Taming of Evolution*. Cornell University Press, Ithaca, New York.

Guthrie, H. A.
1975   *Introductory Nutrition*. 3rd ed. C. V. Mosby, Saint Louis, Missouri.

Hall, R. L.
1978   A test of paleodemographic models. *American Antiquity* 43: 715–729.

Hamilton, M. E.
1982   Sexual dimorphism in skeletal samples. In *Sexual Dimorphism in Homo Sapiens*, ed. R. L. Hall, pp. 107–163. Praeger, New York.

Hammel, E. A., and N. Howell
1987   Research in population and culture: An evolutionary framework. *Current Anthropology* 28: 141–160.

Handwerker, W. P.
1981   Reproductive choices and behavior: A test of two theories of fertility variation with data from Monrovia, Liberia. *Medical Anthropology* 5: 368–381.
1983   The first demographic transition: An analysis of subsistence choices and reproductive consequences. *American Anthropologist* 85: 5–27.

Harner, M. J.
1970   Population pressure and the social evolution of agriculturalists. *Southwestern Journal of Anthropology* 26: 67–86.

Harpending, H. C., and L. Wandsnider
1982   Population structures of Ghanzi and Ngamiland !Kung. In *Current Developments in Anthropological Genetics*, ed. M. H. Crawford and J. Mielke, pp. 29–50. Plenum Press, New York.

Hassan, F. A.
1981   *Demographic Archaeology*. Academic Press, New York.

Hatch, J. W.
1976   Status in death: Principles of ranking in Dallas culture mortuary remains. Ph.D. dissertation, Department of Anthropology, Pennsylvania State University, University Park.

Hatch, J. W., P. S. Willey, and E. E. Hunt, Jr.
1983   Indicators of status-related stress in Dallas society: Transverse lines and cortical thickness in long bones. *Midcontinental Journal of Archaeology* 8: 49–71.

Haviland, W. A.
1967   Stature at Tikal, Guatemala: Implications for ancient Maya demography and social organization. *American Antiquity* 32: 316–325.

Hayden, B.
1975   The carrying capacity dilemma. In *Population Studies in Archaeology and Biological Anthropology: A Symposium*, ed. A. C. Swedlund, pp. 11–21. Memoirs of the Society for American Archaeology, no. 30. Washington, D.C.

Henneberg, M.
1976   Reproductive possibilities and estimations of the biological dynamics of earlier human populations. In *The Demographic Evolution of Human Populations*, ed. R. H. Ward and K. M. Weiss, pp. 41–48. Academic Press, London.

Himes, J. H., R. Martorelli, J.-P. Habicht, C. Yarbrough, R. M. Malina, and R. E. Klein
1975   Patterns of cortical bone growth in malnourished preschool children. *Human Biology* 47: 337–350.

Hirth, K. G.
1978   Teotihuacan regional population administration in eastern Morelos. *World Anthropology* 9: 320–333.

Hirth, K. G., and W. Swezey
1976   The changing nature of the Teotihuacan Classic: A regional perspective from Manzanilla, Puebla. In *Las Fronteras de Mesoamerica: XIV Mesa Redonda*, vol. 2. Sociedad Mexicana de Antropología, Mexico City.

Hodges, D. C.
1987   Health and agricultural intensification in the prehistoric Valley of Oaxaca, Mexico. *American Journal of Physical Anthropology* 73: 323–332.

Hopkins, K.
1967   On the probable age structure of the Roman population. *Population Studies* 20: 245–264.

Hopkins, M. R.
1987   An explication of the plans of some Teotihuacan apartment compounds. In *Teotihuacan: Nuevos Datos, Nuevas Síntesis, Nuevos Problemas*, ed. E. McClung de Tapia and E. Rattray, pp. 369–388. Universidad Nacional Autónoma de México, Mexico City.

Horowitz, S., and G. J. Armelagos with K. Wachter
1988   On generating birth rates from skeletal populations. *American Journal of Physical Anthropology* 76: 189–196.

Howell, N.
1976   Toward a uniformitarian theory of human paleodemography. In *The Demographic Evolution of Human Populations*, ed. R. H. Ward and K. M. Weiss, pp. 25–40. Academic Press, London.
1979   *Demography of the Dobe !Kung.* Academic Press, New York.
1982   Village composition implied by a paleodemographic life table: The Libben site. *American Journal of Physical Anthropology* 59: 263–269.
1986   Demographic anthropology. *Annual Review of Anthropology* 15: 219–46.

Humphreys, S. C.
1981   Introduction: Comparative perspectives on death. In *Mortality and Immortality: The Anthropology and Archaeology of Death*, ed. S. C. Humphreys and H. King, pp. 1–14. Academic Press, London.

Hunt, E. E., Jr., and I. Gleiser
1955   The estimation of age and sex of preadolescent children from bone and teeth. *American Journal of Physical Anthropology* 13: 479–487.

Hunt, E. E., Jr., and J. W. Hatch
1981   The estimation of age at death and ages of formation of transverse lines from measurements of human long bones. *American Journal of Physical Anthropology* 54: 461–469.

Hunter, W. S., and S. M. Garn
1972   Disproportionate sexual dimorphism in the human face. *American Journal of Physical Anthropology* 36: 133–138.

Huss-Ashmore, R., A. Goodman, and G. J. Armelagos
1982   Nutritional inference from paleopathology. In *Advances in Archaeological Method and Theory*, vol. 5, ed. M. B. Schiffer, pp. 395–474. Academic Press, New York.

INCAP [Institute of Nutrition of Central America and Panama]
1961   *Food Composition Table for Use in Latin America*. National Institutes of Health, Bethesda, Maryland.

Iscan, M. Y.
1988   Rise of forensic anthropology. *Yearbook of Physical Anthropology* 31: 203–230.

Iscan, M. Y., and P. Miller-Shavitz
1984   Determination of sex from the tibia. *American Journal of Physical Anthropology* 64: 53–58.

Iscan, M. Y., S. R. Loth, and R. K. Wright
1984   Metamorphosis at the sternal rib end: A new method to estimate age at death in white males. *American Journal of Physical Anthropology* 65: 147–156.
1987   Racial variation in the sternal extremity of the rib and its effect on age determination. *Journal of Forensic Sciences* 32: 452–466.

Jiménez, R., and Z. Lagunas
1989   Los entierros humanos de "El Conchalito," La Paz, Baja California Sur. In *Estudios de Antropología Biológica*, Instituto de Investigaciones Antropológicas, Serie Antropológica, 100, pp. 501–530. Universidad Nacional Autónoma de México, Mexico City.

Johansson, S. R., and S. Horowitz
1986   Estimating mortality in skeletal populations: Influence of the growth rate on the interpretation of levels and trends during the transition to agriculture. *American Journal of Physical Anthropology* 71: 233–250.

Johnson, A., and T. Earle
1987   *The Evolution of Human Society: From Forager Group to Agarian State.* Stanford University Press, Stanford, California.

Johnston, F. E.
1962   Growth of the long bones of infants and young children at Indian Knoll. *American Journal of Physical Anthropology* 20: 249–254.

Katz, D., and J. M. Suchey
1986   Age determination of the male os pubis. *American Journal of Physical Anthropology* 69: 427–436.

Kerley, E. R.
1965   The microscopic determination of age in human bone. *American Journal of Physical Anthropology* 23: 149–163.

Kerley, E. R., and D. H. Ubelaker
1978   Revisions in the microscopic method of estimating age at death in human cortical bone. *American Journal of Physical Anthropology* 49: 545–546.

Klepinger, L. L.
1984   Nutritional assessment from bone. *Annual Review of Anthropology* 13: 75–96.

Kolata, G.
1974   !Kung hunter-gatherers: Feminism, diet and birth control. *Science* 185: 932–934.

Kolb, C. C.
1985   Demographic calculations from Mesoamerican ethnoarchaeology. *Current Anthropology* 26: 581–599.

Kraus, B. S., and R. E. Jordan
1965   *The Human Dentition before Birth.* Lea and Febiger, Philadelphia.

Krogman, W. M.
1962   *The Human Skeleton in Forensic Medicine.* Charles C. Thomas, Springfield, Illinois.

Krotser, P.
1987   Levels of specialization among potters of Teotihuacan. In *Teotihuacan: Nuevos Datos, Nuevas Síntesis, Nuevos Problemas,* ed. E. McClung de Tapia and E. Rattray, pp. 417–428. Universidad Nacional Autónoma de México, México.

Krotser, P., and E. C. Rattray
1980   Manufactura y distribución de tres grupos cerámicos principales de Teotihuacan. *Anales de Antropología* 17 (1): 91–104.

Krzywicki, L.
1934   *Primitive Society and Its Vital Statistics.* Macmillan, London.

Lallo, J. W.
1973   The skeletal biology of three prehistoric American Indian populations from Dickson Mounds. Ph.D. dissertation, Department of Anthropology, University of Massachusetts at Amherst.

Lallo, J., G. J. Armelagos, and R. P. Mensforth
1977   The role of diet, disease and physiology in the origin of porotic hyperostosis. *Human Biology* 49: 471–483.

Lee, R. B.
1979   *The !Kung San: Men, Women and Work in a Foraging Society.* Cambridge University Press, Cambridge.
1980   Lactation, ovulation, infanticide, and women's work: A study of hunter-gatherer population regulation. In *Biosocial Mechanisms of Population Regulation,* ed. M. N. Cohen, R. S. Malpass, and H. G. Klein, pp. 321–348. Yale University Press, New Haven, Connecticut.

Lewis, T. M. N., and M. Kneberg
1946   *Hiwassee Island.* University of Tennessee Press, Knoxville.

Linné, S.
1934   *Archaeological Researches at Teotihuacan, Mexico.* Ethnographic Museum of Sweden, n.s., Publication 1. Stockholm.
1942   *Mexican Highland Cultures.* Ethnographic Museum of Sweden, n.s., Publication 7. Stockholm.

Little, M. A., and P. T. Baker
1976   Environmental adaptations and perspectives. In *Man in the Andes,* ed. P. T. Baker and M. A. Little, pp. 405–428. Dowden, Hutchinson, and Ross, Stroudsburg, Pennsylvania.

Lopez, S., Z. Lagunas, and C. Serrano
1976   *Entierramientos Humanos de la Zona Arqueológica de Cholula, Puebla.* Colección Científica 44. Instituto Nacional de Antropología e Historia, Mexico City.

Loth, S. R., and M. Y. Iscan
1987   The effect of racial variation on sex determination from the sternal rib. *American Journal of Physical Anthropology* 72: 241 (abstract).

Lovejoy, C. O.
1971   Methods for the detection of census error in paleodemography. *American Anthropologist* 73: 101–109.
1985   Dental wear in the Libben population: Its functional pattern and role in the determination of adult skeletal age at death. *American Journal of Physical Anthropology* 68: 47–56.

Lovejoy, C. O., R. S. Meindl, R. P. Mensforth, and T. J. Barton
1985a   Multifactorial determination of skeletal age at death: A method and blind tests of its accuracy. *American Journal of Physical Anthropology* 68: 1–14.

Lovejoy, C. O., R. S. Meindl, T. R. Pryzbeck, and R. P. Mensforth
1985b   Chronological metamorphosis of the auricular surface of the ilium: A new method for the determination of adult skeletal age at death. *American Journal of Physical Anthropology* 68: 15–28.

Lovejoy, C. O., R. S. Meindl, T. R. Pryzbeck, and R. P. Mensforth
1977   Paleodemography of the Libben Site, Ottawa County, Ohio. *Science* 198: 291–293.

Lovell, N. C.
1989   Test of Phenice's technique for determining sex from the os pubis. *American Journal of Physical Anthropology* 79: 117–120.

Lunt, R. C., and D. B. Law
1974   A review of the chronology of calcification of deciduous teeth. *Journal of the American Dental Association* 89: 599–606.

Maat, G. J. R.
1984   Dating and rating of Harris's lines. *American Journal of Physical Anthropology* 63: 291–300.

McClung de Tapia, E.
1987   Patrones de subsistencia urbana en Teotihuacan. In *Teotihuacan: Nuevos Datos, Nuevas Síntesis, Nuevos Problemas*, ed. E. McClung de Tapia and E. Rattray, pp. 57–74. Universidad Nacional Autónoma de México, Mexico City.

MacDonnell, W. R.
1913   On the expectation of life in ancient Rome and in the provinces of Hispania and Lusitania and Africa. *Biometrika* 9: 366–380.

McHenry, H., and P. Schulz
1976   The association between Harris lines and enamel hypoplasia in prehistoric California Indians. *American Journal of Physical Anthropology* 44: 507–512.

McKern, T. W., and T. D. Stewart
1957   *Skeletal Age Changes in Young American Males.* Technical Report EP-45. Headquarters, Quartermaster Research and Development Command, Natick, Massachusetts.

McNeill, W. H.
1976   *Plagues and Peoples.* Anchor Press/Doubleday, Garden City, New York.
1984   Human migration in historical perspective. *Population and Development Review* 10: 1–18.

Mansilla, J.
1980   *Las Condiciones Biológicas de la Población Prehispanica de Cholula, Puebla.* Colección Científica 82. INAH, Mexico City.

Marcy, S. M.
1976   Microorganisms responsible for neonatal diarrhea. In *Infectious Diseases of the Fetus and Newborn Infant*, ed. J. S. Remington and J. O. Klein. W. B. Saunders, Philadelphia.

Maresh, M. M.
1955   Linear growth of long bones of extremities from infancy through adolescence. *American Journal of Diseases of Children* 89: 725–742.

Márquez, M. L.
1984   Distribución de la estatura en colecciones óseas mayas prehispánicas.
In *Estudios de Antropolgía Biológica*, ed. R. Ramos and R. M. Ramos, pp.
253–272. Instituto de Investigaciones Antropológicas, Serie Antropológica, 75. Universidad Nacional Autónoma de México, Mexico
City.

Martin, D. L., and G. J. Armelagos
1979   Morphometrics of compact bone: An example from Sudanese Nubia.
American Journal of Physical Anthropology 51: 571–578.

Martin, D. L., A. H. Goodman, and G. J. Armelagos
1985   Skeletal pathologies as indicators of quality and quantity of diet. In *The
Analysis of Prehistoric Diets*, ed. R. I. Gilbert, Jr., and J. H. Mielke, pp.
227–280. Academic Press, Orlando, Florida.

Martorell, R., and T. Gonzalez-Cossío
1987   Maternal nutrition and birthweight. *Yearbook of Physical Anthropology*
30: 195–220.

Massé, G., and E. E. Hunt, Jr.
1963   Skeletal maturation of the hand and wrist in West African children.
Human Biology 35: 3–25.

Massler, M., I. Schour, and H. G. Poncher
1941   Development pattern of the child as reflected in the calcification pattern of teeth. *American Journal of Diseases of Children* 62: 33–67.

Mays, S. A.
1985   The relationship between Harris line formation and bone growth and
development. *Journal of Archaeological Science* 12: 207–220.

Meindl, R. S., and C. O. Lovejoy
1985   Ectocranial suture closure: A revised method for the determination of
skeletal age at death based on the lateral-anterior sutures. *American
Journal of Physical Anthropology* 68: 57–66.

Meindl, R. S., and A. C. Swedlund
1977   Secular trends in mortality in the Connecticut Valley, 1700–1850.
Human Biology 49: 389–414.

Meindl, R. S., C. O. Lovejoy, R. P. Mensforth, and L. Don Carlos
1985a   Accuracy and direction of error in the sexing of the skeleton: Implications for paleodemography. *American Journal of Physical Anthropology*
68: 79–86.

Meindl, R. S., C. O. Lovejoy, R. P. Mensforth, and R. P. Walker
1985b   A revised method of age determination using the os pubis, with a
review and tests of accuracy of other current methods of pubic symphyseal aging. *American Journal of Physical Anthropology* 68: 29–46.

Menken, J., J. Trussell, and S. Watkins
1981   The nutrition-fertility link: An evaluation of the evidence. *Journal of Interdisciplinary History* 11: 425–441.

Mensforth, R. P., and C. O. Lovejoy
1985   Anatomical, physiological, and epidemiological correlates of the aging process: A confirmation of multifactorial age determination in the Libben skeletal population. *American Journal of Physical Anthropology* 68: 87–106.

Mensforth, R. P., C. O. Lovejoy, J. W. Lallo, and G. J. Armelagos
1978   The role of constitutional factors, diet and infectious disease in the etiology of porotic hyperostosis and periosteal reactions in prehistoric infants and children. *Medical Anthropology* 2: 1–59.

Meyers, J. T.
1971   The origins of agriculture: An evaluation of three hypotheses. In *Prehistoric Agriculture*, ed. S. Struever, pp. 101–121. The Natural History Press, Garden City, New York.

Miles, A. E. W.
1963   Dentition in the assessment of individual age in skeletal material. In *Dental Anthropology*, ed. D. R. Brothwell, pp. 191–209. Pergamon Press, Oxford.

Miller, A.
1973   *The Mural Painting of Teotihuacan.* Dumbarton Oaks, Washington, D.C.

Millon, R.
1973   *Urbanization at Teotihuacan: The Teotihuacan Map*, vol. 1, part 1. University of Texas Press, Austin.

1976   Social relations in ancient Teotihuacan. In *The Valley of Mexico*, ed. E. R. Wolf, pp. 205–248. University of New Mexico Press, Albuquerque.

1981   Teotihuacan: City, state and civilization. In *Supplement to the Handbook of Middle American Indians*, vol. 1, *Archaeology*, ed. J. A. Sabloff, pp. 198–243. University of Texas Press, Austin.

Millon, R., B. Drewitt, and G. L. Cowgill
1973   *Urbanization at Teotihuacan: The Teotihuacan Map*, vol. 1, part 2. University of Texas Press, Austin.

Milner, G. R., D. A. Humpf, and H. C. Harpending
1989   Pattern matching of age-at-death distributions in paleodemographic analysis. *American Journal of Physical Anthropology* 80: 49–58.

Mobley, C. M.
1980   Demographic Structure of Pecos Indians. *American Antiquity* 45: 518–530.

Molnar, S.
1977   Human tooth wear, tooth function and cultural variability. *American Journal of Physical Anthropology* 34: 175–190.

Moore, J. A., A. C. Swedlund, and G. J. Armelagos
1975   The use of life tables in paleodemography. In *Population Studies in Archaeology and Biological Anthropology: A Symposium*, ed. A. C. Swedlund, pp. 57–70. Memoirs of the Society for American Archaeology, no. 30. Washington, D.C.

Moorees, C. F., E. A. Fanning, and E. E. Hunt, Jr.
1963   Age variation of formation stages for ten permanent teeth. *Journal of Dental Research* 42: 1490–1502.

Naeye, R. L.
1970   Structural correlates of fetal undernutrition. In *Fetal Growth and Development*, ed. H.A. Waisman and G.R. Kerr. McGraw-Hill Books, New York.

Nag, M.
1962   *Factors Affecting Human Fertility in Nonindustrial Societies: A Cross-Cultural Study.* Yale University Publications in Anthropology, no. 66. New Haven, Connecticut.

Neel, J. V., and K. M. Weiss
1975   The genetic structure of a tribal population, the Yanamama Indians: XII, Biodemographic studies. *American Journal of Physical Anthropology* 42: 25–52.

Netting, R. McC.
1972   Sacred power and centralization: Aspects of political adaptation in Africa. In *Population Growth: Anthropological Implications*, ed. B. Spooner, pp. 219–244. MIT Press, Cambridge, Massachusetts.
1981   *Balancing on an Alp.* Cambridge University Press, Cambridge.

Newman, M. T.
1977   Aboriginal New World epidemiology and medical care and the impact of Old World disease imports. *American Journal of Physical Anthropology* 45: 667–72.

Nickens, P. R.
1976   Stature reduction as an adaptive response to food production in Mesoamerica. *Journal of Archaeological Science* 3:31–41.

Ortner, D. J., and W. C. J. Putschar
1981   *Identification of Pathological Conditions in Human Skeletal Remains.* Smithsonian Contributions to Anthropology, no. 28. Washington, D.C.

Ounsted, M., and C. Ounsted
1973   *On Fetal Growth Rate: Its Variations and Their Consequences.* J. P. Lippincott, Philadelphia.

Owsley, D. W., and B. Bradtmiller
1983   Mortality of pregnant females in Arikara villages: Osteological evidence. *American Journal of Physical Anthropology* 61: 331–336.

Owsley, D. W., and R. L. Jantz
1983   Formation of the permanent dentition in Arikara Indians: Timing differences that affect dental age assessments. *American Journal of Physical Anthropology* 61: 467–471.

Paine, R. R.
1989   Model life table fitting by maximum likelihood estimation: A procedure to reconstruct paleodemographic characteristics from skeletal age distributions. *American Journal of Physical Anthropology* 79: 51–62.

Palkovich, A. M.
1980   *Pueblo Population and Society: The Arroyo Hondo Skeletal and Mortuary Remains.* Arroyo Hondo Archaeological Series, vol. 3. School of American Research Press, Santa Fe.
1987   Endemic disease patterns in paleopathology: Porotic hyperostosis. *American Journal of Physical Anthropology* 74: 527–538.

Park, E. A.
1964   The imprinting of nutritional disturbances on the growing bone. *Pediatrics* 33 (supplement): 815–862.

Peebles, C. S., and S. M. Kus
1977   Some archaeological correlates of ranked societies. *American Antiquity* 42: 421–448.

Perrenoud, A.
1975   L'inégalité sociale devant la mort à Genève au XVIIieme siècle. *Population* 30 (special number): 221–243.
1978   La mortalité à Genève de 1625 à 1825. *Annales de Démographie Historique*, pp. 209–233. Société de Demographie Historique, Paris.
1982   Croissance or déclin? Les mecanismes du non-renouvellement des populations urbaines. *Histoire Économie et Société* 4: 581–601.

Pfeiffer, S.
1980   Age changes in the external dimensions of adult bone. *American Journal of Physical Anthropology* 52: 529–532.

Phenice, T. W.
1969   A newly developed visual method of sexing the os pubis. *American Journal of Physical Anthropology* 30: 297–301.

Polgar, S., ed.
1971   *Culture and Population.* Carolina Population Center Monograph 9. Schenkman, Cambridge, Massachusetts.

Powell, M. L.
1988   *Status and Health in Prehistory.* Smithsonian Institution Press, Washington, D.C.

Preston, S. H., and N. Bennett
1983   A census-based method for estimating adult mortality. *Population Studies* 37: 91–104.

Preston, S. H., and A. J. Coale
1982   Age structure, growth, attrition, and accession: A new synthesis. *Population Index* 48: 217–259.

Price, B. J.
1982   Cultural materialism: A theoretical review. *American Antiquity* 47: 709–741.

Rathbun, T. A., J. Sexton, and J. Michie
1980   Disease patterns in a formative period South Carolina coastal population. In *The Skeletal Biology of Aboriginal Populations in the Southeastern United States*, ed. P. Willey and F. H. Smith, pp. 52–74. Tennessee Anthropological Association Miscellaneous Paper, no. 5. Knoxville.

Rathje, W. A.
1970   Socio-political implications of lowland Maya burials. *World Archaeology* 1: 359–374.

Ray, A. K., and E. A. Roth
1984   Demography of the Juang Tribal Population of Orissa. *American Journal of Physical Anthropology* 65: 387–389.

Reeves, J. N., and R. P. Mensforth
1986   Multifactorial determination of adult skeletal age at death: Effects of differential age indicator representation. *American Journal of Physical Anthropology* 69: 254 (abstract).

Reinhard, K. J.
1987   Porotic hyperostosis and diet: The coprolite evidence. *American Journal of Physical Anthropology* 72: 246 (abstract).

Richerson, P. J., and R. Boyd
1985   Comments on "Darwinian selection, symbolic variation, and the evolution of culture." *Current Anthropology* 26: 83.

Rindos, D.
1985   Darwinian selection, symbolic variation, and the evolution of culture. *Current Anthropology* 26: 65–77.

Rogers, A., and L. J. Castro
1984a   Age patterns of migration: Cause-specific profiles. In *Migration, Urbanization, and Spatial Population Dynamics*, ed. A. Rogers, pp. 92–126. Westview Press, Boulder, Colorado.
1984b   Model migration schedules. In *Migration, Urbanization, and Spatial Population Dynamics*, ed. A. Rogers, pp. 41–91. Westview Press, Boulder, Colorado.

Rose, J. C., K. W. Condon, and A. H. Goodman
1985   Diet and dentition: Developmental disturbances. In *The Analysis of Prehistoric Diets*, ed. R. I. Gilbert, Jr., and J. H. Mielke, pp. 281–306. Academic Press, Orlando, Florida.

Russell, J. C.
1958   Late ancient and medieval population. *Transactions of the American Philosophical Society*, vol. 48, part 3. Philadelphia.
1985   The control of late ancient and medieval population. *Memoirs of the American Philosophical Society*, vol. 160. Philadelphia.

Sanders, W. T.
1974   Chiefdom to state: Political evolution at Kaminaljuyu, Guatemala. In *Reconstructing Complex Societies: An Archaeological Colloquium*, ed. C. B. Moore, pp. 97–112. Supplement to the Bulletin of the American Schools of Oriental Research, no. 20.
1984   Pre-industrial demography and social evolution. In *On the Evolution of Complex Societies: Essays in Honor of Harry Hoijer*, ed. T. Earle, pp. 7–39. Udena Publications, Malibu, California.

Sanders, W. T., and R. Santley
1983   A tale of three cities. In *Prehistoric Settlement Patterns*, ed. E. Vogt and R. Leventhal, pp. 243–291. University of New Mexico Press, Albuquerque.

Sanders, W. T., and D. Webster
1978   Unilinealism, multilinealism, and the evolution of complex societies. In *Social Archaeology, Beyond Subsistence and Dating*, ed. C. Redman et al, pp. 249–301. Academic Press, New York.
1988   The Mesoamerican urban tradition. *American Anthropologist* 90: 521–526.

Sanders, W. T., J. R. Parsons, and R. S. Santley
1979   *The Basin of Mexico: Ecological Processes in the Evolution of a Civilization*. Academic Press, New York.

Sanders, W. T., D. Nichols, R. Storey, and R. Widmer
1982   A Reconstruction of a Classic Period Landscape in the Teotihuacan Valley. Final Report to the National Science Foundation. Department of Anthropology, Pennsylvania State University, University Park.

Sarnat, B. G., and I. Schour
1941   Enamel hypoplasia (chronological enamel hypoplasia) in relation to systemic disease: A chronologic, morphologic and etiologic classification. *Journal of the American Dental Association* 28: 1989–2000.

Sattenspiel, L., and H. Harpending
1983   Stable population and skeletal age. *American Antiquity* 48: 489–498.

Saul, F. D.
1972   *The Human Skeletal Remains of Altar de Sacrificios: An Osteobiographic Analysis*. Papers of the Peabody Museum of Archaeology and Ethnology, vol. 63, no. 2. Cambridge, Massachusetts.

Saxe, A. A.
1970   Social Dimensions of Mortuary Practices. Ph.D. dissertation, Department of Anthropology, University of Michigan, Ann Arbor.

Scheinvar, L., and J. Gonzalez
1985   Identificacíon de semillas carbonizadas de cactáceas procedentes del sitio arqueológico Tlajinga, Teotihuacan, Estado de México. *Anales Escuela Nacional de Ciencias Biológicas, México* 29: 71–93.

Scheuer, J. L., J. H. Musgrave, and S. P. Evans
1980   The estimation of late fetal and perinatal age from limb bone length by linear and logarithmic regression. *Annals of Human Biology* 7: 257–265.

Scott, E. C.
1978   Dental wear scoring technique. *American Journal of Physical Anthropology* 51: 213–218.

Scott, E. C., and F. E. Johnston
1985   Science, nutrition, fat and policy: Tests of the critical fat hypothesis. *Current Anthropology* 26: 463–475.

Scrimshaw, N. S., C. E. Taylor, and J. E. Gordon
1968   *Interactions of Nutrition and Infection.* World Health Organization, Monograph 57.

Séjourné, L.
1959   *Un Palacio en la Ciudad de los Dioses: Exploraciones en Teotihuacan 1955–58.* Instituto Nacional de Antropología e Historía, Mexico City.
1966   *Architectura y Pintura en Teotihuacan.* Siglo XXI Editores, Mexico City.

Sempowski, M. L.
1987   Differential mortuary treatment: Its implications for social status at three residential compounds in Teotihuacan, México. In *Teotihuacan: Nuevos Datos, Nuevas Síntesis, Nuevos Problemas,* ed. E. McClung de Tapia and E. C. Rattray, pp. 115–132. Universidad Nacional Autónoma de México, Mexico City.

Serrano, C., and Z. Lagunas
1974   Sistema de entierramiento y notas sobre el material osteológico de La Ventilla, Teotihuacán, México. *Anales* 7a: 105–144. Instituto Nacional de Antropología e Historía, Mexico City.

Serrano C., and E. Martinez
1989   Nuevos patrones de mutilación dentaria en Teotihuacan. In *Estudios de Antropología Biológica,* Instituto de Investigaciones Antropológicas, Serie Antropológica, 100, pp. 585–598. Universidad Nacional Autónoma de México, Mexico City.

Sharlin, A.
1978   Natural decrease in early modern cities: A reconsideration. *Past and Present* 79: 126–138.

Shryock. H. S., and J. S. Siegel
1976   *The Methods and Materials of Demography.* Condensed ed. by E. G. Stockwell. Academic Press, New York.

Sjoberg, G.
1960   *The Preindustrial City: Past and Present*. Free Press, New York.

Smith, B. H.
1984   Patterns of molar wear in hunter-gatherers and agriculturalists. *American Journal of Physical Anthropology* 63: 39–56.

Smith, P. E. L.
1972   Changes in population pressure in archaeological explanation. *World Archaeology* 4: 5–18.

Somolinos-D'Ardois, G.
1968   La medicina Teotihuacana. *Gaceta Médica de México* 98: 359–369.

Soustelle, J.
1961   *Daily Life of the Aztecs on the Eve of the Spanish Conquest*. Stanford University Press, Stanford, California.

Spence, M. W.
1971   Skeletal morphology and social organization in Teotihuacan, Mexico. Ph.D. dissertation, Department of Anthropology, Southern Illinois University, Carbondale.
1974   Residential practices and the distribution of skeletal traits in Teotihuacan, Mexico. *Man* 9: 262–273.
1981   Obsidian production and the state in Teotihuacan. *American Antiquity* 46: 769–788.

SPSS Inc. and M. J. Norusis
1986   *SPSS/PC+ for the IBM PC/XT/AT*. SPSS Inc., Chicago.

Starbuck, D. R.
1975   Man-animal relationships in precolumbian central Mexico. Ph.D. dissertation, Department of Anthropology, Yale University, New Haven, Connecticut.
1987   Faunal evidence for the Teotihuacan subsistence base. In *Teotihuacan: Nuevos Datos, Nuevas Síntesis, Nuevos Problemas*, ed. E. McClung de Tapia and E. Rattray, pp. 75–90. Universidad Nacional Autónoma de México, Mexico City.

Steele, D. G.
1976   The estimation of sex on the basis of the talus and calcaneus. *American Journal of Physical Anthropology* 45: 581–588.

Steele, D. G., and C. A. Bramblett
1988   *The Anatomy and Biology of the Human Skeleton*. Texas A&M University Press, College Station.

Steward, J. H.
1955   *Theory of Culture Change*. University of Illinois Press, Urbana.

Stewart, T. D.
1960   A physical anthropologist's view of the peopling of the New World. *Southwestern Journal of Anthropology* 16: 259–273.

Stini, W. A.
1985   Growth rates and sexual dimorphism in evolutionary perspective. In *The Analysis of Prehistoric Diets*, ed. R. I. Gilbert, Jr., and J. H. Mielke, pp. 191–226. Academic Press, Orlando, Florida.

Stolnitz, G. J.
1964   The demographic transition: From high to low birth rates and death rates. In *Population: The Vital Revolution*, ed. R. Freedman, pp. 30–46. Doubleday Press, Garden City, New York.

Storey, R.
1983   The paleodemography of Tlajinga 33: An apartment compound of the pre-Columbian city of Teotihuacan. Ph.D. dissertation, Department of Anthropology, Pennsylvania State University, University Park.
1985   An estimate of mortality in a pre-Columbian urban population. *American Anthropologist* 87: 519–535.
1986   Prenatal mortality at pre-Columbian Teotihuacan. *American Journal of Physical Anthropology* 69: 541–548.

Storey, R., and R. J. Widmer
1989   Household and community structure of a Teotihuacan apartment compound: S3W1:33 of the Tlajinga Barrio. In *Households and Communities*, ed. S. MacEachern, D. J. W. Archer, and R. D. Garvin, pp. 407–415. Archaeological Association of the University of Calgary, Calgary.

Stout, S. D.
1986   The use of histomorphometry in skeletal identification: The case of Francisco Pizarro. *Journal of Forensic Sciences* 31: 296–300.

Stuart-Macadam, P.
1985   Porotic hyperostosis: Representative of a childhood condition. *American Journal of Physical Anthropology* 66: 391–398.

Suchey, J. M.
1979   Problems in aging of females using the os pubis. *American Journal of Physical Anthropology* 51: 467–470.

Sugiyama, S.
1989   Burials dedicated to the old Temple of Quetzalcoatl at Teotihuacan, Mexico. *American Antiquity* 54: 85–106.

Swardstedt, T.
1966   *Odontological Aspects of a Medieval Population in the Province of Jamtland/ Mid-Sweden*. Tiden-Barnangen Tryckerien, Stockholm.

Swedlund, A. C., and G. J. Armelagos
1976   *Demographic Anthropology*. William C. Brown, Dubuque, Iowa.

Tainter, J. A.
1973   The social correlates of mortuary patterning at Kaloko, North Kona, Hawaii. *Archaeology and Physical Anthropology in Oceania* 8: 1–11.

Tanner, J. M.
1978   Fetus Into Man: Physical Growth from Conception to Maturity. Harvard University Press, Cambridge, Massachusetts.

Thomas, D. H.
1986   Refiguring Anthropology. Waveland Press, Prospect Heights, Illinois.

Thomas, R. B.
1973   Human Adaptation to a High Andean Energy Flow System. Occasional Papers in Anthropology, no. 6. Department of Anthropology, Pennsylvania State University, University Park.

Todd, T. W.
1920   Age changes in the pubic bone: I, the male white pubis. American Journal of Physical Anthropology (original series) 3: 286–334.
1921   Age changes in the pubic bone. American Journal of Physical Anthropology (original series) 4: 1–70.

Trotter, M., and G. C. Gleser
1958   A re-evaluation of estimation of stature based on measurements of stature taken during life and of long bones after death. American Journal of Physical Anthropology 16: 79–123.

Turner, M. H.
1987   The lapidaries of Teotihuacan, México. In Teotihuacan: Nuevos Datos, Nuevas Síntesis, Nuevos Problemas, ed. E. McClung de Tapia and E. Rattray, pp. 465–472. Universidad Nacional Autónoma de México, Mexico City.

Ubelaker, D. H.
1974   Reconstruction of Demographic Profiles from Ossuary Skeletal Samples. Smithsonian Contributions to Anthropology, no. 18. Washington, D.C.
1989   Human Skeletal Remains: Excavation, Analysis, Interpretation. 2nd ed. Taraxacum, Washington, D.C.

Ucko, P. J.
1969   Ethnography and the archaeological interpretation of funerary remains. World Archaeology 1: 262–277.

Van Gerven, D. P., and G. J. Armelagos
1983   "Farewell to paleodemography?" Rumors of its death have been greatly exaggerated. Journal of Human Evolution 12: 353–360.

Van Vark, G. N.
1970   Some Statistical Procedures for the Investigation of Prehistoric Human Skeletal Material. Rijksuniversiteit te Groningen, Groningen.

Vidarte, J.
1964   Exploraciones Arqueológicas en el Rancho "La Ventilla." Informe al Instituto Nacional de Antropología e Historía, Mexico City.

Villar, J., and J. M. Belizán
1982   The relative contribution of prematurity and fetal growth retardation to low birthweight in developing and developed societies. *American Journal of Obstetrics and Gynecology* 143: 793–798.

Walker, R. A., and C. O. Lovejoy
1985   Radiographic changes in the clavicle and proximal femur and their use in the determination of skeletal age at death. *American Journal of Physical Anthropology* 68: 67–78.

Watts, B. K., and A. L. Merrill
1962   *Composition of Foods.* Agriculture Handbook, no. 8. U.S. Department of Agriculture, Washington, D.C.

Weaver, D. S.
1980   Sex differences in the ilia of a known sex and age sample of fetal and infant skeletons. *American Journal of Physical Anthropology* 52: 191–195.

Weiss, K. M.
1972   On the systematic bias in skeletal sexing. *American Journal of Physical Anthropology* 37: 239–249.
1973   *Demographic Models for Anthropology.* Memoirs of the Society for American Archaeology, no. 27. Washington, D.C.
1975   Demographic disturbance and the use of life tables in anthropology. In *Population Studies in Archaeology and Biological Anthropology: A Symposium*, ed. A. C. Swedlund, pp. 46–56. Memoirs of the Society for American Archaeology, no. 30. Washington, D.C.

Weiss, K. M., and P. E. Smouse
1976   The demographic stability of small human populations. In *The Demographic Evolution of Human Populations*, ed. R. H. Ward and K. M. Weiss, pp. 59–74. Academic Press, London.

White, L. A.
1959   *The Evolution of Culture.* McGraw-Hill, New York.

Widmer, R. J.
1983   Craft specialization at Tlajinga 33, Teotihuacan. Paper presented at the 48th Annual Meeting of the Society for American Archaeology, Pittsburg, Pennsylvania.
1988   *The Evolution of the Calusa: A Nonagricultural Chiefdom on the Southwest Florida Coast.* University of Alabama Press, Tuscaloosa.

Wiesenfield, S.
1967   Sickle-cell trait in human biological and cultural evolution. *Science* 157: 1134–1140.

Wilkinson, R. G., and R. J. Norelli
1981   A biocultural analysis of social organization at Monte Albán. *American Antiquity* 46: 743–758.

Willey, P., and B. Mann
1986   The skeleton of an elderly woman from the Crow Creek site and its implications for paleodemography. *Plains Anthropologist* 31: 141–152.

Wing, E. S., and A. B. Brown
1979   *Paleonutrition: Method and Theory in Prehistoric Foodways.* Academic Press, New York.

Wrigley, E. A.
1969   *Population and History.* McGraw-Hill, New York.

Zubrow, E. B. W.
1976   Demographic anthropology: An introductory analysis. In *Demographic Anthropology*, ed. E. B. W. Zubrow, pp. 1–25. University of New Mexico Press, Albuquerque.

Index

ABOUT THE AUTHOR

REBECCA STOREY is Associate Professor of Anthropology at the University of Houston. She received her bachelor's degree from Smith College, Massachusetts, her master's degree from Columbia University, and her doctorate from Pennsylvania State University.